NATIVE AMERICAN TRIBES

FIVE CIVILIZED TRIBES OF CHEROKEE, CHOCTAW, CHICKASAW, CREEK & SEMINOLE NATION

5 BOOKS IN 1

BOOK 1
THE CHEROKEE NATION: A HISTORY OF RESILIENCE AND RENEWAL

BOOK 2
CHOCTAW LEGACY: FROM HOMELAND TO REMOVAL

BOOK 3
CHICKASAW HOMELAND: A JOURNEY THROUGH HISTORY

BOOK 4
CREEK NATION CHRONICLES: SURVIVING AND THRIVING

BOOK 5
SEMINOLE NATION SAGA: ADAPTATION AND SURVIVAL

BY A.J. KINGSTON

Published by A. J. Kingston
Library of Congress Cataloging-in-Publication Data
ISBN 978-1-83938-486-8
Cover design by Rizzo

Join Our Productivity Group and Access your Bonus

If you're passionate about history books and want to connect with others who share your love of the subject, joining our Facebook group (search for "History Books by A.J.Kingston") can be a great way to do so. By joining a group dedicated to history books, you'll have the opportunity to connect with like-minded individuals, share your thoughts and ideas, and even discover new books that you might not have come across otherwise. You can also access your FREE BONUS once you joined our Facebook group called "History Books by A.J.Kingston".

One of the biggest advantages of joining our Facebook group is the sense of community it provides. You'll be able to interact with other history book enthusiasts, ask questions, and share your own knowledge and expertise. This can be especially valuable if you're a student or someone who is just starting to explore the world of history books.

If you love audiobooks, then joining our YouTube channel that offers free audiobooks on a weekly basis can be a great way to stay entertained and engaged. By subscribing to our channel, you'll have access to a range of audiobooks across different genres, all for free. Not only this is a great opportunity to enjoy some new audiobooks, but it's also a chance to discover new authors and titles that you might not have come across otherwise.

Lastly, don't forget to follow us on Facebook and YouTube by searching for A.J. Kingston.

TABLE OF CONTENTS – BOOK 1 - THE CHEROKEE NATION: A HISTORY OF RESILIENCE AND RENEWAL

TABLE OF CONTENTS – BOOK 2 - CHOCTAW LEGACY: FROM HOMELAND TO REMOVAL

TABLE OF CONTENTS – BOOK 3 - CHICKASAW HOMELAND: A JOURNEY THROUGH HISTORY

TABLE OF CONTENTS – BOOK 4 - CREEK NATION CHRONICLES: SURVIVING AND THRIVING

TABLE OF CONTENTS – BOOK 5 - SEMINOLE NATION SAGA: ADAPTATION AND SURVIVAL

Introduction

Welcome to "Native American Tribes: Five Civilized Tribes of Cherokee, Choctaw, Chickasaw, Creek & Seminole Nation," a captivating journey through the rich and diverse histories of some of America's most remarkable Indigenous nations. In this book bundle, we invite you to explore the intricate tapestry of cultures, traditions, and resilience that define the Cherokee, Choctaw, Chickasaw, Creek, and Seminole peoples.

Indigenous communities have played a pivotal role in shaping the story of America, yet their narratives are often overlooked or marginalized. This collection seeks to rectify that oversight by delving deep into the heart of these tribes, highlighting their ancient origins, their encounters with European settlers, the struggles they endured during forced removal, and the enduring spirit that has allowed them to adapt, rebuild, and thrive.

Across the five books that comprise this bundle, we will traverse the landscapes of their ancestral homelands, accompany them through the trials of removal and displacement, and witness their tenacity as they reclaim their identities and cultures in unfamiliar territories. Each tribe's story is a testament to the strength of the human spirit, the resilience of Indigenous cultures, and the importance of preserving these histories for future generations.

Book 1 - The Cherokee Nation: A History of Resilience and Renewal immerses us in the world of the Cherokee people, tracing their roots, their encounters with European explorers, and their tragic journey along the Trail of Tears. But it also showcases their remarkable ability to rebound and revive their cultural heritage.

Book 2 - Choctaw Legacy: From Homeland to Removal unfolds the epic saga of the Choctaw Nation, exploring their vibrant pre-European societies, the challenges they faced during removal, and their legacy of adaptability and strength.

Book 3 - Chickasaw Homeland: A Journey Through History invites us to walk in the footsteps of the Chickasaw people, from their ancient origins to their return to their homeland after displacement, exemplifying the enduring power of cultural identity.

Book 4 - Creek Nation Chronicles: Surviving and Thriving takes us on a historical odyssey of the Creek Nation, revealing their ancestral lands, their encounters with European settlers, and the resilience that has defined their journey.

Book 5 - Seminole Nation Saga: Adaptation and Survival explores the unique culture and unwavering resistance of the Seminole people, who faced removal and the challenges of life in new territories with remarkable resilience.

As you embark on this literary voyage through the histories of these five Indigenous nations, we encourage you to keep an open heart and mind. These stories are not just chapters in history; they are living narratives, illuminating the path forward for these tribes and reminding us all of the enduring power of culture, heritage, and the human spirit.

Join us as we delve into the past and present of the Cherokee, Choctaw, Chickasaw, Creek, and Seminole Nations, and together, let us honor and celebrate the diverse and resilient cultures that continue to enrich the fabric of America.

BOOK 1
THE CHEROKEE NATION
A HISTORY OF RESILIENCE AND RENEWAL

BY A.J. KINGSTON

Chapter 1: Ancient Roots and Pre-European Contact

Ancient Origins and Migration are fundamental aspects of human history and have shaped the course of civilizations for millennia. Our understanding of these topics continues to evolve as archaeologists, anthropologists, and historians uncover new evidence and refine existing theories.

The study of Ancient Origins seeks to uncover the earliest traces of human existence on Earth. It delves into the archaeological record to unearth artifacts, fossils, and other remnants of ancient civilizations. These discoveries provide valuable insights into the lives, technologies, and cultures of our distant ancestors.

One of the most remarkable aspects of human history is our species' ability to adapt and migrate across vast distances. Early humans were nomadic by nature, constantly on the move in search of food, water, and shelter. This nomadic lifestyle played a pivotal role in our survival and eventual dominance on the planet.

The migration of ancient peoples is a fascinating area of study. It involves tracing the movement of human populations across continents and regions over thousands of years. Archaeological findings and genetic research have shed light on these migratory patterns, revealing the complex interplay of factors that drove people to explore and settle new lands.

In the distant past, the movement of ancient populations was often driven by environmental factors. Changes in climate, such as the end of the last ice age, could create new opportunities or necessitate migrations to more hospitable regions. For example, the melting of glaciers led to the opening of new land routes that early humans could follow.

Additionally, the availability of resources played a crucial role in migration. Early humans followed the herds of animals they hunted, as well as the seasonal growth of plants they gathered. This nomadic lifestyle led to the gradual spread of our species across the continents.

As humans migrated, they encountered new environments and adapted to diverse landscapes. This process of adaptation led to the development of distinct regional cultures and technologies. For example, those who settled in fertile river valleys like the Nile or the Tigris and Euphrates developed advanced agricultural practices, leading to the rise of early civilizations.

Ancient trade networks also played a significant role in migration. As people moved, they established trade routes that connected distant regions. These routes facilitated the exchange of goods, ideas, and technologies, contributing to the spread of knowledge and cultural diffusion.

One remarkable example of ancient migration is the peopling of the Americas. For thousands of years, the Americas remained uninhabited by humans until a group of early migrants crossed a land bridge connecting Siberia and Alaska. These pioneers ventured further south, populating the entire continent and giving rise to diverse Native American cultures.

In some cases, ancient migrations were driven by conflict and conquest. The expansion of empires, such as the Roman Empire in Europe or the Mongol Empire in Asia, led to the displacement of populations and the merging of cultures. This resulted in the spread of languages, religions, and governance systems.

Another crucial aspect of ancient migrations is the impact on cultural diversity. As people moved, they encountered new societies and adapted to different ways of life. This process often led to the exchange of customs, languages, and traditions. Over time, these interactions enriched human culture and fostered cross-cultural understanding.

The study of ancient migrations is not limited to prehistoric times. It also includes the movements of ancient civilizations and their interactions with neighboring societies. For example, the Silk Road, which connected China with the Mediterranean world, facilitated trade and cultural exchange between East and West.

In summary, Ancient Origins and Migration are essential components of human history. The study of these topics allows us to trace the footsteps of our ancestors, understand their motivations, and appreciate the rich tapestry of cultures that have emerged over millennia. As our knowledge and technology continue to advance, we can look forward to uncovering even more fascinating insights into our ancient past.

Indigenous Societies of the Cherokee Homeland represent a captivating facet of Native American history. These societies thrived in what is now known as the southeastern United States long before the arrival of European settlers, leaving behind a legacy of rich cultural traditions, complex social structures, and deep connections to the land.

The Cherokee Nation, in particular, was one of the prominent Indigenous societies in the southeastern region. Their homeland encompassed parts of present-day Tennessee, North Carolina, Georgia, and Alabama. Within this vast territory, various Cherokee communities and clans established their unique ways of life.

One key aspect of Cherokee society was its matrilineal kinship system. In this system, descent and clan membership were determined through the mother's lineage. Clans played a crucial role in Cherokee life, governing social and political interactions, and often held their own specific responsibilities and duties within the community.

The Cherokee homeland was characterized by a diverse environment, including mountains, forests, rivers, and fertile valleys. This diversity allowed Cherokee societies to develop a wide range of subsistence practices. They were skilled hunters and gatherers, relying on game like deer and turkey, as well as seasonal harvests of fruits, nuts, and plants.

Agriculture was also integral to Cherokee societies. They cultivated crops like corn, beans, and squash, known as the "Three Sisters," which provided a stable food source. The Cherokee's agricultural knowledge and techniques were passed down through generations and allowed them to thrive in their homeland.

Villages were the central units of Cherokee society. These communities were often situated near rivers or streams, providing access to water for daily needs and transportation. Cherokee villages were typically comprised of communal structures, including council houses, homes, and granaries, reflecting the importance of community life.

Council houses held immense significance in Cherokee culture. They served as gathering places for important ceremonies, councils, and decision-making processes. Cherokee society was governed by a council of elders and leaders, and discussions within these council houses played a critical role in shaping their communities.

Ceremony and spirituality were deeply ingrained in the fabric of Cherokee societies. They held various ceremonies, dances, and rituals throughout the year to honor their connections to the land, their ancestors, and the natural world. These ceremonies were often accompanied by intricate songs and dances, showcasing the Cherokee's artistic and cultural richness.

Trade was another vital aspect of Cherokee society. They engaged in a vast trade network, exchanging goods such as furs, hides, and agricultural products with neighboring tribes. These trade connections fostered intertribal relationships and facilitated the exchange of ideas and technologies.

The Cherokee homeland was not isolated; it was a region where different Indigenous societies coexisted and interacted. The Cherokee had interactions and alliances with neighboring tribes like the Creek, Choctaw, and Chickasaw. These interactions influenced their culture, art, and governance systems.

However, the arrival of European settlers in the 17th century began to alter the dynamics of Cherokee society. The introduction of new diseases, the encroachment of European settlers on their lands, and conflicts over territory led to significant changes in the lives of Cherokee people.

Despite the challenges and hardships they faced, the Cherokee Nation's resilience and determination to preserve their cultural heritage remain evident to this day. Their history serves as a testament to the enduring strength of Indigenous societies and their deep-rooted connections to their homeland.

Pre-European Contact and Cultural Practices are integral parts of the history of Indigenous societies in North America. These eras, often referred to as pre-contact or pre-Columbian times, represent a period of rich cultural diversity, sustainable practices, and complex social structures long before the arrival of European explorers and settlers.

Before the arrival of Europeans, Indigenous societies across North America had developed unique and sophisticated ways of life that were deeply connected to their environments. These societies were highly adaptable and had thrived in a wide range of geographical settings, from the Arctic tundra to the desert Southwest to the temperate woodlands of the eastern United States.

One of the defining characteristics of pre-European contact Indigenous societies was their sustainable and harmonious relationship with the natural world. These societies relied on the land and its resources for their survival, and they had developed intricate systems of resource management and conservation.

Agriculture played a significant role in many Indigenous societies. The cultivation of crops like maize (corn), beans, and squash, known as the "Three Sisters," was a cornerstone of agriculture in regions such as the Eastern Woodlands. This agricultural system was sustainable and provided a diverse and nutritious diet.

In addition to agriculture, Indigenous peoples practiced various forms of hunting, fishing, and gathering based on the ecosystems of their respective regions. These practices were not only essential for food but also deeply intertwined with cultural and spiritual beliefs. Many Indigenous societies had a profound respect for the animals they hunted and the plants they gathered, often incorporating them into their rituals and ceremonies.

Social structures in pre-European contact Indigenous societies were diverse and adapted to the specific needs of each community. In many cases, kinship systems played a central role in organizing society. Clan systems, often matrilineal, were common, and individuals identified with and were loyal to their clans.

Cultural practices and belief systems varied widely among Indigenous societies. These cultures were characterized by oral traditions, storytelling, and the transmission of knowledge from one generation to the next. Spiritual beliefs were deeply connected to the land, the seasons, and the natural world, and ceremonies and rituals played a significant role in maintaining balance and harmony.

Artistic expression was also a vital part of Indigenous cultures. Many Indigenous peoples created intricate and beautiful works of art, including pottery, basketry, beadwork, textiles, carvings, and paintings. These art forms often conveyed stories, symbols, and spiritual meanings.

Trade networks were established among Indigenous societies long before the arrival of Europeans. These networks allowed for the exchange of goods, technologies, and cultural practices over vast distances. Items like shells, obsidian, and copper moved through these networks, connecting different regions and fostering intertribal relationships.

The absence of written languages in many Indigenous societies did not diminish the depth of their knowledge and intellectual achievements. Indigenous peoples developed intricate systems of oral history, passing down knowledge, traditions, and stories through generations. These oral traditions were a testament to the complexity of their societies.

Pre-European contact Indigenous societies also exhibited resilience and adaptability in the face of environmental challenges. They developed strategies for coping with changing climates, resource availability, and natural disasters. These strategies often involved mobility, allowing them to move seasonally to access different resources.

In summary, the era of pre-European contact in North America was marked by the diversity, sustainability, and complexity of Indigenous societies. These societies had developed intricate cultural practices, sustainable resource management, and deeply rooted spiritual connections to the land. The legacy of these pre-contact societies continues to influence and enrich Indigenous cultures and communities today.

Chapter 2: Early Encounters with European Explorers

The arrival of European explorers in Cherokee territory marked a significant turning point in the history of the Cherokee Nation and the broader Southeastern United States. European exploration of the Americas began in the late 15th century, with Christopher Columbus's voyages, and continued throughout the subsequent centuries. Here, we will explore the impact of European explorers specifically in Cherokee territory.

Early Encounters: The earliest European explorers to reach Cherokee territory included Spanish expeditions led by Hernando de Soto in the mid-16th century. De Soto's expedition, which explored parts of present-day Tennessee and the southeastern United States, brought the Cherokee people into direct contact with Europeans. These encounters introduced the Cherokees to new technologies, animals, and diseases.

Trade Relations: European explorers, particularly the Spanish and later the French and English, established trade relationships with the Cherokee people. The Cherokee traded furs, hides, and other valuable resources in exchange for European goods such as metal tools, firearms, cloth, and glass beads. This trade had a profound impact on Cherokee culture, introducing new materials and technologies.

Conflict and Alliances: European colonization efforts often led to conflicts in Cherokee territory. As European powers vied for control of North America, the Cherokee found themselves caught in the middle. They sometimes formed alliances with European colonists, such as the English during the late 17th century, in efforts to gain an advantage over rival Indigenous nations.

Disease and Population Decline: Like many Indigenous peoples, the Cherokee were highly susceptible to diseases introduced by European explorers. Diseases such as smallpox, measles, and influenza decimated Cherokee populations, leading to a significant decline in numbers. This demographic impact was profound and had long-lasting consequences.

Land Disputes and Displacement: As European settlements expanded, land disputes arose in Cherokee territory. European colonists and later American settlers encroached on Cherokee lands, leading to conflicts and negotiations over territory. These disputes eventually culminated in the forced removal of the Cherokee people from their ancestral lands in the early 19th century, a tragic event known as the Trail of Tears.

Influence on Cherokee Culture: European contact also influenced Cherokee culture in various ways. This influence can be seen in the adoption of European-style clothing, the incorporation of European farming techniques, and the use of firearms in hunting and warfare. The Cherokee syllabary, developed by Sequoyah in the early 19th century, was influenced by European writing systems.

Impact on Governance: The introduction of European political systems and concepts of governance had an impact on Cherokee leadership and governance structures. The Cherokee Nation adapted to some aspects of European-style governance, particularly during the 19th century.

In summary, the arrival of European explorers in Cherokee territory brought about significant changes and challenges for the Cherokee people. It initiated a complex interplay of trade, conflict, disease, cultural exchange, and ultimately, the displacement of the Cherokee from their ancestral lands. The history of European exploration and contact in Cherokee territory is a crucial chapter in the broader history of Indigenous-European interactions in North America.

The Impact of Contact and the Fur Trade on Indigenous societies in North America represents a crucial and transformative period in history. The fur trade, which emerged in the 17th century, had far-reaching consequences for both Indigenous peoples and European colonists. Here, we will explore the significant impact of contact and the fur trade on Indigenous societies.

Introduction of European Goods: The fur trade introduced Indigenous peoples to a wide range of European goods. Indigenous communities began to acquire metal tools, firearms, cloth, glass beads, and other items through trade with European fur traders. These goods significantly impacted daily life, altering hunting, cooking, clothing, and other aspects of Indigenous culture.

Transformation of Indigenous Economies: The fur trade became a central component of Indigenous economies in regions where fur-bearing animals were abundant. Indigenous hunters and trappers exchanged furs for European goods, creating a new economic system that influenced social hierarchies and trade networks.

Intertribal Trade Networks: The fur trade fostered intertribal trade networks and alliances. Indigenous groups often specialized in the procurement of specific furs, which they then traded with other Indigenous nations. This intertribal trade led to the exchange of goods, ideas, and cultural practices, strengthening relationships among Indigenous peoples.

Cultural Exchange: The fur trade facilitated cultural exchange between Indigenous peoples and European traders. This exchange included language acquisition, religious syncretism, and the sharing of culinary traditions. Some Indigenous communities adopted aspects of European culture, while European traders adopted elements of Indigenous lifestyles.

Impact on Traditional Hunting Practices: The demand for furs, particularly beaver pelts, led to changes in traditional hunting practices. Indigenous hunters shifted their focus to specific animals desired by European markets, which could deplete local animal populations and disrupt ecological balances.

Disease and Population Decline: Contact with European traders also exposed Indigenous populations to diseases to which they had no immunity, such as smallpox, measles, and influenza. These diseases led to devastating epidemics and significant population decline among Indigenous communities.

Conflict and Alliances: Competition among European colonial powers for control of the fur trade sometimes led to conflicts in Indigenous territories. Indigenous groups often played rival European powers against each other to their advantage, forming alliances when it suited their interests.

Impact on Ecosystems: The fur trade had ecological consequences as well. Overexploitation of fur-bearing animals, such as beavers, led to declines in their populations in certain areas. This, in turn, affected the ecosystems and disrupted Indigenous subsistence practices.

Challenges to Indigenous Sovereignty: The fur trade contributed to challenges to Indigenous sovereignty. European colonists and traders frequently sought to establish control over fur-rich regions, leading to disputes and conflicts over territory and resources.

Legacy of the Fur Trade: The legacy of the fur trade continues to shape Indigenous communities and their relationships with the broader society. Many Indigenous peoples today maintain cultural practices, stories, and art related to the fur trade era.

In summary, the impact of contact and the fur trade on Indigenous societies in North America was multifaceted. It brought about economic changes, cultural exchange, population decline, ecological consequences, and challenges to Indigenous sovereignty. The fur trade era remains a pivotal chapter in the complex history of Indigenous-European interactions on the continent.

Early Diplomatic Relations and Alliances during the period of European exploration and colonization in North America played a pivotal role in shaping the course of history for both

Indigenous nations and European colonial powers. This era marked a complex and dynamic interplay of diplomacy, trade, cultural exchange, conflict, and cooperation.

When European explorers first arrived on the shores of North America in the late 15th and early 16th centuries, they encountered a vast array of Indigenous nations, each with its unique cultures, languages, and political structures. These Indigenous nations had established their own complex systems of governance, trade networks, and diplomatic protocols long before European contact.

Diplomacy between Indigenous nations and European explorers was often initiated through the exchange of goods and the establishment of trade relationships. Indigenous peoples possessed valuable resources such as furs, hides, and agricultural products that were highly sought after by Europeans. In return, Indigenous nations acquired European goods like metal tools, firearms, cloth, and glass beads, which significantly impacted their daily lives.

These initial diplomatic encounters were characterized by mutual curiosity and the exchange of gifts. European explorers and Indigenous leaders engaged in negotiations to establish trade agreements. These agreements often laid the foundation for diplomatic relations, as both parties recognized the benefits of continued trade.

However, as European colonization efforts expanded, diplomatic relations became more complex. European colonial powers, including the Spanish, French, Dutch, and English, began to establish permanent settlements in North America. This expansion led to increased competition among European nations for control of territory and resources.

Indigenous nations found themselves in the midst of this competition, and many Indigenous leaders skillfully played European powers against each other to their advantage. Diplomatic alliances were forged strategically, often based on mutual interests and shared goals. Indigenous nations recognized that forming alliances with European colonists could provide military support, access to European trade goods, and a means to resist rival Indigenous nations.

Diplomacy and alliances took various forms. Some Indigenous nations entered into formal treaties with European colonial powers, recognizing their sovereignty and establishing agreements for mutual defense and trade. These treaties often included the exchange of wampum belts, which served as symbols of the agreements and were imbued with deep cultural significance.

Diplomatic councils and gatherings became important venues for negotiations. Indigenous leaders from various nations would convene to discuss matters of mutual concern, including trade, territorial boundaries, and alliances. These councils played a vital role in shaping diplomatic relations in North America.

Cultural exchange was an integral part of early diplomacy. Indigenous peoples shared their languages, knowledge, and customs with European explorers, while Europeans introduced Indigenous nations to new technologies, religious beliefs, and cultural practices. This exchange of ideas and traditions had a profound impact on both Indigenous and European societies.

Despite efforts to establish peaceful alliances, conflicts occasionally arose. Competition for land and resources, misunderstandings, and clashes of cultural norms led to tensions and violence. Many Indigenous nations found themselves facing threats to their sovereignty and ancestral lands as European colonization expanded.

One notable example of diplomacy and alliances was the Treaty of Tordesillas in 1494, which divided the newly discovered lands of the Americas between Spain and Portugal. While this treaty did not directly involve Indigenous nations, it set a precedent for European territorial claims in the Americas.

Another significant diplomatic figure was Powhatan, the paramount chief of the Powhatan Confederacy in Virginia, who maintained complex relations with English colonists, including the famous story of Pocahontas and her interactions with Englishman John Smith.

As European colonization progressed, the dynamics of diplomacy and alliances continued to evolve. Indigenous nations adapted to the changing landscape and sought to protect their interests and cultures. Some alliances were successful in resisting European encroachment, while others faced significant challenges and displacement.

In summary, early diplomatic relations and alliances during the era of European exploration and colonization in North America were marked by a complex interplay of diplomacy, trade, cultural exchange, conflict, and cooperation. Indigenous nations and European colonial powers engaged in negotiations, formed alliances, and navigated the challenges of competing interests and cultural differences. This period of history laid the foundation for the diverse diplomatic and cultural landscape that continues to shape North America today.

Chapter 3: The Cherokee Nation's Cultural Heritage

Language and Writing hold profound significance in human history, serving as vehicles for communication, culture, and the preservation of knowledge. One remarkable example of linguistic innovation and cultural preservation is the Cherokee Syllabary, a script developed by Sequoyah, a Cherokee silversmith and visionary, in the early 19th century.

Before the introduction of the Cherokee Syllabary, the Cherokee people, like many Indigenous nations, relied on oral tradition for the transmission of their language, stories, and history. Their spoken language, Cherokee, is a complex and rich linguistic system, and they had no written script to record it.

Sequoyah, also known as George Guess, recognized the importance of creating a written system for the Cherokee language. Born around 1767 in what is now Tennessee, Sequoyah was raised in a Cherokee-speaking family. His experiences and observations during his travels led him to understand the transformative potential of a written script for his people.

The creation of the Cherokee Syllabary was an astonishing feat of innovation. Sequoyah dedicated years to developing a system that would represent the sounds of the Cherokee language with written characters. He faced numerous challenges, as the Cherokee language has a different structure and sound system than English or other European languages.

Sequoyah's breakthrough came when he realized that the Cherokee language could be represented through a set of symbols, each corresponding to a specific syllable. Unlike alphabetic scripts that use individual letters to represent sounds, the Cherokee Syllabary assigns characters to syllables, making it uniquely suited to the Cherokee language's structure.

The Cherokee Syllabary consists of 85 characters, each representing a different syllable in the Cherokee language. These characters were based on a combination of shapes and symbols from Sequoyah's own experiences, such as elements from nature, the human body, and everyday objects. The process of assigning characters to syllables was meticulous and thoughtful, and it showcased Sequoyah's deep understanding of his language.

Sequoyah's creation of the Cherokee Syllabary was an act of cultural preservation and empowerment. He understood that a written script would not only enable the Cherokee people to record their language but also allow them to document their history, stories, and traditions. This was particularly important in a time of increasing interaction with European settlers and the United States government, as it provided a means for the Cherokee to negotiate, communicate, and assert their identity.

The Cherokee Syllabary's impact was profound and immediate. Sequoyah's invention enabled the Cherokee people to write letters, keep written records, and publish newspapers in their own language. The first Cherokee newspaper, the "Cherokee Phoenix," was published in 1828, and it played a vital role in disseminating news, cultural knowledge, and advocacy for the Cherokee Nation.

One of the most remarkable aspects of the Cherokee Syllabary is its success in achieving widespread literacy among the Cherokee people. Within just a few years of its creation, a significant portion of the Cherokee population had learned to read and write in their own language. This rapid adoption of literacy was unprecedented and demonstrated the practicality and effectiveness of the script.

Sequoyah's legacy extends beyond the Cherokee Nation. His invention of a syllabary influenced other Indigenous nations in North America who sought to develop their writing systems. The Cherokee Syllabary served as an inspiration and a model for these efforts.

In 1825, the Cherokee Nation officially adopted the Cherokee Syllabary as its writing system, recognizing its value and cultural significance. The syllabary's impact on Cherokee society was profound, fostering a sense of cultural pride and identity, even in the face of increasing pressures from European settlers and the U.S. government.

However, the Cherokee people faced significant challenges during this period, including land dispossession, forced removal from their ancestral lands in the southeastern United States, and the Trail of Tears in 1838-1839. Despite these hardships, the Cherokee Syllabary remained a symbol of resilience and cultural preservation.

Today, the Cherokee Syllabary continues to be a vital part of Cherokee culture and identity. It is taught in schools and used in various forms of media, literature, and cultural expression. Efforts to revitalize the Cherokee language and promote literacy in the syllabary remain ongoing, ensuring that Sequoyah's legacy endures for future generations.

Sequoyah's invention of the Cherokee Syllabary stands as a testament to the power of individuals to shape the course of history and preserve their culture. It remains a remarkable example of linguistic innovation and cultural resilience, demonstrating the enduring value of language and writing in the preservation of Indigenous knowledge and identity. The Cherokee Syllabary serves as a reminder that language is not only a means of communication but also a powerful tool for cultural preservation and empowerment.

Religious Beliefs and Practices are fundamental aspects of human culture and have played a pivotal role in shaping societies, worldviews, and individual identities throughout history. Across the globe, diverse religious traditions have emerged, each offering unique perspectives on the spiritual, moral, and ethical dimensions of life. In this exploration, we delve into the multifaceted nature of religious beliefs and practices, examining their significance, diversity, and impact on individuals and communities.

Religious beliefs encompass a wide spectrum of perspectives on the divine, the supernatural, and the meaning of existence. At the core of many religious traditions lies the concept of the divine, which is often characterized as a transcendent and all-encompassing force that shapes the universe and governs the human experience. Believers find solace, guidance, and purpose in their relationship with this divine entity, which may take the form of a single, all-powerful God, a pantheon of deities, or a more abstract and non-personified spiritual presence.

The diversity of religious beliefs is striking, with thousands of distinct traditions practiced worldwide. These encompass major world religions such as Christianity, Islam, Hinduism, Buddhism, Judaism, and Sikhism, as well as countless indigenous, folk, and new religious movements. Each tradition offers its unique interpretation of the divine, creation myths, cosmologies, moral codes, and rituals that guide the lives of its adherents.

Central to religious practices are rituals, ceremonies, and observances that serve as tangible expressions of faith and devotion. These rituals often vary widely between religious traditions, but they commonly serve as a means of establishing a connection with the divine, seeking spiritual insight, and fostering a sense of community. Rituals may include prayer, meditation, worship, pilgrimage, sacrifices, fasting, and rites of passage marking significant life events such as birth, marriage, and death.

In addition to rituals, religious practices often encompass ethical and moral guidelines that inform the conduct of believers. Moral principles guide individuals in making ethical choices and living virtuous lives in accordance with the teachings of their faith. These principles may address issues such as compassion, justice, honesty, kindness, and the treatment of others. The ethical framework provided by religion serves as a moral compass, shaping behavior and fostering a sense of accountability to the divine and one's fellow human beings.

The role of religious leaders and institutions is crucial in many religious traditions. Religious leaders, such as priests, pastors, imams, monks, and shamans, serve as intermediaries between the divine and the faithful. They provide spiritual guidance, officiate ceremonies, and offer interpretations of religious texts. Religious institutions, including churches, mosques, temples, synagogues, and monastic communities, serve as centers of worship, education, and community support. These institutions play a vital role in preserving religious traditions and providing a sense of belonging for believers.

Religious texts and scriptures are foundational to many religious traditions. These sacred writings contain the teachings, stories, and moral guidelines that guide the faith and practice of believers. Examples include the Bible in Christianity, the Quran in Islam, the Bhagavad Gita in Hinduism, the Tripitaka in Buddhism, and the Torah in Judaism. The interpretation and study of religious texts often play a central role in religious education and scholarship, fostering a deeper understanding of the tradition's beliefs and practices.

The impact of religious beliefs and practices on individuals and societies is profound and far-reaching. At the individual level, religion often provides a source of comfort, meaning, and purpose in life. Believers turn to their faith for guidance in times of joy, sorrow, and uncertainty. Religious practices offer a sense of structure and routine, creating opportunities for reflection, meditation, and the cultivation of inner peace.

Religion also plays a vital role in shaping moral values and ethical behavior. The moral principles and teachings of religious traditions influence the decisions and actions of individuals, serving as a framework for addressing ethical dilemmas and promoting social justice. Many religious traditions emphasize compassion, empathy, and the importance of helping those in need, fostering a sense of responsibility to one's community and the broader world.

Furthermore, religious communities often serve as sources of social cohesion and support. They provide a sense of belonging, camaraderie, and shared purpose for their members. Religious institutions are frequently involved in charitable activities, humanitarian efforts, and social outreach, contributing to the welfare of society as a whole.

However, religion's impact is not solely positive, as history has shown instances of religious conflicts, intolerance, and persecution. Differences in religious beliefs and practices have at times led to tensions and conflicts between religious groups. These conflicts underscore the importance of promoting interfaith dialogue, religious tolerance, and respect for diverse beliefs and practices.

In contemporary society, religious pluralism and diversity are increasingly prevalent. Individuals have the freedom to choose their religious beliefs and practices, leading to a rich tapestry of faith traditions coexisting in the same communities. Interfaith dialogue and cooperation have become essential in fostering understanding, respect, and peaceful coexistence among people of different faiths.

In summary, religious beliefs and practices are multifaceted, diverse, and deeply ingrained in human culture and history. They encompass a wide range of perspectives on the divine, ethics, rituals, and community. Religion provides individuals with meaning, guidance, and a sense of belonging while shaping moral values and influencing ethical behavior. The impact of religious beliefs extends to societies, where religious institutions and communities play roles in promoting social cohesion, charitable work, and ethical engagement. In an increasingly pluralistic world, the appreciation of religious diversity and the promotion of interfaith dialogue remain essential for fostering understanding, tolerance, and peaceful coexistence.

Arts, crafts, and ceremonies of the Cherokee people offer a rich and multifaceted glimpse into the culture and heritage of this Indigenous nation. The Cherokee, historically located in the southeastern United States, have a long-standing tradition of artistic expression, skilled craftsmanship, and ceremonial practices that have been passed down through generations.

Art and craftsmanship among the Cherokee encompass a wide range of forms and media, reflecting the creativity and ingenuity of the people. One of the most notable art forms is pottery, which has been crafted by Cherokee artisans for centuries. Cherokee pottery is known for its distinctive designs, often featuring intricate geometric patterns and stylized animal motifs. These designs are created using various techniques, including incising, stamping, and carving, and the pottery is traditionally fired in an open flame or pit.

Basketry is another celebrated craft among the Cherokee. Basket weaving has a long history in Cherokee culture and is considered both a practical and artistic endeavor. Cherokee baskets are renowned for their intricate patterns and natural dyes derived from materials like walnut hulls, bloodroot, and blackberries. These baskets serve a variety of purposes, from carrying and storing goods to being used in ceremonial contexts.

Textile arts are also integral to Cherokee culture. Cherokee women have a tradition of weaving river cane and other materials into textiles, producing items such as mats, belts, and sashes. These textiles often incorporate meaningful designs and colors, reflecting the spiritual and cultural significance of these creations.

Beadwork is another expressive art form within Cherokee culture. Beadwork is used to embellish clothing, accessories, and ceremonial regalia. Traditional Cherokee beadwork often features intricate geometric patterns and vibrant colors, with each bead representing a unique symbol or element of Cherokee cosmology.

Ceremonial regalia holds particular importance in Cherokee culture and is adorned with various artistic elements. Featherwork, for instance, is a notable feature of ceremonial attire. Feathers from birds like eagles and turkeys are carefully selected and arranged to create ornate headdresses and other adornments that hold spiritual significance in Cherokee ceremonies.

In addition to these artistic traditions, storytelling plays a crucial role in Cherokee culture. Oral tradition is central to passing down the history, myths, and teachings of the Cherokee people. Cherokee storytellers, often referred to as "beloved people" or "unolvtana," have preserved the narratives and wisdom of their ancestors through spoken word.

Ceremonies and rituals are deeply embedded in Cherokee life and serve as significant expressions of spirituality and community. One of the most well-known Cherokee ceremonies is the Green Corn Ceremony, also known as the New Moon Ceremony. This annual event marks the beginning of the Cherokee agricultural calendar and involves feasting, dancing, purification rituals, and the offering of thanks to the Creator for the harvest.

The Stomp Dance, also known as the Friendship Dance, is a social and ceremonial dance that has been practiced for generations. It involves rhythmic stomping of the feet, the beating of drums, and the chanting of traditional songs. The Stomp Dance is an occasion for socializing, fostering community bonds, and celebrating Cherokee identity.

The Cherokee Ball Play, known as anetsa, is a traditional game that combines elements of sport and ceremony. Historically played between Cherokee communities or with neighboring tribes, the game involves teams competing to score points by propelling a ball through a goal post. The Cherokee Ball Play has ceremonial aspects, including rituals and prayers associated with the game.

The Brush Arbor Meeting, or the Little Greenbrier, is another significant Cherokee ceremony. This gathering is held in an open-air arbor and involves communal singing, prayer, and the sharing of spiritual experiences. The Brush Arbor Meeting allows Cherokee communities to come together to seek guidance, solace, and spiritual connection.

Sacred fire is central to many Cherokee ceremonies. The lighting and tending of the sacred fire symbolize the presence of the Creator and the connection between the earthly and spiritual realms. The sacred fire is a focal point for prayer, reflection, and purification in Cherokee rituals.

The Seven Clans Dance is a ceremonial dance that pays homage to the seven traditional Cherokee clans: Wolf, Bird, Deer, Paint, Wild Potato, Blue, and Long Hair. Each clan has its own unique dance, and the Seven Clans Dance serves as a way to honor and recognize the ancestral heritage and interconnectedness of the clans.

In summary, the arts, crafts, and ceremonies of the Cherokee people are integral components of their culture and identity. These expressions of creativity, spirituality, and community have been passed down through generations, reflecting the deep-rooted traditions and values of the Cherokee nation. The rich tapestry of Cherokee artistry, craftsmanship, and ceremonial practices continues to thrive and evolve, celebrating the enduring spirit and heritage of this Indigenous nation.

Chapter 4: The Trail of Tears: Tragedy and Survival

The Trail of Tears represents one of the most tragic and devastating episodes in the history of Indigenous peoples in the United States. It was a forced removal of several Indigenous nations, including the Cherokee, Choctaw, Chickasaw, Creek, and Seminole, from their ancestral homelands to lands west of the Mississippi River. The forces behind the Trail of Tears were complex and multifaceted, involving a combination of political, economic, social, and cultural factors.

Land Hunger and Expansionism: One of the primary driving forces behind the Trail of Tears was the insatiable land hunger of European-American settlers and the U.S. government. As settlers moved westward in search of fertile land for agriculture and resources like gold, they encroached on Indigenous territories. The U.S. government, influenced by the ideology of Manifest Destiny, aimed to expand its territory from coast to coast, further intensifying pressure on Indigenous lands.

Political Policies and Legislation: The U.S. government implemented a series of policies and legislation that paved the way for the forced removal of Indigenous nations. The Indian Removal Act of 1830, signed into law by President Andrew Jackson, authorized the removal of Indigenous nations from their lands in the southeastern United States. This legislation provided the legal framework for the subsequent removals.

Economic Interests: Economic factors played a significant role in the forced removals. The lands inhabited by the Indigenous nations in the southeastern U.S. were highly desirable for agriculture, particularly the cultivation of cotton, which was a lucrative crop in the 19th century. The economic interests of planters and land speculators drove the push for Indigenous removal.

Conflict and Treaty Negotiations: Many Indigenous nations had established treaties with the U.S. government, but these treaties were often broken or manipulated to favor American expansion. Conflicts and tensions between Indigenous nations and settlers escalated, leading to negotiations for new treaties that were often coercive and unfair.

Racism and Prejudice: Deep-seated racism and prejudice against Indigenous peoples played a role in the forced removals. Many Americans viewed Indigenous nations as inferior and believed that their removal was necessary for the expansion and prosperity of the United States.

Militarization and Coercion: In some cases, the U.S. government used military force and coercion to enforce the removals. The removal of the Cherokee Nation, for example, involved the use of federal troops to round up and forcibly relocate Cherokee people.

Erosion of Indigenous Sovereignty: The forced removals represented a significant erosion of Indigenous sovereignty and autonomy. The U.S. government disregarded the rights and self-determination of Indigenous nations, further marginalizing their voices and agency.

Humanitarian Concerns: Despite the harsh and inhumane conditions of the removals, there were individuals and groups, including some non-Indigenous Americans, who opposed the forced removals on humanitarian grounds. They recognized the suffering and injustices inflicted upon Indigenous peoples during the removal process.

Resistance and Resilience: It is crucial to acknowledge the resistance and resilience of Indigenous nations in the face of the Trail of Tears. Many Indigenous leaders and communities resisted removal, both through diplomatic means and through acts of defiance and resistance.

Long-Term Impact: The Trail of Tears had profound and lasting impacts on Indigenous nations, including loss of land, cultural disruption, and trauma. It is an event that continues to shape the experiences and identity of Indigenous peoples in the United States.

In summary, the forces behind the Trail of Tears were a complex interplay of political, economic, social, and cultural factors. The expansionist desires of settlers, political policies, economic interests, racism, and the erosion of Indigenous sovereignty all contributed to this tragic chapter in American history. The Trail of Tears serves as a stark reminder of the injustices faced by Indigenous peoples and the enduring importance of acknowledging and addressing these historical wounds.

The Devastating Journey Westward, commonly known as the Trail of Tears, stands as a harrowing testament to the suffering endured by Indigenous nations in the United States during the forced removals of the 19th century. This journey, marked by hardship, loss, and tragedy, was a result of the U.S. government's policies and actions that forcibly relocated Indigenous peoples from their ancestral homelands to lands west of the Mississippi River. The devastating journey westward was marked by several key elements:

Forced Relocations: The U.S. government, through a series of policies and legislation, compelled several Indigenous nations, including the Cherokee, Choctaw, Chickasaw, Creek, and Seminole, to leave their ancestral lands. These removals were characterized by coercion, threats, and, in some cases, military force.

Long and Arduous Journeys: The journeys westward were incredibly grueling and often spanned hundreds of miles. Indigenous nations were forced to travel on foot, often in harsh weather conditions, through unfamiliar territories. Families were torn apart, and many lacked proper clothing, food, and shelter.

Inadequate Preparations: The U.S. government made inadequate preparations for the removals. There were insufficient supplies, food, and medical care provided to those undertaking the journey. Many Indigenous people faced extreme hunger, exposure to the elements, and disease.

Loss of Life: Tragically, many Indigenous people lost their lives during the journey. Estimates of the death toll vary, but it is widely believed that thousands perished due to exposure, disease, and starvation. These losses represent a profound tragedy and a deep scar in the collective memory of Indigenous nations.

Impact on Communities: The forced removals had a devastating impact on Indigenous communities. Families were torn apart, and entire communities were uprooted from their ancestral lands. The social and cultural fabric of these nations was profoundly disrupted.

Cultural Loss: The journey westward also resulted in the loss of cultural heritage. Indigenous nations were forced to leave behind sacred sites, burial grounds, and cultural artifacts. This disruption had long-lasting consequences on the preservation of Indigenous traditions and languages.

Resilience and Survival: Despite the immense suffering, many Indigenous people demonstrated incredible resilience and survival skills during the journey. They supported one another, shared what resources they had, and found ways to maintain their cultural practices and identities.

Mixed Motivations: It is important to note that not all Indigenous people complied with the forced removals willingly. Some resisted removal through legal means, while others engaged in acts of defiance and resistance.

Impact on Future Generations: The legacy of the Trail of Tears continues to impact Indigenous nations and their descendants today. It is a painful and traumatic chapter in their history that has left enduring wounds and challenges.

Historical Acknowledgment: In recent years, there has been a growing recognition of the historical injustices of the Trail of Tears. Efforts to acknowledge and memorialize this history have included the establishment of historical sites, educational programs, and official apologies from the U.S. government.

In summary, the Devastating Journey Westward, or the Trail of Tears, represents a dark chapter in American history characterized by the forced removal of Indigenous nations from their ancestral lands. The journey was marked by suffering, loss, and tragedy, with enduring impacts on Indigenous communities and their descendants. It serves as a poignant reminder of the need to acknowledge and confront the historical injustices faced by Indigenous peoples and to work towards reconciliation and healing.

Resilience and rebuilding amidst adversity are central themes in the history of Indigenous nations, particularly in the face of colonization, forced removals, and cultural disruption. Throughout history, Indigenous communities in various parts of the world have demonstrated remarkable resilience and a profound ability to adapt and rebuild in the wake of immense challenges.

One of the most striking examples of resilience is the experience of Indigenous nations in the Americas, including the Cherokee, Choctaw, Chickasaw, Creek, and Seminole, who endured the devastating forced removals collectively known as the Trail of Tears in the 19th century. These Indigenous nations faced a myriad of challenges, including the loss of their ancestral lands, the disruption of their communities, and the trauma of the journey westward.

Despite the immense adversity they faced, these nations exhibited incredible strength and resilience in the aftermath of the Trail of Tears. They rebuilt their communities in new territories and worked diligently to preserve their cultural heritage and identity.

Resilience in this context can be seen in various aspects:

Cultural Preservation: Indigenous nations took deliberate steps to preserve their cultural traditions and languages. They recognized the importance of passing down their cultural heritage to future generations. Language revitalization efforts, storytelling, traditional ceremonies, and the preservation of art and crafts played significant roles in this process.

Community Bonds: Despite the fragmentation caused by removal, Indigenous communities worked to rebuild their social fabric. Families and communities came together to provide support and maintain their interconnectedness. Traditional social structures were adapted to the new circumstances.

Sovereignty and Governance: Indigenous nations established new governments and governance structures in their new territories. They adapted their systems of leadership to address the challenges they faced and to assert their sovereignty in the face of external pressures.

Economic Resilience: Indigenous nations developed new economic strategies in their new environments. They engaged in agriculture, trade, and other economic activities to sustain their communities. This economic resilience allowed them to gradually rebuild their livelihoods.

Educational Initiatives: Indigenous nations recognized the importance of education in preserving their identity and self-determination. They established schools and educational programs that incorporated Indigenous languages and cultural teachings, ensuring that their youth had access to their heritage.

Diplomacy and Advocacy: Indigenous nations engaged in diplomatic efforts to protect their rights and advocate for their interests. They sought recognition of their treaties and land rights, often facing resistance and discrimination from the U.S. government.

Cultural Expression: The arts, including pottery, basketry, beadwork, and storytelling, continued to be essential means of cultural expression and resilience. These artistic traditions served as outlets for preserving cultural narratives and creating a sense of continuity.

Intertribal Alliances: Indigenous nations often formed alliances and coalitions with one another, recognizing the strength in unity. These alliances allowed them to advocate for their common interests and share strategies for survival and rebuilding.

The experiences of Indigenous nations in the Americas are just one example of resilience and rebuilding amidst adversity. Indigenous peoples in other parts of the world, such as the Maori in New Zealand, the Aboriginal peoples in Australia, and various Indigenous communities in Africa and Asia, have similarly demonstrated resilience in the face of colonization, displacement, and cultural suppression.

In contemporary times, the resilience of Indigenous communities continues to be evident. Efforts to revitalize languages, promote cultural practices, assert sovereignty, and address social and economic challenges are ongoing. Indigenous leaders and advocates work tirelessly to ensure that the legacy of resilience endures and that future generations can thrive while maintaining their cultural identities.

The resilience of Indigenous nations serves as a testament to the strength of human spirit and the enduring connection between people, their cultures, and their homelands. It is a reminder that, even in the face of profound adversity and historical injustices, communities can rebuild, preserve their heritage, and continue to thrive while facing the challenges of the modern world.

Chapter 5: Reconstruction and the Post-Civil War Era

Rebuilding after the Civil War, also known as the Reconstruction era, marked a critical period in American history characterized by significant challenges and transformative efforts to reunify the nation. In the aftermath of the devastating conflict between the Union and the Confederacy, the United States faced the monumental task of rebuilding a fractured society, reconstructing the South, and addressing issues related to civil rights, racial equality, and the integration of formerly enslaved individuals into American society.

The end of the Civil War in 1865 brought about a new chapter in American history, but it also left a deeply divided nation grappling with the physical, economic, and social devastation wrought by the conflict. The Reconstruction era, which lasted from approximately 1865 to 1877, was a complex and tumultuous period characterized by a range of efforts to heal the wounds of war and rebuild the nation.

One of the most significant aspects of the Reconstruction era was the effort to rebuild the South, which had suffered extensive damage during the war. Cities and towns lay in ruins, infrastructure was in disrepair, and the economy was in shambles. The task of reconstruction involved not only physical rebuilding but also the establishment of new governments and systems to replace the old Confederate order.

The federal government, under President Abraham Lincoln and later under President Andrew Johnson, initiated a series of policies to reintegrate the Southern states into the Union. These policies included presidential pardons for former Confederates, the readmission of Southern states to the Union, and the creation of provisional governments.

However, the Reconstruction era also witnessed the passage of the Thirteenth Amendment to the U.S. Constitution, which abolished slavery throughout the nation. This landmark legislation represented a monumental step towards addressing the fundamental issue of freedom and civil rights for formerly enslaved African Americans.

The period also saw the enactment of the Fourteenth Amendment, which granted citizenship and equal protection under the law to all persons born or naturalized in the United States. This amendment sought to provide legal safeguards against discrimination and to establish a foundation for civil rights.

The Reconstruction era was further shaped by the passage of the Fifteenth Amendment, which prohibited the denial of the right to vote on the basis of race, color, or previous condition of servitude. This constitutional amendment aimed to ensure the political inclusion and representation of African American citizens.

Despite these progressive constitutional amendments and federal efforts to rebuild the South, the Reconstruction era faced significant challenges and setbacks. Opposition to these changes was widespread in the South, leading to the emergence of white supremacist organizations such as the Ku Klux Klan. These groups engaged in violence and intimidation tactics aimed at suppressing the political and civil rights of African Americans.

The Reconstruction era also witnessed the rise of a political faction known as the Redeemers, who sought to overthrow the Republican governments established during Reconstruction and restore white control in the South. They used various means, including voter suppression, to regain power.

By the late 1870s, the federal government's commitment to Reconstruction waned, and Northern public sentiment shifted. This shift resulted in the withdrawal of federal troops from the South, effectively ending the era of Reconstruction. The Reconstruction era's official end came with the Compromise of 1877, which resolved the disputed presidential election of 1876 and led to the removal of federal troops from the South in exchange for the election of Rutherford B. Hayes as President.

The end of Reconstruction had significant consequences for the South. The withdrawal of federal oversight allowed for the implementation of Jim Crow laws, segregation, and the disenfranchisement of African American voters. The gains made during the Reconstruction era in terms of civil rights and political representation were eroded, leading to decades of racial discrimination and inequality in the South.

However, it is essential to recognize that the Reconstruction era was not without achievements. It laid the foundation for future civil rights efforts and established the legal framework for addressing issues related to equality and citizenship. The Thirteenth, Fourteenth, and Fifteenth Amendments remain cornerstones of civil rights legislation and continue to shape debates on civil liberties and racial equality in the United States.

Furthermore, the Reconstruction era left a legacy of resilience and determination. African Americans who had been enslaved persevered in the face of immense adversity, working to establish communities, churches, and educational institutions. They played active roles in politics, often at great personal risk, and contributed to the ongoing struggle for civil rights.

In summary, the period of Reconstruction after the Civil War was a complex and transformative era in American history. It involved efforts to rebuild the South physically, politically, and economically, as well as to address fundamental issues of civil rights and racial equality. While the era faced significant challenges and ultimately ended with a withdrawal of federal support, it left a lasting legacy of constitutional amendments and a commitment to civil rights that would shape the nation's future struggles for justice and equality.

The Dawes Act, officially known as the General Allotment Act of 1887, stands as a pivotal piece of legislation in the history of

Indigenous land ownership and the United States' policy towards Indigenous nations. This act, signed into law by President Grover Cleveland, sought to address issues related to land ownership, assimilation, and the division of Indigenous lands into individual parcels, or allotments. The Dawes Act had profound and lasting implications for Indigenous communities and their relationship with their ancestral lands.

At the heart of the Dawes Act was the concept of land allotment, which aimed to break up the communal landholding system of many Indigenous nations and replace it with private ownership by individual tribal members. Under the act, Indigenous lands were to be surveyed and divided into individual allotments, typically ranging from 40 to 160 acres in size. These allotments were to be distributed to Indigenous households, with the goal of promoting agricultural practices, sedentary lifestyles, and assimilation into mainstream American society.

The proponents of the Dawes Act argued that the communal landholding system of many Indigenous nations was inefficient and hindered agricultural development. They believed that by converting Indigenous people into individual landowners, they would encourage them to adopt European-American farming practices, become self-sufficient, and assimilate into American society.

However, the implementation of the Dawes Act had far-reaching and detrimental consequences for Indigenous communities. It resulted in the loss of vast tracts of Indigenous lands. As lands were allotted to individual tribal members, any surplus land was declared "surplus" and often opened up for non-Indigenous settlement through mechanisms like the Homestead Act. This process led to the dispossession of Indigenous peoples from their traditional territories and the fragmentation of Indigenous lands.

Moreover, the land allotted to Indigenous individuals often proved inadequate for sustainable agriculture. Many allotments were situated on less fertile or arid lands, making successful farming challenging. Additionally, the lack of access to essential resources and support systems, such as credit, agricultural extension services, and markets, further hindered Indigenous landowners' success in agriculture.

The Dawes Act also had significant cultural and social implications. It disrupted the traditional communal way of life of many Indigenous nations, where land was held collectively and used for the benefit of the entire community. The concept of private land ownership was foreign to many Indigenous cultures, and the division of lands caused internal strife and conflicts within tribal communities.

Furthermore, the Dawes Act did not address the root causes of Indigenous poverty and marginalization. Instead of addressing the systemic issues of discrimination, lack of access to education, and economic opportunities, it placed the burden of assimilation on Indigenous individuals by tying their economic well-being to land ownership.

The Dawes Act also aimed to assimilate Indigenous people into American society by encouraging the abandonment of Indigenous languages, cultures, and practices. Indigenous children were often sent to boarding schools, where they were forced to adopt European-American customs and abandon their Indigenous identities. This policy of cultural assimilation had devastating consequences on Indigenous cultures and languages, many of which are endangered or extinct today.

Despite its negative impacts, the Dawes Act did not achieve its intended goals of promoting agricultural development and assimilation. Instead, it exacerbated the dispossession of Indigenous lands, poverty, and cultural loss. Indigenous resistance to the act was strong, and many tribal leaders and communities fought against the forced division of their lands.

In the decades following the passage of the Dawes Act, there was a growing recognition of its failures and injustices. Efforts to reverse some of its provisions and restore tribal lands gained momentum. The Indian Reorganization Act of 1934, also known as the Wheeler-Howard Act, allowed tribes to reorganize and regain control over their lands and governments.

In recent years, there has been a greater emphasis on Indigenous self-determination and the restoration of tribal sovereignty. Land restoration efforts have sought to return lands to Indigenous control and address the historical injustices of land dispossession.

In summary, the Dawes Act and the policy of land allotment had far-reaching and detrimental consequences for Indigenous communities in the United States. It led to the loss of Indigenous lands, disrupted traditional ways of life, and imposed assimilationist policies on Indigenous individuals and communities. Despite the challenges it created, Indigenous resilience and the ongoing struggle for self-determination have played a crucial role in the efforts to address the historical injustices of the Dawes Act and work towards a more just and equitable future for Indigenous peoples.

Challenges and adaptations in the late 19th century marked a transformative period in American history, characterized by a multitude of social, economic, and technological changes that reshaped the nation. As the United States moved beyond the Civil War and Reconstruction, it faced a wide range of challenges and opportunities that required adaptation and innovation.

One of the significant challenges of the late 19th century was the process of Reconstruction following the Civil War. The nation grappled with the task of rebuilding the South and addressing the economic and social consequences of the conflict. Reconstruction policies aimed to integrate formerly enslaved individuals into American society, protect their civil rights, and establish a new political order in the South. However, these efforts faced opposition and resistance from white supremacists, leading to the eventual withdrawal of federal troops from the region.

Economic challenges were also prevalent during this period. The United States experienced significant shifts in its economy, moving from an agrarian society to an industrial powerhouse. The transition from agrarianism to industrialization posed challenges for workers and led to labor disputes, including strikes and protests. Workers sought better wages, working conditions, and labor rights, leading to the formation of labor unions as a means of collective bargaining.

Technological advancements played a pivotal role in shaping the late 19th-century landscape. The era saw innovations such as the telegraph, the transcontinental railroad, and the telephone. These technological marvels transformed communication, transportation, and connectivity across the nation. The completion of the transcontinental railroad in 1869, connecting the East and West coasts, opened up new opportunities for trade, commerce, and westward expansion.

Urbanization was another key feature of the late 19th century, as people flocked to cities in search of employment and opportunities. This rapid urbanization presented both challenges and adaptations. Cities faced issues of overcrowding, inadequate infrastructure, and unsanitary living conditions. However, they also became hubs of cultural and economic activity, with the rise of industries, businesses, and cultural institutions.

The late 19th century also witnessed significant immigration to the United States, with millions of people arriving from Europe, Asia, and other parts of the world. This wave of immigration brought diversity to the nation and contributed to the development of a multicultural society. However, it also led to tensions and challenges related to assimilation, nativism, and labor competition.

The evolving role of women in society was another central theme of the late 19th century. Women's suffrage movements gained momentum as women advocated for their right to vote and greater participation in civic life. The Seneca Falls Convention in 1848 marked the beginning of the organized women's suffrage movement, and it was followed by decades of activism and advocacy.

Social challenges related to racial inequality persisted in the late 19th century, despite the abolition of slavery. African Americans faced discrimination, segregation, and violence. The era witnessed the rise of Jim Crow laws in the South, which enforced racial segregation in public facilities and institutions. African American leaders and activists like Booker T. Washington and W.E.B. Du Bois emerged to address these challenges and advocate for civil rights.

Environmental challenges also emerged as the nation expanded westward. The settlement of the western frontier brought about issues related to land use, conservation, and resource management. Concerns about the depletion of natural resources, such as forests and wildlife, led to the early conservation movement and the establishment of national parks and forests.

In response to these challenges, the late 19th century witnessed various adaptations and reforms. Social and political movements, including the Progressive Era, aimed to address issues of social justice, political corruption, and economic inequality. Progressive leaders like Theodore Roosevelt and Woodrow Wilson advocated for regulatory reforms, antitrust laws, and social welfare programs.

The late 19th century also saw the emergence of new cultural movements and literary trends. The Gilded Age, characterized by wealth and excess, inspired critical commentary and satire in literature. Authors like Mark Twain and Henry James explored the complexities of American society and culture during this era.

In the realm of education, there was a growing emphasis on public schooling and the expansion of higher education institutions. Land-grant universities were established to promote agricultural and technical education, contributing to the development of the nation's workforce and infrastructure.

Technological innovations continued to shape the late 19th century, with the proliferation of electricity, the development of the phonograph, and advancements in transportation. These innovations improved the quality of life, entertainment, and communication for many Americans.

In summary, the late 19th century in the United States was a period of profound challenges and adaptations. It was marked by the aftermath of the Civil War, economic and technological transformations, urbanization, immigration, and social and political movements. Despite the numerous challenges, the era also saw significant progress in areas such as women's suffrage, civil rights, labor rights, and environmental conservation. The late 19th century laid the groundwork for the complex and dynamic society that would continue to evolve in the 20th century.

Chapter 6: The Cherokee Nation Today: Governance and Identity

Modern Cherokee government structures reflect the evolution of governance within the Cherokee Nation, a sovereign Indigenous nation with a rich history in what is now the United States. Today, the Cherokee Nation has a government that is recognized as a tribal government under U.S. law. The modern Cherokee government is characterized by its commitment to self-determination, cultural preservation, and providing services to its citizens.

Principal Chief and Deputy Principal Chief: At the top of the Cherokee Nation's government is the Principal Chief, who serves as the head of the executive branch. The Principal Chief is elected by Cherokee citizens and is responsible for the administration of tribal affairs. The Deputy Principal Chief assists the Principal Chief in carrying out these duties.

Cherokee Nation Council: The legislative branch of the Cherokee Nation is the Cherokee Nation Council, which is composed of elected representatives from 15 districts. These representatives, known as councilors, are responsible for passing laws and resolutions that govern the Cherokee Nation. The council plays a vital role in shaping tribal policies and ensuring the well-being of Cherokee citizens.

Judicial Branch: The Cherokee Nation has a judicial branch that includes a Supreme Court and various lower courts. The Supreme Court is the highest court in the Cherokee Nation and has the authority to interpret tribal laws and resolve disputes. The judicial branch plays a crucial role in upholding the rule of law and ensuring justice within the Cherokee Nation.

Tribal Citizenship: Citizenship in the Cherokee Nation is a significant aspect of modern Cherokee governance. Cherokee citizens have the right to vote in tribal elections, access tribal services, and participate in cultural and community activities. The Cherokee Nation has specific criteria for tribal citizenship, which may include documentation of Cherokee ancestry.

Services and Programs: The Cherokee Nation operates a wide range of programs and services to meet the needs of its citizens. These services encompass healthcare, education, housing, employment assistance, and cultural preservation. The Cherokee Nation is committed to improving the quality of life for its citizens and ensuring their access to essential resources.

Cultural Preservation: Cultural preservation is a central focus of the modern Cherokee government. The Cherokee Nation works to protect and promote Cherokee language, arts, crafts, and traditions. Initiatives include language immersion programs, cultural events, and the operation of cultural centers and museums.

Economic Development: Economic development is a priority for the Cherokee Nation. The nation has diversified its economy through various ventures, including gaming, agriculture, manufacturing, and retail. These efforts generate revenue that supports tribal programs and services and promotes economic self-sufficiency.

Education: The Cherokee Nation places a strong emphasis on education. It operates tribal schools, scholarships, and educational programs that provide educational opportunities for Cherokee students. These initiatives aim to empower Cherokee youth with knowledge and skills for the future.

Healthcare: Healthcare is a critical component of the Cherokee Nation's government services. The tribe operates a comprehensive healthcare system that includes hospitals, clinics, and wellness programs. Access to quality healthcare is essential for the well-being of Cherokee citizens.

Partnerships: The Cherokee Nation collaborates with federal, state, and local governments to address common issues and pursue shared goals. These partnerships help leverage resources and support initiatives that benefit both Cherokee citizens and the broader community.

Tribal Sovereignty: Tribal sovereignty is a foundational principle of modern Cherokee government. The Cherokee Nation asserts its right to self-governance and self-determination, including the ability to make decisions about its internal affairs and the welfare of its citizens.

In summary, modern Cherokee government structures are built upon the principles of self-determination, cultural preservation, and the provision of essential services to Cherokee citizens. These structures include executive, legislative, and judicial branches, as well as a focus on tribal citizenship, cultural preservation, economic development, education, and healthcare. The Cherokee Nation's commitment to sovereignty and collaboration with external partners underscores its dedication to improving the lives of its citizens and maintaining its unique cultural heritage.

Cultural identity and revival among Indigenous nations, including the Cherokee Nation, played a vital role in the 20th century. This period was marked by significant efforts to preserve and revitalize traditional cultural practices, languages, and ways of life that had been under threat due to centuries of colonization and assimilation policies. For the Cherokee Nation and many other Indigenous communities, cultural identity became a cornerstone of resilience and self-determination.

Language Revitalization: One of the most critical aspects of cultural revival in the 20th century was the effort to preserve and revitalize Indigenous languages. Cherokee is a prominent example, with the Cherokee Nation implementing language immersion programs, language classes, and language preservation initiatives. These efforts sought to ensure that future generations could speak, read, and write in their ancestral language.

Cultural Centers and Museums: The establishment of cultural centers and museums became instrumental in preserving and showcasing Indigenous cultures. These institutions, often run by Indigenous communities, provided spaces to exhibit traditional art, crafts, clothing, and historical artifacts. They also served as venues for cultural events, workshops, and educational programs.

Traditional Arts and Crafts: The 20th century saw a resurgence in traditional Indigenous arts and crafts, including basketry, pottery, beadwork, and textiles. Indigenous artists and artisans often blended traditional techniques with contemporary styles, creating a vibrant market for Indigenous art and generating income for communities.

Cultural Festivals and Powwows: Cultural festivals and powwows became important gatherings where Indigenous people could celebrate their heritage through dance, music, storytelling, and traditional foods. These events fostered a sense of community and pride in cultural identity.

Oral History and Storytelling: Elders and knowledge keepers played a crucial role in passing down traditional knowledge, oral history, and stories to younger generations. Storytelling became a means of preserving cultural narratives and values.

Tribal Government Support: Tribal governments, including the Cherokee Nation, played an active role in supporting cultural revival efforts. They allocated resources, established cultural preservation departments, and promoted cultural initiatives.

Education Initiatives: Indigenous education initiatives aimed to integrate cultural teachings and Indigenous history into mainstream education systems. These efforts ensured that Indigenous youth had access to their heritage and cultural knowledge.

Intertribal Collaboration: Indigenous communities often collaborated with one another to share cultural practices and traditions. Intertribal gatherings and partnerships allowed for the exchange of knowledge and cultural revival strategies.

Cultural Preservation Legislation: In the United States, legislation such as the Native American Graves Protection and Repatriation Act (NAGPRA) and the American Indian Religious Freedom Act (AIRFA) were enacted to protect Indigenous cultural heritage and sacred sites. These laws provided legal mechanisms for the repatriation of ancestral remains and the practice of traditional religious ceremonies.

Media and Publications: The 20th century also witnessed the use of media, including books, films, and radio, to document and promote Indigenous cultures. Indigenous authors, filmmakers, and journalists played a pivotal role in sharing their stories and perspectives with a broader audience.

Political Activism: Political activism often went hand in hand with cultural revival. Indigenous leaders and advocates used political platforms to raise awareness about cultural issues, advocate for policy changes, and secure recognition and rights for Indigenous communities.

Cultural Resilience: Above all, cultural revival in the 20th century demonstrated the resilience of Indigenous communities. Despite centuries of adversity and efforts to suppress their cultures, Indigenous people demonstrated their commitment to preserving their unique identities and passing them on to future generations.

In summary, cultural identity and revival were central themes in the 20th century for Indigenous nations, including the Cherokee Nation. These efforts encompassed language revitalization, the establishment of cultural institutions, the promotion of traditional arts and crafts, cultural festivals, education initiatives, and political advocacy. The resilience and determination of Indigenous communities in preserving their cultural identities served as a testament to the enduring strength of Indigenous cultures and their commitment to self-determination.

Economic development and tribal sovereignty are intricately

linked concepts that have played a central role in the modern history of Indigenous nations, including the Cherokee Nation. Throughout the 20th and 21st centuries, Indigenous communities have pursued economic development initiatives as a means to assert their sovereignty, improve the well-being of their citizens, and achieve self-determination.

The concept of tribal sovereignty is rooted in the inherent right of Indigenous nations to self-governance and self-determination. It recognizes that Indigenous nations possess the authority to make decisions about their internal affairs, cultural preservation, and the welfare of their citizens. Tribal sovereignty is a fundamental aspect of the government-to-government relationship between Indigenous nations and the federal government of the United States.

One of the key ways in which tribal sovereignty has been exercised is through economic development. Economic self-sufficiency is seen as a critical component of sovereignty, as it reduces dependence on external entities and allows Indigenous nations to make decisions that align with their cultural values and long-term goals. Economic development initiatives have taken various forms within the Cherokee Nation and other Indigenous communities:

Gaming Enterprises: The gaming industry, including the operation of casinos and resorts, has been a significant driver of economic development for many Indigenous nations. The Indian Gaming Regulatory Act of 1988 (IGRA) provided a framework for tribes to engage in gaming activities on their lands. The Cherokee Nation and other tribes have leveraged gaming revenues to fund essential services, such as healthcare, education, and infrastructure, and to promote economic diversification.

Agriculture and Agribusiness: Agriculture and agribusiness have been areas of economic focus for the Cherokee Nation. Efforts to revitalize traditional farming practices, such as the cultivation of Cherokee heirloom crops, have supported local food production and agricultural sustainability. Additionally, the Cherokee Nation has ventured into agribusiness enterprises, including meat processing and distribution.

Manufacturing and Retail: Economic diversification strategies have led to the establishment of manufacturing facilities and retail businesses. These enterprises not only generate revenue but also create job opportunities for tribal citizens. The Cherokee Nation's commitment to economic growth has extended to industries like aerospace, healthcare, and technology.

Tourism and Cultural Heritage: Cultural tourism initiatives have become a means of economic development and cultural preservation. The Cherokee Nation operates cultural centers, museums, and historical sites that showcase Cherokee history, arts, and traditions. Tourism also includes events, such as cultural festivals and powwows, which promote cultural exchange and economic activity.

Tribal Enterprises and Partnerships: The Cherokee Nation has ventured into various tribal enterprises, often through partnerships and collaborations. These enterprises may include retail operations, healthcare facilities, construction companies, and more. Strategic partnerships allow the Cherokee Nation to expand its economic footprint and enhance service delivery.

Small Business Development: Supporting small businesses owned by tribal citizens has been a priority for the Cherokee Nation. Economic development programs provide resources, training, and financial assistance to aspiring entrepreneurs. These initiatives stimulate local economies and empower individuals to pursue economic self-sufficiency.

Investment in Education: Economic development initiatives often involve investments in education and workforce development. The Cherokee Nation recognizes that a skilled workforce is essential for the success of economic ventures. Scholarships, vocational training, and educational programs prepare tribal citizens for careers in various industries.

Infrastructure and Housing: Economic development goes hand in hand with infrastructure development. Investments in infrastructure, including roads, utilities, and housing, create a foundation for economic growth and improved living conditions for tribal citizens.

Cultural and Environmental Stewardship: The Cherokee Nation places a strong emphasis on cultural and environmental stewardship within its economic development efforts. Sustainable practices and the preservation of cultural and natural resources are integral to the Cherokee Nation's approach to economic growth.

In summary, economic development and tribal sovereignty are interwoven principles that have guided the Cherokee Nation and other Indigenous communities in their pursuit of self-determination and improved living conditions. Economic development initiatives have allowed Indigenous nations to exercise greater control over their destinies, reduce reliance on external entities, and promote the well-being of their citizens. As Indigenous nations continue to navigate the challenges and opportunities of the 21st century, economic development remains a vital tool for advancing tribal sovereignty and preserving cultural identities.

Chapter 7: Cultural Revival and Preservation Efforts

Language revitalization and education are fundamental components of preserving cultural heritage, fostering community identity, and ensuring the continuity of Indigenous languages within the Cherokee Nation and other Indigenous communities across the United States. These efforts have been integral to maintaining the unique linguistic diversity that contributes to the rich tapestry of Indigenous cultures.

Within the Cherokee Nation, the revitalization of the Cherokee language, also known as Tsalagi, has been a paramount undertaking. This language is a pivotal aspect of Cherokee identity, encapsulating the tribe's deep-rooted connection to their ancestral lands, traditions, and history. The Cherokee language, like many Indigenous languages, faced the threat of extinction due to historical factors such as colonization, forced assimilation, and the erosion of traditional language transmission within communities.

Language revitalization initiatives within the Cherokee Nation and similar efforts in other Indigenous communities have involved a multifaceted approach that encompasses various educational, cultural, and community-based strategies. These initiatives are aimed at revitalizing Indigenous languages and ensuring their transmission to future generations.

One key aspect of language revitalization is the establishment of language immersion programs. These programs immerse students in the language from an early age, creating a conducive environment for language acquisition. In the Cherokee Nation, immersion schools and language programs have been established to promote fluency and encourage children to become proficient speakers of Cherokee.

Furthermore, adult language classes and community language learning opportunities are available to people of all ages. These courses are designed to engage both beginners and those with varying degrees of proficiency, fostering a sense of inclusivity and encouraging learners to take pride in their language heritage.

Cultural institutions, such as cultural centers and museums, also play a pivotal role in language revitalization. These institutions serve as repositories of linguistic and cultural knowledge, offering resources and materials to support language learners and educators. They provide a physical space where cultural traditions and language can be celebrated and preserved.

Elders and fluent speakers within Indigenous communities have been instrumental in passing down linguistic knowledge through oral tradition. Their role as language keepers and mentors is indispensable in language revitalization efforts. Elders and fluent speakers often serve as teachers, sharing their knowledge, stories, and wisdom with younger generations.

Additionally, Indigenous communities have worked to develop language curricula, textbooks, and educational resources tailored to their specific languages. These materials are used in schools, immersion programs, and community settings, enabling structured language instruction while accommodating different learning styles.

Language revitalization is closely intertwined with education, and Indigenous educational institutions have played a crucial role in this endeavor. Tribal schools, colleges, and universities have integrated language courses into their curricula, ensuring that language revitalization is embedded in the broader educational experience. Moreover, scholarships and grants have been made available to support students pursuing language studies and related fields.

Language revitalization efforts extend beyond formal educational settings. Language nests, where young children and caregivers interact in the Indigenous language, are a common approach. These settings provide opportunities for children to acquire language skills organically while fostering bonds between generations.

Furthermore, cultural events and gatherings, such as powwows and language immersion camps, offer immersive language experiences. These events create an environment where participants can practice their language skills, connect with other speakers, and celebrate their cultural heritage.

The use of technology has also played a role in language revitalization. Indigenous communities have developed language apps, online courses, and multimedia resources that make language learning accessible to a broader audience. These digital tools have proven valuable in reaching individuals who may not have access to traditional classroom settings.

Language revitalization is more than just learning vocabulary and grammar; it is about reconnecting with cultural identity and heritage. Indigenous languages encapsulate unique worldviews, histories, and relationships with the land and environment. Revitalizing these languages is essential for preserving the full depth and richness of Indigenous cultures.

Moreover, language revitalization contributes to the overall well-being and resilience of Indigenous communities. Speaking one's Indigenous language is an act of cultural sovereignty and resistance against the historical forces that sought to eradicate these languages. Language is a powerful tool for self-expression, communication, and community cohesion.

In summary, language revitalization and education are indispensable components of preserving and celebrating the linguistic and cultural heritage of Indigenous communities, including the Cherokee Nation. These efforts encompass immersion programs, language classes, cultural institutions, intergenerational knowledge transfer, educational materials, and technological tools. Language revitalization is not only about linguistic proficiency but also about fostering a deep sense of cultural pride and ensuring the continued vibrancy of Indigenous cultures for generations to come.

The revival of traditional arts and crafts within Indigenous communities, including the Cherokee Nation, has been a dynamic and culturally enriching movement that spans generations. These artistic traditions hold a deep significance, as they reflect the creativity, history, and cultural identity of Indigenous peoples. The resurgence of traditional arts and crafts in the Cherokee Nation and similar Indigenous communities has been a testament to the enduring spirit of creativity and the commitment to preserving cultural heritage.

In the Cherokee Nation, traditional arts and crafts encompass a diverse array of artistic expressions, including pottery, basketry, beadwork, textile arts, and woodcarving, among others. Each of these art forms carries its own cultural significance and symbolism, often rooted in the tribe's deep connection to the natural world, ancestral traditions, and storytelling.

One of the essential aspects of the revival of traditional arts and crafts is the passing down of knowledge from one generation to the next. Elders and master artists within the Cherokee Nation have played a crucial role as mentors, imparting their expertise and cultural wisdom to younger artists. This intergenerational exchange of knowledge not only ensures the continuity of artistic traditions but also fosters a sense of community and connection to the past.

Traditional arts and crafts are deeply intertwined with cultural and spiritual practices within the Cherokee Nation. For example, pottery-making has been a tradition for centuries, with clay vessels used for both practical and ceremonial purposes. The intricate designs and motifs on Cherokee pottery often incorporate symbols representing elements of the natural world, such as animals, plants, and celestial bodies. Pottery serves as a medium through which cultural stories are told and preserved.

Basketry is another traditional art form that holds cultural significance within the Cherokee Nation. Cherokee basketry encompasses a wide range of styles and techniques, including doubleweave and river cane basketry. These baskets are not only utilitarian but also embody intricate patterns and designs passed down through generations. Basketry is a testament to the Cherokee people's relationship with the land and the natural materials found within their ancestral territories.

Beadwork is another thriving traditional art form within the Cherokee Nation. Beadwork artists create intricate designs using colorful glass beads, often depicting stories, symbols, and cultural motifs. Beadwork has evolved over time, incorporating both traditional designs and contemporary elements. Beaded regalia and accessories are worn during ceremonies, powwows, and other cultural events, symbolizing a connection to heritage and identity.

Textile arts, such as quilting and weaving, have also experienced a revival within the Cherokee Nation. Quilting, in particular, has a rich history, with Cherokee women creating quilts that tell stories, preserve cultural knowledge, and reflect their artistic abilities. These quilts serve as tangible connections to the past and as means of passing down cultural teachings.

Woodcarving is yet another traditional art form that showcases the skill and craftsmanship of Cherokee artists. Woodcarvers create intricate sculptures, masks, and other wooden objects that often feature traditional designs, animals, and cultural symbols. Woodcarving represents a form of artistic storytelling, capturing the essence of Cherokee cultural narratives.

The revival of traditional arts and crafts has not only preserved cultural heritage but also fostered economic opportunities within the Cherokee Nation. Many artists and artisans have turned their skills into livelihoods by selling their creations, participating in art markets, and showcasing their work in galleries and exhibitions. This economic aspect has allowed artists to continue their craft while supporting their families and communities.

Cultural institutions and organizations have played a vital role in supporting the revival of traditional arts and crafts. The Cherokee Nation operates cultural centers and museums that serve as hubs for artistic expression and cultural preservation. These institutions provide spaces for artists to showcase their work, offer workshops and educational programs, and promote the continuation of artistic traditions.

Collaborative efforts between artists and cultural institutions have resulted in the creation of cultural festivals and events that celebrate traditional arts and crafts. These gatherings not only provide opportunities for artists to showcase their work but also allow the broader community to engage with and appreciate Indigenous artistic traditions.

Moreover, the promotion of traditional arts and crafts has extended to the digital realm. Many artists within the Cherokee Nation and other Indigenous communities use digital platforms to share their work with a global audience. Social media, websites, and online marketplaces have allowed artists to connect with buyers and admirers of Indigenous art worldwide.

In summary, the revival of traditional arts and crafts within the Cherokee Nation and Indigenous communities at large has been a dynamic and culturally significant movement. These artistic traditions embody the creativity, heritage, and cultural identity of Indigenous peoples, reflecting a deep connection to the natural world, storytelling, and ancestral traditions. The passing down of knowledge from elders to younger generations, the economic opportunities for artists, and the support of cultural institutions have all played crucial roles in preserving and celebrating these traditions. Traditional arts and crafts continue to thrive, contributing to the cultural vibrancy and resilience of Indigenous communities.

Ceremonial practices and cultural centers are integral components of Indigenous cultures, including the Cherokee Nation. These elements play a vital role in preserving and transmitting cultural heritage, fostering community cohesion, and celebrating the spiritual and ceremonial traditions that have been passed down through generations.

Ceremonial practices within the Cherokee Nation are deeply rooted in the tribe's cultural and spiritual beliefs. These practices encompass a wide range of rituals, ceremonies, and observances that honor the natural world, ancestral spirits, and the Cherokee way of life. Ceremonies are often tied to the cycles of nature, reflecting the Cherokee people's close relationship with the environment.

One of the most well-known Cherokee ceremonies is the Green Corn Ceremony, also known as the Busk. This annual event marks the beginning of the new year and is a time of purification, renewal, and thanksgiving. Participants fast and engage in traditional dances, songs, and prayers. The Green Corn Ceremony is a significant cultural and spiritual practice that reaffirms the Cherokee people's connection to the land and their ancestors.

Another important Cherokee ceremony is the Stomp Dance, which is performed throughout the year during various gatherings and events. The Stomp Dance involves rhythmic dancing to the beat of drums, accompanied by singing and chanting. This communal dance reflects the importance of community and unity among the Cherokee people.

Sweat lodges, also known as purification lodges, are used for spiritual and physical cleansing. These small structures are heated with hot stones, and participants engage in sweat ceremonies to purify the body and spirit. Sweat lodges are often conducted before important ceremonies or events.

The Strawberry Ceremony is another Cherokee tradition that celebrates the harvest of strawberries, an important cultural and culinary symbol. During this ceremony, strawberries are shared among community members, and songs and dances are performed. The Strawberry Ceremony embodies the Cherokee people's gratitude for the gifts of the land.

In addition to these specific ceremonies, storytelling is an essential ceremonial practice within the Cherokee Nation. Elders and knowledge keepers pass down oral traditions, myths, and legends through storytelling. These narratives convey cultural teachings, moral lessons, and the Cherokee worldview.

Cultural centers within the Cherokee Nation serve as hubs for the preservation and celebration of these ceremonial practices. These centers are physical spaces that house artifacts, exhibits, and educational resources related to Cherokee culture, history, and traditions. They serve as living repositories of cultural knowledge and are open to both tribal citizens and the broader community.

Cultural centers often offer educational programs and workshops that teach traditional skills, such as basketry, pottery, and beadwork. These programs provide opportunities for community members, especially youth, to engage with their cultural heritage and learn from skilled artisans and practitioners.

Furthermore, cultural centers host cultural events and festivals that showcase ceremonial practices, traditional arts, and storytelling. These events bring the community together and provide a platform for the wider public to appreciate and learn about Cherokee culture.

Language revitalization is another critical aspect of cultural centers within the Cherokee Nation. Language classes, immersion programs, and resources are often available to help tribal citizens learn and preserve the Cherokee language, which is an integral part of ceremonial practices and cultural identity.

Traditional medicine and healing practices are also often associated with ceremonial practices within Indigenous communities. Cultural centers may offer programs that explore traditional healing methods, herbal medicine, and the role of spirituality in well-being.

Ceremonial practices and cultural centers serve as a means of cultural revitalization, strengthening the connection between past, present, and future generations. They provide spaces where tribal citizens can come together to celebrate their shared heritage, participate in sacred rituals, and pass down traditional knowledge to younger members of the community.

Moreover, ceremonial practices and cultural centers are instrumental in promoting intergenerational relationships. Elders play a central role in passing down ceremonial knowledge, ensuring that cultural practices are preserved and carried forward. The respect and reverence for elders within Cherokee culture are reflected in the transmission of ceremonial teachings.

The Cherokee Nation has recognized the significance of ceremonial practices and cultural centers in fostering cultural resilience and self-determination. These practices and institutions are not static but continue to evolve and adapt to the changing needs and aspirations of the Cherokee people. They embody the ongoing commitment to preserving, celebrating, and sharing the rich cultural tapestry of the Cherokee Nation with both tribal citizens and the broader world.

In summary, ceremonial practices and cultural centers are vital components of Indigenous cultures, including the Cherokee Nation. These practices encompass a range of rituals and observances that honor cultural traditions, spirituality, and the Cherokee way of life. Cultural centers serve as spaces for preserving, celebrating, and passing down cultural knowledge, strengthening community ties, and promoting intergenerational relationships. They play a central role in the ongoing cultural resilience and self-determination of Indigenous communities.

Chapter 8: Challenges and Hopes for the Future

The Cherokee Nation, like many Indigenous communities, faces a range of contemporary challenges that impact its people, culture, and sovereignty. These challenges reflect a complex interplay of historical legacies, government policies, and modern socioeconomic factors. Despite these challenges, the Cherokee Nation remains resilient and committed to addressing these issues for the well-being of its citizens and the preservation of its cultural heritage.

Health Disparities: Health disparities are a significant challenge within the Cherokee Nation. Factors such as limited access to healthcare services, higher rates of chronic diseases, and historical trauma contribute to health disparities among tribal citizens. The Cherokee Nation has implemented healthcare initiatives, including clinics and hospitals, to improve access to quality care and address these disparities.

Substance Abuse and Addiction: Substance abuse and addiction, particularly opioid addiction, have had a devastating impact on Indigenous communities, including the Cherokee Nation. Substance abuse contributes to social and economic challenges, including family disruption and criminal justice involvement. The tribe has launched prevention and treatment programs to combat addiction and support those in recovery.

Education Disparities: Education disparities persist in Indigenous communities, affecting academic achievement and opportunities for future success. Limited access to quality educational resources, high dropout rates, and cultural insensitivity in curriculum are challenges the Cherokee Nation seeks to address through investments in education and advocacy for culturally relevant curriculum.

Economic Development: While the Cherokee Nation has made significant strides in economic development, there is a continued need for job creation and economic diversification. Sustainable economic growth is essential to reduce poverty, improve living conditions, and provide opportunities for tribal citizens.

Land and Resource Management: The management of land and natural resources is a complex challenge, particularly as tribal nations seek to balance economic development with environmental preservation. The Cherokee Nation is engaged in efforts to responsibly manage its land and resources while preserving the environment.

Cultural Preservation: Preserving and revitalizing Cherokee culture and language remain a priority. Cultural preservation is challenged by assimilation pressures, the erosion of traditional practices, and the loss of fluent Cherokee speakers. The Cherokee Nation invests in language programs, cultural centers, and educational initiatives to address this challenge.

Sovereignty and Federal Relations: The Cherokee Nation, like other tribal nations, navigates complex federal-tribal relations. Issues related to tribal sovereignty, treaty rights, and self-governance are central to the tribe's political and legal efforts.

Environmental and Climate Challenges: Indigenous communities, including the Cherokee Nation, are increasingly facing the impacts of environmental changes and climate-related challenges. These include threats to traditional lands, natural resources, and cultural sites. The tribe is engaged in climate resilience and environmental protection efforts.

Housing and Infrastructure: Access to safe and affordable housing remains a concern within the Cherokee Nation. Many tribal citizens face housing shortages and inadequate infrastructure, including clean water and sanitation facilities. Efforts to improve housing and infrastructure are ongoing.

Criminal Justice and Public Safety: Addressing crime and ensuring public safety are critical priorities. The Cherokee Nation operates its own criminal justice system, including law enforcement, courts, and corrections, to address these issues and promote community safety.

Tribal Citizenship and Enrollment: Issues related to tribal citizenship and enrollment can be contentious and challenging. Decisions about who qualifies as a tribal citizen are central to issues of identity, access to tribal benefits, and representation within tribal government.

Digital Divide: Access to reliable high-speed internet and technology infrastructure is a concern in many Indigenous communities, including the Cherokee Nation. Bridging the digital divide is critical for education, economic development, and communication.

Cultural Appropriation and Misrepresentation: Indigenous communities often face issues of cultural appropriation and misrepresentation in mainstream media and popular culture. These challenges can perpetuate harmful stereotypes and undermine efforts to preserve and promote authentic Indigenous cultures.

Despite these challenges, the Cherokee Nation continues to assert its sovereignty and work towards self-determination. The tribe collaborates with federal and state governments, engages in legal advocacy, and implements community-driven initiatives to address these contemporary issues. Moreover, the Cherokee Nation draws upon its cultural resilience, strong sense of community, and commitment to preserving its unique heritage as it navigates these challenges and builds a brighter future for its citizens.

Environmental conservation and stewardship are critical priorities for the Cherokee Nation, as they reflect the tribe's deep connection to the land, natural resources, and cultural heritage. The Cherokee Nation, like many Indigenous communities, recognizes the importance of preserving the environment for current and future generations and is actively engaged in efforts to protect and sustain the natural world.

Protection of Ancestral Lands: The Cherokee Nation places a strong emphasis on protecting its ancestral lands from environmental degradation, encroachment, and development. These lands hold cultural and historical significance, and the tribe seeks to maintain their integrity through land management and conservation efforts.

Sustainable Resource Management: The Cherokee Nation practices sustainable resource management to ensure the long-term health of ecosystems and natural resources. This includes responsible forestry practices, wildlife management, and conservation of plant species used in traditional medicine and cultural practices.

Water Quality and Conservation: Water is a precious resource, and the tribe is committed to preserving water quality in rivers, streams, and lakes within its territory. Conservation efforts focus on reducing pollution, safeguarding aquatic habitats, and ensuring access to clean water for tribal citizens.

Climate Resilience: Indigenous communities, including the Cherokee Nation, are increasingly affected by climate change. The tribe engages in climate resilience efforts, such as adapting to changing weather patterns, addressing the impacts of extreme weather events, and promoting sustainable agricultural practices.

Cultural and Environmental Education: The Cherokee Nation recognizes the importance of educating tribal citizens and the broader community about environmental conservation and cultural connections to the land. Cultural centers and educational programs offer resources and opportunities to learn about traditional environmental knowledge and stewardship practices.

Environmental Advocacy: The tribe engages in environmental advocacy efforts at the local, state, and federal levels to protect natural resources and uphold its treaty rights. Advocacy often involves legal actions, policy initiatives, and collaboration with other organizations dedicated to environmental conservation.

Wildlife Protection: The Cherokee Nation is actively involved in wildlife protection and conservation efforts. This includes habitat restoration, wildlife monitoring, and initiatives to protect endangered or threatened species that are culturally significant.

Traditional Ecological Knowledge: Traditional ecological knowledge, passed down through generations, plays a crucial role in environmental conservation. The Cherokee Nation integrates this knowledge into its conservation practices, recognizing the value of Indigenous wisdom in maintaining ecological balance.

Environmental Cleanup: The tribe is committed to addressing environmental contamination and pollution within its territory. Cleanup efforts focus on restoring lands and waterways affected by industrial activities and pollution, ensuring a healthier environment for all.

Community-Based Conservation: Environmental conservation is a community endeavor within the Cherokee Nation. The tribe engages tribal citizens in conservation activities, such as tree planting, clean-up events, and habitat restoration, fostering a sense of responsibility and connection to the environment.

Traditional Agriculture: The Cherokee Nation promotes traditional agricultural practices that are environmentally sustainable, such as planting heirloom crops and employing organic farming methods. These practices contribute to food sovereignty and cultural preservation.

Cultural Landmarks and Sacred Sites: Preservation of cultural landmarks and sacred sites is integral to environmental conservation. The Cherokee Nation works to protect these sites from development and degradation, ensuring their continued cultural and spiritual significance.

Collaboration and Partnerships: The tribe collaborates with federal, state, and local governments, as well as non-governmental organizations, to address environmental conservation challenges. Partnerships facilitate the sharing of resources, expertise, and strategies to protect the environment.

Traditional Fire Management: Traditional fire management practices, such as controlled burns, are employed to maintain healthy ecosystems, prevent wildfires, and promote biodiversity. These practices draw upon Indigenous ecological knowledge.

Eco-Tourism and Cultural Tourism: The Cherokee Nation leverages eco-tourism and cultural tourism as opportunities to promote environmental conservation. By showcasing the natural beauty and cultural heritage of its lands, the tribe encourages responsible tourism that respects the environment.

In summary, environmental conservation and stewardship are deeply embedded in the values and practices of the Cherokee Nation. The tribe recognizes the intrinsic connection between cultural heritage and the natural world, and its efforts reflect a commitment to preserving both. Through sustainable resource management, education, advocacy, and community engagement, the Cherokee Nation actively contributes to the protection and sustainability of the environment for current and future generations.

The prospects and aspirations for future generations within the Cherokee Nation are rooted in a profound commitment to cultural preservation, self-determination, and holistic well-being. These aspirations reflect the tribe's enduring resilience and a vision of a brighter future where Cherokee culture thrives, tribal sovereignty is upheld, and the needs and aspirations of tribal citizens are met.

Cultural Continuity: At the heart of the Cherokee Nation's aspirations is the desire to ensure the continuity of Cherokee culture and traditions for future generations. Efforts to revitalize the Cherokee language, preserve traditional arts and crafts, and pass down ancestral knowledge through storytelling are central to this goal. The tribe envisions a future where Cherokee children grow up immersed in their cultural heritage, grounded in their identity, and equipped with the skills to carry it forward.

Language Revival: The Cherokee language, Tsalagi, is a cornerstone of Cherokee identity. The tribe aspires to see the Cherokee language spoken fluently by younger generations, ensuring its survival as a living, vibrant tongue. Language immersion programs, educational resources, and community support contribute to this vision of linguistic revitalization.

Educational Excellence: The Cherokee Nation aspires to provide world-class educational opportunities for its youth. This includes fostering an educational environment that embraces cultural relevance and values, integrating Cherokee history and traditions into curricula, and supporting students in pursuing higher education and career paths that benefit both the individual and the tribe.

Health and Well-being: The well-being of future generations is a paramount concern for the Cherokee Nation. The tribe envisions a future where access to quality healthcare, mental health services, and preventive care is readily available to all tribal citizens. Addressing health disparities, reducing substance abuse, and promoting healthy lifestyles are vital components of this aspiration.

Economic Prosperity: Economic development is a key driver of self-sufficiency and self-determination for the Cherokee Nation. Aspiring to expand economic opportunities, the tribe envisions a future with diverse industries, sustainable businesses, and job growth. This economic prosperity extends to tribal citizens, creating pathways to financial security and economic independence.

Environmental Stewardship: The Cherokee Nation's commitment to environmental conservation and stewardship extends to future generations. The tribe aspires to pass on a healthy, vibrant environment where clean water, pristine landscapes, and sustainable natural resources are preserved. This includes addressing climate challenges, protecting ancestral lands, and practicing responsible resource management.

Cultural Centers and Education: The Cherokee Nation envisions cultural centers and educational institutions as vibrant hubs for cultural exchange and knowledge transmission. These centers serve as places of inspiration and learning for future generations, fostering a deep appreciation for Cherokee culture, history, and traditions.

Sovereignty and Self-Governance: The Cherokee Nation aspires to see its sovereignty upheld and respected, both within the United States and on the international stage. This includes the continued exercise of self-governance, the protection of treaty rights, and the recognition of the tribe's inherent right to determine its own future.

Community Resilience: Future generations are expected to inherit communities characterized by resilience, social cohesion, and a strong sense of collective responsibility. Aspiration for strong, thriving communities includes community-based programs, support networks, and opportunities for civic engagement.

Cultural Revival: The Cherokee Nation envisions a future where traditional arts, crafts, ceremonies, and storytelling thrive, drawing strength from the past while adapting to the present. Cultural revival contributes to a sense of pride, identity, and unity among tribal citizens.

Cultural Diplomacy: Beyond the boundaries of the Cherokee Nation, there is an aspiration to share Cherokee culture and heritage with the wider world. Cultural diplomacy efforts aim to foster understanding, respect, and appreciation for Cherokee traditions, values, and contributions.

Environmental Resilience: In the face of environmental challenges, the Cherokee Nation aspires to be resilient and adaptive. This includes strategies to mitigate the impacts of climate change, protect natural habitats, and ensure a sustainable relationship with the land.

Tribal Citizenship and Inclusion: The Cherokee Nation values an inclusive approach to tribal citizenship, where future generations have the opportunity to connect with their Cherokee heritage and access the benefits and responsibilities of tribal citizenship. This inclusivity reflects the tribe's commitment to unity and cultural preservation.

Cultural Exchange: The Cherokee Nation aspires to engage in cultural exchange with other Indigenous nations and communities, fostering solidarity, mutual learning, and shared experiences. This exchange contributes to a broader Indigenous renaissance and cultural resurgence.

Interconnectedness: Ultimately, the Cherokee Nation envisions a future where all aspects of its aspirations are interconnected, creating a holistic vision of well-being, cultural preservation, and self-determination. This interconnectedness reflects the tribe's holistic worldview and the belief that a thriving future depends on nurturing all aspects of Cherokee life. In summary, the prospects and aspirations for future generations within the Cherokee Nation reflect a multifaceted commitment to cultural continuity, self-determination, and holistic well-being. These aspirations encompass cultural preservation, education, health, economic prosperity, environmental stewardship, and the exercise of sovereignty. The Cherokee Nation looks forward to a future where these aspirations are realized, creating a vibrant and thriving community for generations to come.

BOOK 2
CHOCTAW LEGACY
FROM HOMELAND TO REMOVAL

BY A.J. KINGSTON

Chapter 1: Ancient Roots and the Choctaw Homeland

Before the arrival of European explorers and settlers, the Choctaw Nation, like many other Indigenous societies in North America, had a rich and complex social, cultural, and political structure that was deeply rooted in their ancestral lands of the Southeastern United States. Understanding pre-European Choctaw society requires delving into their history, beliefs, customs, and way of life.

At the heart of Choctaw society was a profound connection to the land. The Choctaw people inhabited the region that is now Mississippi, Louisiana, Alabama, and parts of Florida and Tennessee. They were part of a larger cultural group known as the Muskogean people, which included other tribes like the Creek, Chickasaw, and Seminole. The Choctaw homeland was characterized by lush forests, fertile river valleys, and abundant wildlife, providing the basis for their subsistence and way of life.

The Choctaw were organized into a matrilineal kinship system, where descent and clan membership were traced through the mother's line. This system shaped social relationships, inheritance, and clan identity. Choctaw clans, known as "imis," played a significant role in their society, and each clan had its own leadership structure and responsibilities. Clans often functioned as extended families, providing support, protection, and a sense of belonging.

Within Choctaw communities, a council of elders, often referred to as "minko," held a central role in decision-making and governance. These leaders were chosen for their wisdom, experience, and ability to guide the community. While leadership was often hereditary, the council of elders also considered an individual's character, accomplishments, and contributions to the community.

Spirituality and belief systems were integral to Choctaw life. The Choctaw practiced a traditional Indigenous religion that emphasized a deep connection to the natural world. They believed in a Creator, ancestral spirits, and a complex system of supernatural forces that influenced daily life. Spiritual leaders, known as "chasukla," played a crucial role in facilitating communication with the spirit world through rituals, ceremonies, and storytelling.

The Choctaw calendar was closely tied to the cycles of nature, with ceremonies marking important events such as the changing of seasons, the planting and harvest of crops, and rites of passage. The Green Corn Ceremony, a major annual event, celebrated the first corn harvest and served as a time of renewal, purification, and thanksgiving. It was a time for forgiveness, healing, and the strengthening of community bonds.

Sustenance in pre-European Choctaw society came primarily from agriculture, hunting, and gathering. Corn, beans, and squash were staple crops, known as the "Three Sisters," and formed the basis of their diet. Agriculture was women's work, and Choctaw women were skilled farmers who tended to the fields, while men took on the roles of hunters and protectors of the community.

Hunting was a vital part of Choctaw life, with deer being a particularly important source of food, clothing, and tools. The Choctaw were skilled hunters who used bows and arrows, as well as various trapping techniques. They also gathered wild plants, herbs, and roots, adding to the diversity of their diet and medicinal practices.

Trade networks were essential for the Choctaw, allowing them to exchange goods and resources with neighboring tribes. The Choctaw were known for their craftsmanship, producing items like pottery, baskets, and textiles, which were highly sought after in trade. Their proximity to the Mississippi River and its tributaries facilitated trade routes and interactions with other Indigenous nations.

Social gatherings and communal activities were a vital part of Choctaw life. Towns and villages were organized around central meeting places where community members could come together for storytelling, dance, games, and celebrations. These gatherings reinforced social bonds, shared traditions, and cultural identity.

Conflict and warfare were also part of Choctaw society, as they had to defend their territory from neighboring tribes and, later, European encroachment. Choctaw warriors, often known as "holmes," played a critical role in protecting their communities and way of life. Warfare was guided by a complex system of protocols and rituals.

The arrival of Europeans, particularly the French and later the English, brought significant changes to Choctaw society. The fur trade, introduced by European colonists, created economic opportunities and new intertribal alliances. However, it also exposed the Choctaw to diseases, firearms, and alcohol, which had profound and often devastating effects on their population and way of life.

In summary, pre-European Choctaw society was characterized by a deep connection to the land, a matrilineal kinship system, a council of elders, a rich spiritual belief system, and a reliance on agriculture, hunting, and trade. The Choctaw people thrived in their ancestral homelands, fostering a vibrant and resilient culture that was intricately woven into the natural world. Their history is a testament to their adaptability, strength, and enduring commitment to their cultural heritage.

The Cherokee Nation, one of the most prominent and well-known Native American tribes, has a rich history deeply intertwined with its homeland territories and settlements. Spanning across the southeastern region of what is now the United States, the Cherokee people established a complex and interconnected network of communities and settlements that played a pivotal role in their cultural, political, and economic life.

The heart of the Cherokee Nation's homeland was located in the Appalachian region, encompassing parts of present-day Georgia, Tennessee, North Carolina, and South Carolina. This territory was characterized by its lush forests, fertile valleys, and abundant wildlife, providing the Cherokee with the resources they needed for sustenance and cultural practices.

Within their homeland, the Cherokee established a series of towns and settlements that served as the foundation of their society. These towns were strategically situated near rivers and waterways, facilitating transportation, trade, and access to essential resources. The towns were typically composed of communal houses, ceremonial grounds, and agricultural fields.

One of the most significant towns within Cherokee territory was Chota, located in what is now eastern Tennessee. Chota served as a political and ceremonial center for the Cherokee Nation and was the site of important council meetings and diplomatic negotiations. It was a hub of cultural exchange and played a crucial role in maintaining Cherokee governance and unity.

Another notable settlement was Kituwah, often regarded as the "mother town" of the Cherokee. Kituwah held deep spiritual significance and was considered the place where the Cherokee people were first created. It was a sacred site where important ceremonies, such as the Green Corn Ceremony, were conducted.

The town of New Echota holds a unique place in Cherokee history as the capital of the Cherokee Nation during the early 19th century. It was here that the Cherokee Nation established a written constitution, adopted a legal code, and published a newspaper, The Cherokee Phoenix. New Echota was a symbol of Cherokee modernization and efforts to engage with the United States as a sovereign nation.

In addition to these prominent settlements, the Cherokee Nation was composed of numerous smaller towns and villages scattered throughout their territory. Each of these settlements had its own leadership, often referred to as "minko" or chiefs, who were responsible for the governance and well-being of their community. These leaders played a vital role in local decision-making and maintaining order.

The Cherokee people were known for their agricultural practices, and their settlements were surrounded by cultivated fields where they grew crops such as corn, beans, squash, and sunflowers. These agricultural practices not only provided sustenance but also played a central role in Cherokee culture and spirituality.

Trade was another essential aspect of Cherokee life, and their settlements were strategically positioned along trade routes that connected them to neighboring tribes, such as the Creek and Chickasaw, as well as European settlers. The Cherokee engaged in trade, exchanging goods such as deerskins, fur, pottery, and agricultural produce for items like firearms, metal tools, and cloth.

As European settlers expanded into the southeastern United States, conflicts and encroachments on Cherokee territory became increasingly common. The 1830 Indian Removal Act, signed into law by President Andrew Jackson, led to the forced removal of the Cherokee people from their ancestral lands. This tragic event, known as the Trail of Tears, resulted in the displacement and suffering of thousands of Cherokee citizens.

Despite the forced removal, the Cherokee Nation's connection to its homeland territories and settlements persisted. Many Cherokee people, both those who were forcibly removed and those who managed to remain in their ancestral homeland, continued to cherish and maintain their cultural ties to the land.

In the present day, the Cherokee Nation has reestablished a significant presence in parts of its ancestral territory, particularly in northeastern Oklahoma. Tahlequah, Oklahoma, serves as the capital of the Cherokee Nation and is a vibrant center of Cherokee culture, governance, and education.

The Cherokee Nation's commitment to preserving its cultural heritage and connection to its homeland territories is evident in ongoing efforts to protect and reclaim ancestral lands, maintain cultural practices, and ensure that future generations continue to have a strong sense of their Cherokee identity.

In summary, the homeland territories and settlements of the Cherokee Nation were at the core of their cultural, political, and economic life. These towns and communities were not just places of habitation but also centers of cultural exchange, governance, and spirituality. Despite the challenges of forced removal, the Cherokee people have persevered in maintaining their deep connection to their ancestral lands and continue to thrive as a sovereign nation with a rich and resilient cultural heritage.

The development of agriculture marked a significant turning point in human history, and early agricultural practices played a pivotal role in the growth and evolution of human societies. As humans transitioned from nomadic hunter-gatherer lifestyles to settled agricultural communities, they began to cultivate plants and domesticate animals, fundamentally altering their way of life.

In the millennia preceding the advent of agriculture, early human societies relied on hunting, gathering, and foraging for their sustenance. These activities required constant mobility as humans followed the seasonal availability of food sources, such as wild game, fruits, nuts, and edible plants. While these societies had a deep understanding of their environments, they were constrained by the unpredictability of nature and the limited carrying capacity of their territories.

The shift towards agriculture, often referred to as the Neolithic Revolution, began around 10,000 years ago in various regions of the world, including the Fertile Crescent in the Middle East, the Nile Valley in Egypt, the Indus Valley in South Asia, and Mesoamerica. Early agricultural practices differed across these regions, but they shared common characteristics that laid the foundation for the development of complex civilizations.

One of the key innovations in early agriculture was the cultivation of cereal crops, such as wheat, barley, rice, and maize (corn). These crops provided a stable and reliable source of food that could be grown in specific locations, allowing communities to settle in one place for longer periods. The cultivation of grains required the development of tools, such as plows and sickles, to prepare the soil, plant seeds, and harvest the crops.

In addition to cereals, early agriculturalists also domesticated a variety of other plants, including legumes like lentils and chickpeas, oilseeds like flax and sesame, and root crops like potatoes and yams. This diversification of crops provided a more balanced diet and reduced the risk of crop failure due to disease or adverse weather conditions.

The practice of irrigation played a crucial role in early agriculture, particularly in regions with arid or seasonal climates. Irrigation systems were developed to control the flow of water to fields, allowing crops to thrive even in areas with limited rainfall. Ancient civilizations, such as the Sumerians in Mesopotamia, built intricate canal networks to support their agricultural endeavors.

Another significant development in early agriculture was the domestication of animals. Humans began to selectively breed and raise animals for various purposes, including food, labor, and transportation. The earliest domesticated animals included cattle, sheep, goats, pigs, and chickens. These animals provided not only meat and dairy products but also labor for plowing fields and pulling carts.

The transition to agriculture had profound social and economic implications. As communities settled in one place, they could accumulate surplus food, leading to the development of trade and commerce. This surplus also enabled population growth, as more individuals could be supported by agriculture than by hunting and gathering.

Early agricultural practices were closely tied to the cycles of nature and the changing seasons. Planting and harvesting times were determined by observations of celestial events, such as the rising and setting of stars and the solstices. Religious and cultural rituals often revolved around agricultural milestones, reinforcing the importance of farming to these societies.

With the development of agriculture came the emergence of complex societies and social hierarchies. The surplus of food allowed for the specialization of labor, leading to the rise of artisans, craftsmen, and leaders. Early agricultural societies also began to build permanent structures, such as houses, granaries, and temples, to accommodate their growing populations and store surplus crops.

The social organization of early agricultural societies varied widely, from egalitarian communities to hierarchical chiefdoms and early states. In some cases, the surplus of food and other resources led to social inequality, as a ruling elite emerged to control and distribute these resources. The emergence of writing systems, such as cuneiform in Mesopotamia and hieroglyphs in Egypt, was closely linked to the need for record-keeping and administration in complex agricultural societies.

The spread of agriculture had profound effects on the environment as well. As forests were cleared for farming and irrigation systems altered natural water flows, ecosystems underwent significant changes. Early agricultural practices could lead to soil erosion and depletion, which required strategies like crop rotation and fallowing to maintain soil fertility.

In summary, early agricultural practices represented a monumental shift in human history, marking the transition from nomadic hunter-gatherer lifestyles to settled agricultural communities. The cultivation of crops, domestication of animals, and development of irrigation systems allowed for the growth of surplus food and the emergence of complex societies. These practices laid the foundation for the development of agriculture-based civilizations and had far-reaching cultural, social, economic, and environmental implications that continue to shape our world today.

Chapter 2: Encounters with European Settlers

The arrival of European explorers in Choctaw lands marked a significant and transformative chapter in the history of the Choctaw Nation. As the Age of Exploration unfolded, European nations sought to expand their territories and exert control over the newly discovered lands of the Americas. In doing so, they encountered Indigenous peoples like the Choctaw, forever altering the course of history for both Native Americans and European explorers.

The early encounters between European explorers and the Choctaw people were characterized by curiosity, mutual misunderstandings, and complex interactions. The Choctaw were one of the numerous Indigenous nations residing in the Southeastern United States when the first European explorers set foot on their ancestral lands.

One of the earliest recorded encounters between Europeans and the Choctaw occurred in the early 16th century when Spanish explorer Hernando de Soto ventured into the region. De Soto's expedition, driven by the quest for riches and territorial expansion, led him to the Mississippi Valley, where the Choctaw were among the Indigenous nations he encountered.

De Soto's arrival in Choctaw territory in 1540 marked a momentous occasion. The Choctaw, like other Indigenous societies, had never encountered European technologies, animals, or diseases. De Soto's expedition introduced the Choctaw to horses, pigs, and firearms, forever altering their way of life. While the Choctaw initially regarded these newcomers with curiosity and sought to establish trade and peaceful relations, tensions later arose due to resource competition and misunderstandings.

The encounter with European diseases, such as smallpox, had a devastating impact on the Choctaw population. Like many Indigenous nations, the Choctaw lacked immunity to these diseases, leading to widespread illness and loss of life. The introduction of European diseases had demographic consequences that reverberated throughout Choctaw history.

In the decades following De Soto's expedition, European interest in the Southeastern United States continued to grow. Spanish, French, and English explorers and settlers sought to establish footholds in the region, often coming into contact with the Choctaw and other Indigenous nations.

The Choctaw, who had a well-established agricultural society and trade networks, found themselves caught in the crossfire of European rivalries. European powers, including the Spanish, French, and English, vied for control over the Southeastern territories, leading to a complex web of alliances and conflicts between European nations and Indigenous peoples.

During the 18th century, the Choctaw, like many Indigenous nations, became strategic allies in the ongoing conflicts between European powers. The French and Indian War (1754-1763) and the American Revolutionary War (1775-1783) saw the Choctaw aligning with different European nations based on their own interests and grievances.

The Treaty of Paris in 1783 marked the end of the American Revolutionary War and led to the recognition of the United States as an independent nation. It also set the stage for further interactions between the Choctaw Nation and the United States government. In the years that followed, the United States sought to expand westward, encroaching on Choctaw lands.

The U.S. government's approach to land acquisition and territorial expansion often clashed with the sovereignty and territorial rights of Indigenous nations like the Choctaw. The Treaty of Hopewell in 1786 and the Treaty of San Lorenzo in 1795 attempted to establish peaceful relations between the

United States and the Choctaw, but tensions continued to mount as American settlers encroached on Choctaw lands.

The early 19th century brought a new wave of challenges for the Choctaw Nation as the United States government pursued a policy of Indian removal. The Indian Removal Act of 1830, signed into law by President Andrew Jackson, authorized the forced removal of Indigenous nations from their ancestral lands to lands west of the Mississippi River. This tragic event, known as the Trail of Tears, had a profound and devastating impact on the Choctaw people, resulting in the loss of lives, land, and cultural heritage.

In summary, the arrival of European explorers in Choctaw lands set in motion a series of interactions, conflicts, and alliances that shaped the course of Choctaw history. The encounter with Europeans brought both opportunities and challenges, including the introduction of new technologies and diseases, the disruption of traditional ways of life, and ultimately, the forced removal from their ancestral lands. The history of the Choctaw Nation serves as a poignant reminder of the complex and often tumultuous interactions between Indigenous nations and European powers during the age of exploration and colonization.

The fur trade and cultural exchange were central elements of early interactions between European settlers and Indigenous peoples in North America. These exchanges had profound impacts on both Indigenous cultures and European colonial ventures, reshaping economies, societies, and cultural landscapes.

The fur trade was driven by the demand for valuable furs in Europe, particularly beaver pelts, which were highly prized for their use in fashionable hats. European fashion trends created a lucrative market for fur pelts, leading European traders to seek out sources of fur in North America. This quest brought them into contact with Indigenous nations who had long been engaged in the fur trade for their own purposes.

Indigenous nations, including the Cree, Ojibwe, Huron, Iroquois, and many others, had been hunting, trapping, and trading furs for centuries before European arrival. Fur-bearing animals like beavers, muskrats, and minks were abundant in North America, and Indigenous peoples had developed sophisticated hunting and trapping techniques to harvest them. Furs served as both practical items for clothing and trade goods for intertribal exchange.

The fur trade created a system of economic exchange that became intertwined with Indigenous cultures. Indigenous trappers and hunters would exchange furs with European traders in return for a variety of European goods, including metal tools, firearms, textiles, and, later, alcohol. These goods had a significant impact on Indigenous societies, improving their quality of life while also altering traditional ways of life.

The fur trade was not just about economic exchange; it also facilitated cultural interaction and the exchange of ideas, beliefs, and practices. European traders and Indigenous peoples came into contact, often living in close proximity to one another in trading posts and settlements. This proximity led to cultural exchanges that influenced both groups.

One notable aspect of cultural exchange was the sharing of technological knowledge. Indigenous peoples introduced European traders to their hunting and trapping techniques, including the use of the canoe, snowshoes, and moccasins. These innovations were crucial for European fur trappers navigating North America's vast and often challenging wilderness.

Conversely, European traders introduced Indigenous peoples to new technologies, including firearms and metal tools. Firearms, in particular, transformed Indigenous hunting practices, making it easier to harvest furs and defend against rival nations. The introduction of metal tools also improved efficiency in various aspects of daily life, from farming to crafting.

Language and communication were integral to the fur trade and cultural exchange. Indigenous peoples and European traders developed pidgin languages and trade jargon to facilitate communication. These languages incorporated elements of Indigenous languages, European languages, and a shared lexicon for trade. Pidgin languages played a crucial role in negotiating fur trades and conducting business.

Religious and spiritual exchanges also occurred during this period. Indigenous spiritual practices and beliefs often influenced the syncretic spiritual traditions that emerged among Métis and other mixed-ancestry Indigenous groups. European missionaries and religious practices, particularly Christianity, also made inroads into Indigenous communities, leading to the syncretism of Indigenous and European religious elements.

The fur trade had complex effects on Indigenous societies. While it brought economic benefits, it also disrupted traditional economies and social structures. The focus on fur trapping and trade led some Indigenous communities to shift away from traditional subsistence activities like farming and fishing. Additionally, the reliance on European trade goods created dependencies that made Indigenous peoples vulnerable to fluctuations in the fur market.

The fur trade also played a role in intertribal conflicts and alliances. Competition for access to European traders and their goods sometimes led to tensions and rivalries among Indigenous nations. Conversely, the fur trade also fostered alliances as Indigenous nations recognized the benefits of cooperation in their dealings with European powers.

One of the most significant impacts of the fur trade was the transformation of Indigenous lands. As European fur traders and settlers expanded further into North America, they established trading posts and settlements, which often disrupted Indigenous territories and ways of life. Indigenous peoples were gradually pushed westward and onto reservations as European colonization advanced.

The fur trade also had environmental consequences. The intense demand for fur pelts led to overhunting of certain species, especially beavers, which had a cascading impact on ecosystems. The decline of beaver populations disrupted wetlands and waterways, affecting the habitats of numerous other species.

In summary, the fur trade and cultural exchange were complex and multifaceted aspects of early interactions between European settlers and Indigenous peoples in North America. These exchanges were driven by economic interests but also had profound cultural, social, and environmental impacts. They transformed Indigenous societies, influenced the development of mixed-ancestry Indigenous communities, and shaped the course of North American history. The legacy of the fur trade and cultural exchange continues to be felt in the cultural diversity and historical narratives of North America today.

The early interactions between European colonizers and Indigenous peoples in North America were marked by a complex web of conflicts, negotiations, and diplomacy. As European settlers sought to establish colonies and expand their territories, they encountered numerous Indigenous nations, each with its own distinct cultures, languages, and systems of governance. These interactions laid the foundation for centuries of diplomatic exchanges and conflicts.

One of the earliest challenges faced by European settlers was the diversity of Indigenous nations inhabiting North America. The continent was home to hundreds of Indigenous tribes and nations, each with its own territorial claims and ways of life. European colonizers often struggled to comprehend the intricate political and cultural landscapes they encountered.

Initial conflicts arose primarily from the clash of worldviews, economic interests, and territorial ambitions. European settlers, driven by the desire for land and resources, frequently encroached upon Indigenous territories, leading to tensions and confrontations. Indigenous peoples, rightfully protective of their ancestral lands, often resisted these encroachments.

The arrival of European diseases, such as smallpox, measles, and influenza, had devastating consequences for Indigenous populations. These diseases, to which Indigenous peoples had little immunity, spread rapidly and caused widespread death and suffering. The loss of large segments of their populations weakened Indigenous nations, making them more vulnerable to European colonization.

Despite the challenges and conflicts, early interactions also saw attempts at diplomacy and peaceful coexistence. Indigenous nations recognized the advantages of establishing trade relationships with European colonizers, exchanging furs, food, and other resources for European goods, including metal tools, cloth, and firearms. These trade networks led to diplomatic exchanges and alliances between Indigenous nations and European powers.

Diplomacy often took the form of treaties and agreements, where Indigenous nations negotiated with European colonizers to define boundaries, establish trade relationships, and address disputes. The Treaty of Tordesillas in 1494, for example, divided the newly discovered lands of the Americas between Spain and Portugal, while subsequent treaties delineated specific territorial boundaries.

The concept of sovereignty and land ownership differed significantly between European colonizers and Indigenous nations. European powers viewed the land as a resource to be claimed and exploited, while Indigenous peoples viewed it as an integral part of their cultural and spiritual identity. These differing worldviews often led to misunderstandings and conflicts.

One significant diplomatic effort during the early colonial period was the establishment of the Wampum Belt Treaty, a symbol of peace and friendship between Indigenous nations and European settlers. Wampum belts, made from intricately woven beads, were used to commemorate important agreements and alliances. These belts represented the principles of mutual respect and peaceful coexistence.

Despite diplomatic efforts, conflicts frequently erupted as European settlers continued to expand westward. The colonization of North America was driven by a desire for land, resources, and economic opportunities. Indigenous nations found themselves increasingly marginalized and displaced from their ancestral territories.

The fur trade, which played a significant role in early colonial economies, often brought Indigenous nations into contact with European traders and settlers. This trade led to alliances, rivalries, and conflicts as Indigenous nations sought to secure advantageous trading relationships.

The expansion of European colonies and the westward movement of settlers intensified conflicts over land and resources. Indigenous nations, faced with encroachment on their territories, engaged in various forms of resistance, including armed confrontations and guerrilla warfare. Prominent conflicts like King Philip's War in New England and Pontiac's Rebellion in the Great Lakes region highlighted the tensions between Indigenous nations and European settlers.

Diplomatic efforts continued in parallel with conflicts, as both Indigenous nations and European colonizers recognized the advantages of negotiation and treaty-making. The Treaty of Paris in 1763, which ended the French and Indian War, redrew the map of North America and established new boundaries and territorial claims.

The American Revolution further complicated diplomatic relations, as Indigenous nations navigated the conflicting interests of British and American forces. Some Indigenous nations aligned with the British Crown in hopes of protecting their territories, while others remained neutral or supported the American Revolution.

The Treaty of Fort Stanwix in 1768 and the Treaty of Hopewell in 1785 were early attempts by the United States government to formalize agreements with Indigenous nations. These treaties aimed to establish peaceful relations, define territorial boundaries, and facilitate trade. However, many Indigenous leaders viewed these treaties with skepticism, as they often favored American interests and did not fully respect Indigenous sovereignty.

The late 18th and early 19th centuries brought significant challenges for Indigenous nations as the United States government pursued a policy of westward expansion. The Indian Removal Act of 1830 and subsequent events, such as the Trail of Tears, saw the forced removal of Indigenous nations from their ancestral lands to lands west of the Mississippi River. These events marked a tragic chapter in Indigenous history and further strained diplomatic relations.

In summary, the early interactions between European colonizers and Indigenous nations in North America were marked by a complex interplay of conflicts, diplomacy, and negotiations. These interactions shaped the course of history, influencing the destinies of Indigenous nations and European settlers alike. The legacy of these early interactions continues to be felt in contemporary Indigenous struggles for sovereignty, land rights, and cultural preservation.

Chapter 3: Choctaw Culture and Society

The Choctaw Nation, like many Indigenous societies, had a well-defined social structure and system of governance that played a crucial role in their cultural and political life. Understanding the Choctaw social structure and government provides insight into the complex organization of their communities.

The Choctaw social structure was organized into clans, which were extended family units that formed the basis of Choctaw society. Clans were matrilineal, meaning that descent and membership were traced through the mother's line. Each clan had its own distinct name and identity, often associated with a particular animal or natural element. Clans played a central role in Choctaw life, influencing social relationships, responsibilities, and cultural practices.

Within Choctaw clans, there were various roles and positions that individuals could hold. The Miko (Chief) was the highest-ranking authority within a clan and held significant influence over clan decisions and governance. Below the Miko were various other positions, including the Itta Homma (War Chief), who was responsible for matters related to defense and conflict, and the Apela (Speaker), who acted as a spokesperson and mediator for the clan.

The Choctaw social structure extended beyond the clan level to encompass larger tribal divisions. The Choctaw Nation was traditionally divided into three main regional groups: the Okla Falaya (People of the Long Hair), Okla Tannap (People of the Opposite Side), and Okla Hannalia (Sixtown People). These regional divisions reflected historical migrations and alliances and influenced Choctaw political organization.

At the tribal level, the Choctaw Nation was governed by a system of councils and chiefs. Each tribal division had its own

Miko and council, responsible for making decisions on matters that affected the division as a whole. The tribal councils played a significant role in maintaining social order, resolving disputes, and representing their division in intertribal and diplomatic affairs.

The Choctaw Nation had a complex system of laws and governance that predated European contact. Choctaw law was based on a system of justice and fairness, with principles of restitution and conflict resolution at its core. Disputes were often resolved through mediation and negotiation, with the goal of restoring harmony within the community.

The arrival of European colonizers introduced new challenges and complexities to Choctaw governance. As European powers established colonies in North America, they sought to establish relationships with Indigenous nations, often through treaties and agreements. The Choctaw Nation engaged in diplomatic negotiations with European powers, including the French and later the Spanish and British.

The Treaty of San Lorenzo in 1795, also known as Pinckney's Treaty, marked a significant diplomatic achievement for the Choctaw Nation. This treaty, negotiated with Spain, recognized Choctaw territorial rights and established peaceful relations with the Spanish government.

However, as European settlers continued to encroach on Choctaw lands, tensions and conflicts increased. The Treaty of Doak's Stand in 1820 saw the Choctaw Nation cede a significant portion of their ancestral lands to the United States. This marked the beginning of a series of removal treaties that ultimately led to the forced removal of the Choctaw people from their homeland to Indian Territory (present-day Oklahoma) in the 1830s, a tragic event known as the Trail of Tears.

Despite the hardships of removal, the Choctaw Nation endured and adapted to their new circumstances in Indian Territory. They established a government in exile and worked to rebuild their communities. In 1855, the Choctaw Nation adopted a new constitution, which provided for a bicameral legislature and an elected chief. This constitution laid the groundwork for the modern Choctaw Nation government.

In the late 19th and early 20th centuries, the Choctaw Nation underwent further changes in response to the United States' policies of allotment and assimilation. The Dawes Act of 1887 sought to break up tribal land holdings and encourage individual land ownership. As a result, the Choctaw Nation's communal land was divided into individual allotments, leading to the loss of much tribal land.

The Choctaw Nation persisted in its efforts to adapt to these changes and protect its sovereignty. In 1983, the Choctaw Nation adopted a new constitution, establishing a government with three branches: legislative, executive, and judicial. The Chief of the Choctaw Nation serves as the elected leader and representative of the tribe.

Today, the Choctaw Nation is a vibrant and thriving Indigenous nation with a rich cultural heritage. It operates as a sovereign government with its own laws, institutions, and services for its citizens. The Choctaw Nation's social structure and government have evolved over centuries, reflecting both traditional values and the challenges posed by European colonization and U.S. policies. Despite the hardships and disruptions of history, the Choctaw people continue to preserve and celebrate their unique culture and identity.

Language and communication were integral aspects of Choctaw culture, facilitating interpersonal relationships, storytelling, and the transmission of cultural knowledge. The Choctaw Nation, like many Indigenous societies, had a rich and complex linguistic tradition that played a central role in their way of life.

The Choctaw language, known as Chahta Anumpa, belongs to the Muskogean language family, which also includes languages like Creek, Chickasaw, and Seminole. It is a unique and distinct language with its own grammar, syntax, and vocabulary. The Choctaw language was traditionally oral and was passed down through generations via spoken word and storytelling.

Oral tradition was a fundamental part of Choctaw culture. Choctaw elders and storytellers played a vital role in preserving and passing down the tribe's history, myths, and cultural values through spoken narratives. These oral traditions included creation stories, legends, and teachings that provided a sense of identity and connectedness to the Choctaw people.

Choctaw elders, often referred to as "storytellers" or "keepers of knowledge," held a revered position within the community. They were responsible for not only transmitting stories but also teaching the language and cultural practices to younger generations. This intergenerational transmission of knowledge was critical for the preservation of Choctaw identity and cultural continuity.

The Choctaw language was also used as a means of daily communication within the community. It allowed individuals to convey their thoughts, emotions, and needs, fostering a sense of belonging and shared experience. Conversations in Choctaw often took place in various settings, from homes to community gatherings, reinforcing the language's role in maintaining social bonds.

In addition to spoken language, Choctaw culture incorporated non-verbal forms of communication, such as gestures, facial expressions, and body language. These non-verbal cues were used to convey emotions, intentions, and nuances of communication. They were particularly important in contexts where silence or subtlety was valued, such as during ceremonies or discussions of sensitive topics.

The Choctaw language also played a role in trade and intertribal interactions. As the Choctaw people engaged in trade networks with neighboring tribes, a common trade language called Mobilian Jargon emerged. Mobilian Jargon was a simplified form of communication that incorporated elements of Choctaw, Creek, Chickasaw, and other languages, facilitating trade and diplomacy among diverse Indigenous nations.

European contact introduced new linguistic influences to the Choctaw language. European traders and settlers introduced loanwords and phrases into Choctaw, reflecting the cultural exchange that occurred during this period. The Choctaw language adapted to incorporate these new elements while preserving its core structure and vocabulary.

The 19th century brought significant challenges to the Choctaw language and communication patterns. The forced removal of the Choctaw people from their ancestral lands to Indian Territory (present-day Oklahoma) disrupted traditional ways of life and cultural practices. Many Choctaw individuals and families faced linguistic challenges as they resettled in a new environment.

In the late 19th and early 20th centuries, the United States government implemented policies aimed at assimilating Indigenous peoples into mainstream American society. Boarding schools and English-only policies were part of this effort, leading to the suppression of Indigenous languages, including Choctaw. Many Choctaw children were sent to boarding schools where they were discouraged or forbidden from speaking their native language, resulting in a decline in language proficiency among younger generations.

Despite these challenges, efforts to revitalize the Choctaw language have been ongoing. Language preservation initiatives, language immersion programs, and language revitalization efforts have played a crucial role in preserving and promoting the Choctaw language. These efforts aim to ensure that future generations of Choctaw people have the opportunity to learn and speak their ancestral language.

In 2008, the Mississippi Band of Choctaw Indians, one of the federally recognized Choctaw tribes, became the first tribe in the United States to establish a tribal school where the Choctaw language is the primary language of instruction. Such initiatives are vital for the preservation and revitalization of the Choctaw language and cultural identity.

In summary, language and communication were integral to Choctaw culture, serving as a means of conveying knowledge, preserving cultural heritage, and strengthening social bonds. The Choctaw language, like many Indigenous languages, faced challenges throughout history, but ongoing efforts to revitalize and promote it are helping to ensure that it continues to be a vibrant and vital part of Choctaw identity and heritage.

The religious beliefs and ceremonies of the Choctaw Nation were deeply intertwined with their cultural identity and worldview. These spiritual practices played a vital role in the lives of the Choctaw people, providing a framework for understanding the natural world, fostering community cohesion, and maintaining a sense of connection to their ancestral lands.

The Choctaw religious belief system was characterized by animism, the belief that all natural elements, including animals, plants, rivers, and celestial bodies, possessed spiritual significance and consciousness. This belief system emphasized the interconnectedness of all living beings and their relationship with the Great Spirit, a central figure in Choctaw cosmology.

The Choctaw Great Spirit, often referred to as Ababinili or Ababinili Yut, was considered the supreme and benevolent creator of the universe. The Great Spirit was believed to provide guidance, protection, and blessings to the Choctaw people and all living creatures. Choctaw spirituality emphasized the importance of maintaining harmony and balance within the natural world, recognizing the inherent value of all living beings.

Choctaw religious practitioners included spiritual leaders, medicine people, and storytellers who played essential roles in guiding the community's spiritual life. These individuals possessed specialized knowledge of traditional practices, rituals, and ceremonies and acted as intermediaries between the human and spiritual realms.

Ceremonies and rituals were central to Choctaw religious life and often marked significant life events, seasonal changes, or communal gatherings. Some of the key religious ceremonies and practices of the Choctaw Nation included:

Green Corn Ceremony (Chakchiuma Okla): This important annual ceremony celebrated the harvest of the first corn crop, symbolizing renewal and the cycle of life. It included feasting, dancing, and purification rituals, and it served as a time of community healing and spiritual reflection.

Ball Game Ceremony: The Choctaw ball game, known as "ishtaboli" or "stickball," was more than just a sport; it had spiritual and ceremonial significance. The game was often accompanied by rituals, prayers, and songs, and it could serve as a form of conflict resolution or diplomacy among different tribes.

Stomp Dance (Tushka Homma): The stomp dance was a vibrant and communal dance ceremony featuring rhythmic drumming and chanting. It celebrated the connection between the physical and spiritual worlds and was often held in conjunction with other ceremonies.

Vision Quests: Young Choctaw individuals seeking guidance and spiritual insight would embark on vision quests, which involved fasting, isolation, and meditation in a secluded area of nature. During these quests, they hoped to receive visions or messages from the spiritual realm.

Purification Rituals: Choctaw purification rituals, such as sweat lodges, were used to cleanse the body, mind, and spirit. These ceremonies were often performed before important events or as part of the Green Corn Ceremony.

Ancestral Veneration: The Choctaw people held deep respect for their ancestors and believed that their spirits continued to influence the living. Ancestral veneration involved making offerings and showing reverence to the spirits of deceased relatives.

The arrival of European colonizers and the influence of Christianity introduced new religious elements to Choctaw culture. Choctaw spiritual practices often adapted to incorporate Christian beliefs, leading to a syncretic form of spirituality that combined traditional Indigenous beliefs with elements of Christianity. Choctaw churches and religious leaders played significant roles in the spiritual life of the community.

Despite the challenges and disruptions brought about by colonization, Choctaw religious beliefs and ceremonies have persisted through the centuries. Today, many Choctaw individuals and communities continue to embrace and revitalize their traditional spiritual practices, ensuring that their cultural and spiritual heritage remains an integral part of their identity and connection to their ancestral lands.

Chapter 4: The Impact of the Trail of Tears

The forced removal of the Choctaw Nation, along with other Indigenous nations, from their ancestral lands in the southeastern United States to Indian Territory (present-day Oklahoma) in the 1830s is a tragic chapter in American history known as the Trail of Tears. This event was influenced by a complex web of historical, political, economic, and social factors, which are essential to understanding its context and causes.

European Colonization and Expansion: The arrival of European colonizers in the Americas in the 16th century marked the beginning of significant changes for Indigenous nations like the Choctaw. European settlers sought to establish colonies and expand westward, encroaching upon Indigenous territories and resources.

Treaty Negotiations and Land Cessions: Throughout the 18th and 19th centuries, Indigenous nations were coerced or pressured into signing a series of treaties with the United States government. These treaties often involved the cession of vast amounts of land in exchange for promises of protection, financial compensation, or reserved territories. However, many treaties were negotiated under duress or with limited understanding on the part of Indigenous leaders.

Economic Pressures: The expansion of cotton cultivation in the southeastern United States created a demand for fertile land and labor, which led to increased pressure on Indigenous nations to cede their lands. European settlers, including those of European descent and African Americans, moved into these regions to engage in cotton farming, which became economically vital to the South.

Political Factors: The U.S. government's policies toward Indigenous nations evolved over time. President Andrew

Jackson's administration, in particular, pursued a policy of Indian removal, which aimed to relocate Indigenous peoples to lands west of the Mississippi River to open up new territories for white settlement. Jackson's presidency saw the passage of the Indian Removal Act of 1830, which provided the legal framework for the forced removal of Indigenous nations.

Gold Rushes and Resource Extraction: The discovery of valuable resources, such as gold in Georgia, further escalated the pressure on Indigenous nations. The Georgia Gold Rush of the 1830s led to a surge of settlers into Cherokee lands, intensifying conflicts and the push for removal.

Legal Challenges and Resistance: Some Indigenous nations, including the Cherokee, Choctaw, and Creek, sought legal remedies to protect their lands and sovereignty. The U.S. Supreme Court's rulings in cases like Worcester v. Georgia (1832) upheld the sovereignty of Indigenous nations and their rights to self-governance. However, these decisions were not always enforced by the federal government, and removal continued.

Coercion and Forced Relocation: Despite legal challenges and resistance, the U.S. government pursued a policy of forced removal. Federal and state authorities used various tactics, including military force, to compel Indigenous nations to leave their lands. The Choctaw Nation, in particular, faced a harrowing journey westward as they were forcibly removed from their homeland.

Devastating Consequences: The Trail of Tears, as the removal is commonly known, resulted in immense suffering and loss of life among the Choctaw and other Indigenous nations. Thousands of people died from exposure, disease, and starvation during the arduous journey westward.

Legacy and Impacts: The forced removal had profound and long-lasting effects on the Choctaw Nation and other Indigenous nations. It resulted in the loss of ancestral lands, cultural disruption, and the fragmentation of communities.

Despite these challenges, many Indigenous nations, including the Choctaw, persevered and rebuilt their communities in Indian Territory.

The forced removal of the Choctaw Nation and other Indigenous nations remains a somber reminder of the injustices and hardships faced by Indigenous peoples throughout American history. It also underscores the resilience and strength of Indigenous communities in the face of adversity as they continue to preserve their cultural heritage and advocate for their rights and sovereignty.

The journey westward, often referred to as the Trail of Tears, was a harrowing and devastating ordeal endured by the Choctaw Nation and other Indigenous nations in the 1830s as they were forcibly removed from their ancestral lands in the southeastern United States to Indian Territory (present-day Oklahoma). This tragic episode in American history resulted in immense suffering and loss of life, leaving an indelible mark on the Choctaw and other Indigenous communities.

Forced Removal Orders: The Choctaw and other Indigenous nations faced relentless pressure and threats from the U.S. government and state authorities to vacate their lands. The Indian Removal Act of 1830, signed into law by President Andrew Jackson, provided the legal basis for the forced removal. Removal orders were issued, and Indigenous nations were given a limited timeframe to leave their homelands.

Displacement and Loss of Homes: Families and communities were uprooted from their ancestral lands, often leaving behind homes, farms, and sacred sites. The abrupt displacement caused emotional and cultural trauma, as generations had deep connections to the land.

Forced Marches: The journeys westward were grueling and arduous. Indigenous people were forced to travel long distances on foot, horseback, or in wagons, often without sufficient provisions, in the midst of harsh weather conditions. The forced marches extended for hundreds of miles.

Disease and Starvation: The conditions during the forced removal were deplorable. Indigenous people faced exposure to the elements, inadequate food supplies, and contaminated water sources. Disease outbreaks, including cholera and smallpox, ravaged the groups, leading to a high mortality rate.

Loss of Lives: The toll on human life was staggering. Thousands of Indigenous individuals, including men, women, children, and the elderly, perished during the journey. Mass graves were created along the routes westward, serving as tragic reminders of the suffering endured.

Separation and Disintegration of Communities: Families were torn apart, and entire communities were scattered across unfamiliar territories. The forced removal disrupted social structures and traditional ways of life, leading to the loss of cultural knowledge and community cohesion.

Trauma and Grief: The forced removal left deep psychological scars on survivors and their descendants. The trauma and grief of the journey westward persisted for generations, impacting mental and emotional well-being.

Survival and Resilience: Despite the overwhelming challenges, many Indigenous individuals and families displayed remarkable resilience and determination to survive. They relied on their cultural strengths, knowledge of the land, and communal bonds to endure the journey.

Arrival in Indian Territory: Those who survived the journey arrived in Indian Territory, where they faced the daunting task of rebuilding their communities and adapting to a new environment. Land allotment policies and the loss of traditional homelands further complicated their efforts.

Ongoing Legacy: The legacy of the Trail of Tears endures within the Choctaw Nation and other Indigenous communities. It serves as a painful reminder of the injustices and hardships endured by Indigenous peoples throughout American history. It also underscores the resilience and strength of Indigenous communities in the face of adversity as they continue to preserve their cultural heritage and advocate for their rights and sovereignty.

The Trail of Tears remains a powerful symbol of the enduring strength and determination of the Choctaw and other Indigenous nations to overcome immense challenges and maintain their cultural identity and heritage despite the devastating hardships they endured.

Upon their arrival in Indian Territory (present-day Oklahoma) after the forced removal, the Choctaw Nation and other Indigenous communities faced the daunting task of establishing new lives in unfamiliar lands. Life in these new territories marked a significant transition and required profound cultural adaptation. This period of history is characterized by resilience, determination, and the preservation of cultural heritage.

The Choctaw people, like many other Indigenous nations, had been forcibly displaced from their ancestral lands in the southeastern United States. The removal had taken a tremendous toll, resulting in the loss of lives, disruption of communities, and the abandonment of homes and farms. As they entered Indian Territory, Choctaw families and communities encountered a vastly different landscape and environment.

One of the immediate challenges was the need to secure food, shelter, and resources in their new surroundings. The Choctaw people relied on their traditional knowledge of hunting, fishing, and agriculture to adapt to the local ecosystem. They began cultivating crops such as corn, beans, and squash in the fertile soil of Indian Territory, employing agricultural practices that had sustained their ancestors for generations.

The Choctaw also adapted to the local wildlife, utilizing hunting and fishing techniques that were effective in the new environment. Bison, deer, and various fish species became essential sources of sustenance. These hunting and fishing traditions became not only a means of survival but also integral aspects of Choctaw culture, connecting them to the land and its resources.

In their new territories, Choctaw communities faced the challenge of reestablishing social structures and governance systems. The forced removal had disrupted traditional leadership and community organization. Over time, Choctaw leaders worked to rebuild tribal institutions and governance structures, adapting them to the realities of Indian Territory.

One significant development during this period was the adoption of a new constitution for the Choctaw Nation in 1855. This constitution established a government with a bicameral legislature, an elected chief, and a judicial system. The Choctaw Nation thus reaffirmed its sovereignty and commitment to self-governance, even in the face of considerable adversity.

The preservation of cultural heritage and traditional practices remained a top priority for the Choctaw people. Despite the challenges of removal and resettlement, they continued to pass down their cultural knowledge and values to younger generations. Elders played a crucial role in this process, serving as keepers of knowledge and storytellers who shared the tribe's history, myths, and teachings.

Language, in particular, played a vital role in maintaining cultural continuity. The Choctaw language, Chahta Anumpa, was a source of identity and connection to their ancestors. Efforts were made to ensure that the language was passed down to younger generations through oral tradition and, later, through written materials.

Education became increasingly important as Choctaw leaders recognized the need to adapt to changing circumstances. Missionary schools and, later, tribal schools were established to provide education to Choctaw children. These institutions played a role in preserving cultural values and transmitting the Choctaw language.

As the United States continued its westward expansion and settlement, the Choctaw Nation, like other Indigenous nations, faced further challenges to their sovereignty and land rights. The policy of allotment, introduced through the Dawes Act of 1887, sought to break up tribal land holdings and encourage individual land ownership among Native Americans. This policy led to the loss of communal land and further fragmentation of tribal communities.

Despite these challenges, the Choctaw Nation persisted in its efforts to adapt and thrive. The late 19th and early 20th centuries witnessed a growing sense of identity and unity among the Choctaw people. They continued to engage in trade, establish businesses, and participate in the broader economic landscape.

The Choctaw people also contributed significantly to the development of Indian Territory and, later, the state of Oklahoma. They played vital roles in agriculture, business, and government, contributing to the growth of their communities and the region as a whole.

In the face of adversity, the Choctaw Nation remained committed to preserving its cultural heritage. Traditional arts and crafts, such as basketry, beadwork, and pottery, continued to be practiced and passed down through generations. These artistic traditions not only upheld cultural values but also provided economic opportunities for Choctaw artisans.

Religion and spirituality remained integral aspects of Choctaw life. The Choctaw stomp dance, known as Tushka Homma, continued to be practiced, fostering a sense of community and connection to the spiritual realm. Choctaw churches and spiritual leaders played important roles in providing guidance and support to their congregations.

Throughout the 20th century and into the present, the Choctaw Nation has experienced a resurgence in cultural revitalization and economic development. The tribe's government has expanded its services to meet the needs of its citizens, and initiatives have been undertaken to promote language revitalization and education.

One of the most significant developments has been the success of the Choctaw Nation's businesses and enterprises. These include gaming operations, manufacturing, healthcare facilities, and educational institutions. The revenue generated from these enterprises has allowed the Choctaw Nation to reinvest in its communities, provide services, and support cultural preservation efforts.

In recent years, the Choctaw Nation has also engaged in philanthropic endeavors, extending a helping hand to others in need. This spirit of giving back is exemplified by the Choctaw Nation's historic donation to the Irish during the Great Famine in the 19th century and its ongoing efforts to support charitable causes around the world.

In summary, life in new territories following the forced removal was marked by significant challenges and adaptations for the Choctaw Nation. Despite the hardships endured during the Trail of Tears and the subsequent resettlement, the Choctaw people demonstrated remarkable resilience, determination, and a commitment to preserving their cultural heritage. Their ability to adapt to changing circumstances while maintaining their identity reflects the enduring strength of Indigenous communities in the face of adversity. Today, the Choctaw Nation stands as a testament to the importance of cultural continuity, self-governance, and economic development in sustaining Indigenous communities and preserving their unique heritage.

Chapter 5: Struggles and Survival in New Territories

Adapting to new environments and communities has been a central theme in the history of Indigenous nations like the Choctaw. The forced removal of the Choctaw Nation to Indian Territory in the 1830s marked a profound shift in their way of life, as they navigated the challenges of settling in unfamiliar lands and interacting with diverse Indigenous groups and non-Indigenous settlers.

Upon their arrival in Indian Territory, the Choctaw people faced the task of establishing communities and reimagining their way of life in a new environment. The territory, characterized by its rich and fertile lands, provided both opportunities and challenges for adaptation.

One of the immediate priorities was securing shelter and sustenance. Choctaw families employed their agricultural knowledge to cultivate crops like corn, beans, and squash, adapting their farming practices to the local soil and climate. They also relied on hunting and fishing to supplement their diet, demonstrating a profound understanding of the local ecosystem.

As the Choctaw Nation settled into Indian Territory, they encountered a diverse array of Indigenous communities from various nations, each with its own distinct languages, cultures, and traditions. Interactions with neighboring tribes, such as the Chickasaw, Creek, Seminole, and Cherokee, presented both opportunities for cultural exchange and the need to establish diplomatic relationships.

Diplomacy and mutual cooperation became crucial aspects of adaptation to the new environment. The Choctaw people engaged in trade and alliances with neighboring tribes, forming networks that facilitated economic exchanges and security arrangements. These interactions allowed them to navigate the complex web of Indigenous nations in the region.

The preservation of cultural heritage remained a top priority for the Choctaw people. Despite the disruptions caused by the forced removal, they continued to pass down their cultural knowledge and values to younger generations. Elders played a pivotal role as keepers of knowledge, sharing the tribe's history, myths, and teachings through oral tradition.

Language preservation was particularly important in maintaining cultural continuity. The Choctaw language, Chahta Anumpa, held a central place in their identity and connection to their ancestors. Efforts were made to ensure that the language was passed down to younger generations through spoken narratives and, later, through written materials.

Education emerged as a means of adapting to changing circumstances. Missionary schools and later tribal schools were established to provide education to Choctaw children. These institutions played a role in preserving cultural values and transmitting the Choctaw language, ensuring that younger generations remained connected to their heritage.

While the forced removal had disrupted traditional leadership and community organization, Choctaw leaders worked diligently to rebuild tribal institutions and governance structures. The adoption of a new constitution in 1855 was a significant development, reaffirming the Choctaw Nation's commitment to self-governance and sovereignty.

Economic adaptation was another crucial aspect of life in Indian Territory. Choctaw individuals and communities engaged in trade, established businesses, and participated in the broader economic landscape. They contributed significantly to the development of the region and played vital roles in agriculture, business, and government.

The late 19th century brought further challenges to the Choctaw Nation's sovereignty and land rights. The Dawes Act of 1887 introduced a policy of allotment, aimed at breaking up tribal land holdings and encouraging individual land ownership among Native Americans. This policy led to the loss of communal land and the further fragmentation of tribal communities.

Despite these challenges, the Choctaw Nation persisted in its efforts to adapt and thrive. The 20th century witnessed a growing sense of identity and unity among the Choctaw people. They continued to engage in economic development, establishing businesses, enterprises, and healthcare facilities that benefited their communities.

Religion and spirituality remained integral aspects of Choctaw life. The Choctaw stomp dance, known as Tushka Homma, continued to be practiced, fostering a sense of community and connection to the spiritual realm. Choctaw churches and spiritual leaders played vital roles in providing guidance and support to their congregations.

In recent decades, the Choctaw Nation has experienced a resurgence in cultural revitalization and economic development. The tribe's government has expanded its services to meet the needs of its citizens, and initiatives have been undertaken to promote language revitalization and education.

One of the most significant developments has been the success of the Choctaw Nation's businesses and enterprises, including gaming operations, manufacturing, and educational institutions. The revenue generated from these enterprises has allowed the Choctaw Nation to reinvest in its communities, provide services, and support cultural preservation efforts.

In summary, adapting to new environments and communities has been a dynamic and ongoing process for the Choctaw Nation. Despite the hardships endured during the forced removal and the challenges of resettlement, the Choctaw people have demonstrated remarkable resilience, determination, and a commitment to preserving their cultural heritage. Their ability to adapt to changing circumstances while maintaining their identity reflects the enduring strength of

Indigenous communities in the face of adversity. Today, the Choctaw Nation stands as a testament to the importance of cultural continuity, self-governance, and economic development in sustaining Indigenous communities and preserving their unique heritage.

Economic challenges and land issues have played a significant role in the history of Indigenous nations like the Choctaw. The forced removal of the Choctaw Nation to Indian Territory in the 1830s and subsequent events brought about complex economic struggles and land-related disputes that continue to shape the tribe's economic landscape and relationship with their lands.

Upon their arrival in Indian Territory, the Choctaw people faced the need to rebuild their communities and secure their economic livelihoods. The fertile lands of the territory provided opportunities for agricultural endeavors, and Choctaw families turned to farming as a means of sustenance and economic stability. Corn, beans, squash, and other crops were cultivated to provide food for the community.

Hunting and fishing also played a vital role in the Choctaw economy. The abundant wildlife and water resources in Indian Territory allowed Choctaw individuals and families to supplement their diet and contribute to the local economy through the sale of animal pelts and furs.

Trade and economic partnerships with neighboring tribes, such as the Chickasaw, Creek, Seminole, and Cherokee, facilitated economic exchanges and contributed to the resilience of the Choctaw Nation. These alliances allowed for the movement of goods and resources across tribal boundaries, supporting economic cooperation and diplomatic relationships.

However, the late 19th century brought significant challenges to the Choctaw Nation's economic stability and land rights. The Dawes Act of 1887, also known as the General Allotment Act, was a federal policy aimed at breaking up tribal land holdings and encouraging individual land ownership among Native Americans. Under this policy, tribal lands were divided into smaller allotments, which were assigned to individual tribal members.

The Dawes Act had profound implications for the Choctaw Nation. It resulted in the loss of communal land and the further fragmentation of tribal communities. Many Choctaw individuals received allotments of land that were often insufficient for sustaining agricultural practices or generating income. As a result, valuable tribal land was gradually eroded.

The allotment policy also introduced the concept of "surplus land," which was land deemed excess to the needs of the tribe and subject to sale to non-Indigenous settlers. This led to the loss of additional tribal land and further exacerbated economic challenges for the Choctaw Nation.

The impact of the Dawes Act was deeply felt by the Choctaw people. Traditional communal land use practices, which had sustained the tribe for generations, were disrupted. Families were forced to adapt to smaller land allotments, often struggling to maintain their agricultural traditions and economic self-sufficiency.

Despite the challenges brought about by allotment, the Choctaw people persevered and sought ways to adapt to changing economic circumstances. Many Choctaw individuals continued to engage in farming and ranching, while others explored opportunities in trade, commerce, and entrepreneurship.

One of the most significant economic developments for the Choctaw Nation occurred in the late 20th century with the advent of gaming operations. The passage of the Indian Gaming Regulatory Act in 1988 provided a legal framework for tribal gaming enterprises, opening the door to economic opportunities for Indigenous communities across the United States.

The Choctaw Nation embraced the gaming industry and established successful casino operations, becoming a major player in the regional and national gaming market. These enterprises generated substantial revenue for the tribe, which has been reinvested in community development, social services, education, and cultural preservation.

In addition to gaming, the Choctaw Nation has diversified its economic portfolio, venturing into manufacturing, healthcare, construction, and education. These initiatives have provided employment opportunities for tribal citizens and contributed to the economic growth of the region.

Land issues, however, continue to be a complex and evolving aspect of the Choctaw Nation's economic landscape. The tribe has pursued efforts to regain control over its lands and address the historical injustices related to allotment and land loss.

One notable initiative is the Choctaw Nation's land acquisition program, aimed at repurchasing lands within the tribe's historic boundaries. These efforts seek to restore tribal lands and strengthen the Choctaw Nation's economic and cultural ties to its ancestral territories.

The Choctaw Nation's economic development also encompasses social responsibility and philanthropy. The tribe has a strong tradition of giving back to its communities and supporting charitable causes. This spirit of philanthropy is exemplified by the Choctaw Nation's historic donation to the Irish during the Great Famine in the 19th century and its ongoing efforts to support charitable endeavors around the world.

In summary, economic challenges and land issues have been central themes in the history of the Choctaw Nation. The forced removal, the impact of the Dawes Act, and the subsequent economic adaptations have shaped the tribe's economic trajectory. Despite historical injustices and economic hardships, the Choctaw Nation has demonstrated resilience and adaptability, embracing economic opportunities in gaming, manufacturing, and various industries. Efforts to address land issues and promote economic self-sufficiency continue to be priorities, as the tribe works to secure a prosperous future for its citizens and preserve its cultural heritage.

Family and community resilience are at the heart of the Choctaw Nation's history and identity. Across centuries marked by challenges, including forced removal, economic hardships, and cultural disruptions, the Choctaw people have demonstrated a remarkable capacity to adapt, persevere, and support one another.

Families form the cornerstone of Choctaw society, with deep-rooted ties that extend across generations. Traditional Choctaw families were known for their strong bonds and mutual support systems, which played a crucial role in the survival of the tribe throughout its history.

The forced removal of the Choctaw Nation in the 1830s disrupted these familial bonds, as families were uprooted from their ancestral lands and scattered across unfamiliar territories. The journey westward, known as the Trail of Tears, presented immense challenges for families, as they grappled with the loss of homes, loved ones, and their traditional way of life.

Despite these hardships, Choctaw families demonstrated resilience, determination, and a commitment to preserving their cultural identity. Elders played a vital role in passing down cultural knowledge, traditions, and stories to younger generations, ensuring the continuity of Choctaw heritage.

Family networks served as support systems during the challenging years of resettlement in Indian Territory. Families relied on one another for emotional support, sustenance, and mutual aid. The practice of communal living, with extended families residing together, helped mitigate the hardships of the new environment.

As Choctaw communities took root in Indian Territory, the reestablishment of strong familial ties became a priority.

Families worked together to rebuild their homes, farms, and communities. The cultivation of crops, hunting, and fishing, along with the sharing of resources, ensured that families had the means to sustain themselves and prosper.

The importance of family extended to the broader community, as Choctaw society emphasized communal well-being and mutual responsibility. Community resilience was built on the foundation of interdependence and cooperation, as Choctaw families and communities worked together to address challenges and seize opportunities.

Traditional Choctaw governance structures also played a role in fostering community resilience. Leaders, both hereditary and elected, worked to rebuild tribal institutions and adapt them to the changing circumstances of Indian Territory. The adoption of a new constitution in 1855 marked an important step in reaffirming the Choctaw Nation's commitment to self-governance and sovereignty.

Economic challenges, including land loss resulting from the Dawes Act of 1887, presented new obstacles for Choctaw families and communities. The policy of allotment sought to break up tribal land holdings and encourage individual land ownership among Native Americans, leading to the loss of communal land and economic disruption.

Despite these economic challenges, Choctaw families adapted to changing circumstances. Many individuals and families engaged in farming, ranching, and other economic pursuits. They diversified their sources of income and sought opportunities for entrepreneurship.

The late 19th and early 20th centuries witnessed a growing sense of identity and unity among the Choctaw people. As they navigated economic hardships and land loss, they continued to prioritize cultural preservation. Language, in particular, remained a focal point, with efforts made to ensure that the Choctaw language was passed down to younger generations.

Education emerged as a means of preserving cultural values and transmitting the Choctaw language. Missionary schools and tribal schools were established to provide education to Choctaw children, further strengthening the bonds between families and their cultural heritage.

The role of women in Choctaw families and communities has been instrumental in preserving culture and supporting resilience. Choctaw women were often the keepers of traditional knowledge, skilled in crafts such as basketry and beadwork, and central figures in cultural practices.

Religion and spirituality also played a significant role in fostering resilience within Choctaw communities. The Choctaw stomp dance, known as Tushka Homma, continued to be practiced, providing a sense of community, connection to the spiritual realm, and an outlet for cultural expression.

In the 20th century, the Choctaw Nation experienced a resurgence in cultural revitalization and economic development. The success of gaming operations, initiated under the Indian Gaming Regulatory Act of 1988, generated substantial revenue for the tribe. This economic growth allowed the Choctaw Nation to reinvest in its communities, provide services, and support cultural preservation efforts.

Family and community resilience continue to be core values for the Choctaw people in the present day. The tribe's government has expanded its services to meet the needs of its citizens, ensuring access to healthcare, education, and social support. Initiatives have been undertaken to promote language revitalization and education, preserving the cultural heritage that binds families and communities together.

One of the most notable aspects of the Choctaw Nation's resilience is its commitment to philanthropy and giving back. The Choctaw Nation has a long history of assisting others in times of need, exemplified by its historic donation to the Irish during the Great Famine in the 19th century. This tradition of generosity extends to charitable causes around the world.

In summary, family and community resilience are foundational principles that have guided the Choctaw Nation throughout its history. Despite the challenges of forced removal, economic hardships, and cultural disruptions, Choctaw families have demonstrated their unwavering commitment to preserving their cultural identity and supporting one another. The enduring strength of Choctaw communities lies in their deep-seated connections to family, culture, and a shared sense of responsibility, allowing them to adapt and thrive in the face of adversity.

Chapter 6: Rebuilding a Choctaw Identity

Efforts to preserve language and traditions are integral to the identity and cultural resilience of the Choctaw Nation. The Choctaw people have a deep-rooted commitment to safeguarding their unique heritage, which includes the preservation of the Choctaw language, traditional practices, and cultural traditions that have been passed down through generations.

Language holds a central place in the preservation of Choctaw culture. The Choctaw language, known as Chahta Anumpa, is more than just a means of communication; it is a repository of cultural knowledge, history, and identity. Efforts to preserve and revitalize the language have been a top priority for the Choctaw Nation.

The transmission of the Choctaw language from one generation to the next primarily occurs within families and communities. Elders and fluent speakers play a critical role in teaching the language to younger generations through oral tradition. Storytelling, conversations, and family gatherings are occasions where the language is actively used and passed down.

In addition to oral tradition, the Choctaw Nation has recognized the importance of written materials in language preservation. Efforts have been made to develop written resources, textbooks, and educational materials in the Choctaw language. Schools and educational institutions within the tribe have incorporated language programs to ensure that Choctaw children have the opportunity to learn their native language.

Language immersion programs have been established to create immersive environments where Choctaw children and learners can become fluent speakers. These programs offer a unique opportunity for learners to engage with the language in everyday contexts, fostering a deeper connection to their cultural identity.

Language preservation extends to efforts to document and archive the Choctaw language. Linguists, scholars, and community members have worked together to compile dictionaries, grammars, and resources that serve as references for future generations. These resources are invaluable in maintaining the integrity of the language.

Traditional practices and cultural traditions are equally important in the preservation of Choctaw culture. Choctaw communities continue to engage in practices that have been handed down through generations. These practices include the Choctaw stomp dance, known as Tushka Homma, which serves as a vibrant expression of cultural identity and spirituality.

The stomp dance brings together Choctaw families and communities in a celebration of heritage. It provides a sense of belonging, connection to ancestors, and an opportunity for cultural expression. The Choctaw Nation hosts stomp dance gatherings, where the dance is performed, and cultural traditions are upheld.

Arts and crafts are another vital aspect of Choctaw culture that is actively preserved. Choctaw artisans create traditional items such as baskets, beadwork, pottery, and clothing, which are not only beautiful works of art but also symbolic of cultural heritage. These crafts are passed down through families, and the Choctaw Nation supports the continuation of these artistic traditions.

Religious beliefs and ceremonies are integral to Choctaw culture and are also preserved as a part of their traditions. The Choctaw people have their own spiritual practices and ceremonies that are deeply connected to the land and the natural world. These ceremonies are passed down through generations and continue to be practiced by Choctaw communities.

The Choctaw Nation recognizes that the preservation of cultural traditions is closely tied to education and the involvement of youth. Efforts have been made to involve young Choctaw members in cultural activities, language learning, and traditional practices. Youth programs and initiatives are designed to instill a sense of pride in their cultural heritage and encourage active participation in cultural activities.

In recent years, the Choctaw Nation has expanded its cultural outreach efforts beyond its borders, engaging with the broader public to share the richness of Choctaw culture. Cultural festivals, exhibitions, and events provide opportunities for people from different backgrounds to learn about and appreciate Choctaw traditions.

The Choctaw Nation's commitment to cultural preservation is a testament to its resilience and determination to ensure that future generations continue to embrace their unique heritage. The tribe's efforts to preserve language, traditions, and cultural practices are not only a means of honoring their ancestors but also a way of fostering a strong and vibrant Choctaw identity for generations to come. Through these endeavors, the Choctaw Nation stands as a model for the importance of cultural preservation in the face of changing times.

Emerging Choctaw leadership is a vital and evolving aspect of the Choctaw Nation's ongoing development. As the tribe faces contemporary challenges and opportunities, new generations of Choctaw leaders are stepping forward to guide their community into the future. These emerging leaders are building on the legacy of their ancestors while adapting to the complexities of the modern world.

The Choctaw Nation values the principles of self-governance and sovereignty, which provide a framework for leadership and decision-making within the tribe. Emerging leaders within the Choctaw Nation often begin their journeys by actively participating in tribal governance and community organizations. They engage in tribal elections, serve on tribal councils, and contribute to the development of policies and programs that address the needs of their people.

One of the key arenas where emerging Choctaw leadership is nurtured is through educational opportunities. The tribe places a strong emphasis on education and supports Choctaw students in pursuing academic and professional goals. Many emerging leaders have pursued higher education and returned to their communities equipped with the knowledge and skills needed to serve their tribe effectively.

Choctaw leaders are encouraged to actively engage with tribal members and seek input from the community. Open communication and transparency are valued attributes in Choctaw leadership, as leaders work collaboratively with their constituents to address a wide range of issues, including healthcare, education, economic development, and cultural preservation.

Youth leadership development is a priority for the Choctaw Nation. The tribe recognizes the importance of empowering young Choctaw members to become future leaders. Various youth programs, mentorship initiatives, and leadership training opportunities are offered to nurture the potential of young leaders. These programs instill a sense of responsibility, cultural pride, and a commitment to serving the Choctaw community.

The Choctaw Nation also places a strong emphasis on the preservation of cultural heritage. Emerging leaders are encouraged to actively participate in cultural activities, learn traditional practices, and contribute to the continuation of Choctaw traditions. This cultural grounding informs their leadership style and fosters a deep sense of cultural identity.

As emerging Choctaw leaders navigate the challenges of the modern world, they are often called upon to address issues related to tribal sovereignty, land and resource management, economic development, and healthcare. These leaders work to balance the needs of their community with the responsibilities of self-governance and the protection of tribal rights.

Economic development is a significant focus for emerging Choctaw leadership. The tribe has diversified its economic portfolio, with successful gaming operations, manufacturing ventures, and various business enterprises. Emerging leaders play a role in shaping economic policies and initiatives that promote job creation, revenue generation, and community development.

Healthcare is another critical area of concern for Choctaw leaders. Access to quality healthcare services is a priority, and leaders work to ensure that tribal members have access to healthcare facilities, programs, and resources that meet their needs. This includes addressing health disparities, promoting wellness, and responding to public health challenges.

Emerging Choctaw leaders are also involved in efforts to address environmental conservation and stewardship. As caretakers of their ancestral lands, they are committed to preserving the natural resources and ecosystems that sustain their communities. Initiatives related to environmental sustainability and resource management are integral to their leadership roles.

In addition to addressing the immediate needs of the Choctaw Nation, emerging leaders are focused on long-term planning and strategic development. They recognize the importance of intergenerational leadership continuity and are actively engaged in succession planning to ensure that the tribe's values, traditions, and sovereignty endure.

Collaboration with other tribal nations and external partners is another hallmark of emerging Choctaw leadership. Leaders engage in diplomacy, negotiate agreements, and build partnerships to advance the interests of the Choctaw Nation on regional, national, and international levels. In summary, emerging Choctaw leadership represents the future of the tribe, carrying forward the legacy of their ancestors while adapting to the complexities of the modern world. These leaders are guided by the principles of self-governance, sovereignty, cultural preservation, and community service. Their commitment to the well-being and prosperity of the Choctaw Nation ensures that the tribe remains resilient, adaptive, and empowered to face the challenges and opportunities of the 21st century.

Chapter 7: The Choctaw Nation Today: Governance and Identity

Modern Choctaw government and tribal sovereignty are fundamental aspects of the Choctaw Nation's identity and self-determination. As a sovereign nation, the Choctaw Nation exercises its inherent right to govern its affairs, make decisions, and chart its own course in the contemporary world. The tribe's government reflects the values of self-governance, cultural preservation, and the well-being of its citizens.

The Choctaw Nation's government is structured to ensure representation, accountability, and participation of tribal members in the decision-making process. At its core, the government is guided by a constitution that outlines the structure of the tribal government, its branches, and the powers and responsibilities of its leaders.

The government of the Choctaw Nation is divided into three branches: the Executive Branch, the Legislative Branch, and the Judicial Branch. Each branch plays a distinct role in governing the tribe and upholding the principles of democracy and justice.

Executive Branch: The Executive Branch is led by the Principal Chief, who serves as the head of the Choctaw Nation's government. The Principal Chief is elected by tribal citizens and is responsible for executing the laws, overseeing tribal departments and agencies, and representing the tribe in external matters. The Executive Branch also includes other elected officials and administrative staff who assist in the daily operations of tribal government.

Legislative Branch: The Legislative Branch consists of the Tribal Council, which is composed of elected representatives from different districts within the Choctaw Nation. The Tribal Council is responsible for creating and passing tribal laws, resolutions, and budgets. It serves as the legislative body that represents the interests and voices of tribal citizens.

Judicial Branch: The Judicial Branch includes the Choctaw Nation Judicial System, which is responsible for interpreting and applying tribal laws. The judicial system ensures that justice is administered fairly and in accordance with tribal laws and customs. It also includes the Choctaw Nation Supreme Court, which is the highest court of appeals within the tribe.

Tribal sovereignty is a foundational principle of the Choctaw Nation's government. Sovereignty recognizes the inherent authority of tribal nations to govern their internal affairs, make decisions about their citizens, and manage their lands and resources. The Choctaw Nation exercises this sovereignty by enacting laws, establishing policies, and entering into agreements with other governments and entities.

One of the key aspects of tribal sovereignty is the ability to engage in government-to-government relations with the federal and state governments. This means that the Choctaw Nation can negotiate treaties, agreements, and partnerships that respect the tribe's unique status and interests. These government-to-government relationships are essential for addressing issues such as land rights, resource management, and jurisdiction.

The Choctaw Nation's government also plays a vital role in providing essential services and programs to its citizens. These services include healthcare, education, housing, social services, and cultural preservation efforts. Tribal leaders work diligently to ensure that tribal members have access to these services, which are designed to promote the well-being and prosperity of the Choctaw Nation's citizens.

Economic development is another critical component of modern Choctaw government and sovereignty. The tribe has diversified its economic portfolio, with successful ventures in gaming, manufacturing, healthcare, and various businesses. The revenue generated from these enterprises is reinvested in the community, supporting job creation, infrastructure development, and social programs.

The Choctaw Nation actively engages in efforts to preserve and revitalize its cultural heritage. Cultural preservation initiatives are supported by tribal government, which recognizes the importance of maintaining cultural practices, language, and traditions. These efforts not only strengthen the cultural identity of the tribe but also contribute to the well-being of tribal citizens.

In summary, modern Choctaw government and tribal sovereignty are central to the Choctaw Nation's continued self-determination and prosperity. The government's structure, democratic processes, and commitment to cultural preservation reflect the values and aspirations of the Choctaw people. As a sovereign nation, the Choctaw Nation exercises its rights and responsibilities to ensure the welfare and future success of its citizens and the preservation of its rich heritage.

Economic development and community progress are pivotal components of the Choctaw Nation's mission to enhance the well-being of its citizens, promote self-sufficiency, and build a prosperous future. Through strategic initiatives and partnerships, the Choctaw Nation has made significant strides in fostering economic growth, creating employment opportunities, and advancing the overall progress of its communities.

Diversified Economic Portfolio: The Choctaw Nation has diversified its economic portfolio to reduce dependency on any single industry. This diversification includes ventures in gaming, manufacturing, healthcare, retail, agriculture, and various businesses. By spreading economic activities across multiple sectors, the tribe has enhanced its financial stability and resilience.

Gaming Operations: The Choctaw Nation operates successful gaming and entertainment facilities that have not only generated revenue for the tribe but have also become significant employers in the region. These gaming enterprises offer a wide range of job opportunities, from gaming and hospitality to administration and management.

Manufacturing and Industry: The tribe has ventured into manufacturing, creating jobs and economic value in areas such as aerospace, defense, and technology. Manufacturing operations have not only contributed to local economic development but have also expanded the Choctaw Nation's role in national and international markets.

Healthcare Services: The Choctaw Nation provides comprehensive healthcare services to its citizens, including medical facilities, clinics, and wellness programs. Access to quality healthcare is a crucial component of community progress, ensuring the health and well-being of tribal members.

Education and Workforce Development: The tribe places a strong emphasis on education and workforce development. Scholarships, educational programs, and vocational training opportunities are provided to empower tribal members to pursue higher education and develop skills that are in demand in various industries.

Housing Initiatives: Housing programs and initiatives have been established to improve housing conditions for Choctaw families. Affordable and safe housing is essential for community stability and progress.

Infrastructure and Community Development: The Choctaw Nation invests in infrastructure projects, including road improvements, community facilities, and utility services. These investments not only enhance the quality of life for tribal members but also promote economic development in Choctaw communities.

Small Business Development: The tribe supports small business development among its citizens, fostering entrepreneurship and local economic growth. Small businesses contribute to job creation and community vitality.

Cultural Preservation and Tourism: Cultural preservation efforts, including the promotion of Choctaw traditions, arts, and crafts, also play a role in economic development. Cultural tourism initiatives attract visitors and provide economic opportunities for tribal members.

Community Engagement and Partnerships: The Choctaw Nation actively engages with tribal citizens, community leaders, and external partners to identify opportunities for growth and progress. Collaboration with federal and state governments, as well as private sector entities, is essential for advancing economic development initiatives.

Environmental Stewardship: Sustainable practices and environmental stewardship are integral to economic development. The Choctaw Nation strives to balance economic growth with responsible resource management and environmental conservation.

Philanthropic Initiatives: The Choctaw Nation has a long tradition of philanthropy, giving back to the broader community and supporting charitable causes. These initiatives reflect the tribe's commitment to social responsibility and community progress beyond its borders.

In summary, economic development and community progress are intertwined in the Choctaw Nation's vision for a prosperous future. Through a multifaceted approach that includes economic diversification, education, healthcare, infrastructure development, and cultural preservation, the tribe seeks to create opportunities, improve the quality of life for its citizens, and build a resilient and thriving community. The Choctaw Nation's commitment to economic growth and community progress underscores its dedication to the well-being and advancement of its people.

Choctaw identity and cultural expression are deeply interwoven, forming a vibrant tapestry that reflects the tribe's rich history, values, and resilience. The Choctaw Nation has a long and storied heritage, and its members take great pride in preserving and celebrating their unique cultural identity.

At the heart of Choctaw identity is a profound connection to their ancestral lands, which encompass a vast region stretching across the southeastern United States. The Choctaw people have a strong sense of place, rooted in their homeland, and their cultural expression often revolves around their deep connection to the land.

Language, as a cornerstone of identity, plays a pivotal role in Choctaw cultural expression. The Choctaw language, known as Chahta Anumpa, serves as a vessel for preserving traditional knowledge, stories, and customs. It encapsulates the wisdom of generations and holds within its words the essence of Choctaw identity. Efforts to revitalize and pass down the Choctaw language to younger generations are central to cultural preservation.

The Choctaw Nation places great importance on storytelling as a means of cultural expression. Elders and storytellers within the tribe are revered for their ability to share the history, myths, and oral traditions that have been handed down through the ages. These stories serve not only as a source of knowledge but also as a way to reinforce Choctaw values and teachings.

Music and dance are integral components of Choctaw cultural expression. The Choctaw stomp dance, known as Tushka Homma, is a lively and spirited tradition that brings the community together in celebration. The rhythmic beat of the drums, the intricate footwork, and the colorful regalia worn by dancers all contribute to a vibrant cultural tapestry that speaks to the resilience and unity of the Choctaw people.

Visual arts and craftsmanship are also vital forms of cultural expression. Choctaw artisans create intricate beadwork, pottery, basketry, and other crafts that are not only beautiful works of art but also symbolic of their cultural heritage. These traditional crafts are passed down through families, preserving the artistry and skills of past generations.

Cultural ceremonies and gatherings provide opportunities for Choctaw community members to come together and express their shared identity. Events such as stickball games, powwows, and traditional feasts serve as occasions for cultural expression, fostering a sense of belonging and connection among tribal members.

Religious beliefs and spirituality are deeply intertwined with Choctaw identity and are expressed through ceremonies and rituals. Choctaw ceremonies often center around the natural world, reflecting a profound respect for the land, water, and all living beings. These spiritual practices are a testament to the tribe's connection to the environment and their enduring reverence for it.

Cultural preservation efforts extend to education and outreach. The Choctaw Nation is dedicated to passing down cultural knowledge to younger generations through educational programs, language immersion, and cultural classes. These initiatives empower Choctaw youth to embrace their heritage and take pride in their cultural identity.

Interactions with neighboring tribes and nations have also influenced Choctaw cultural expression. Trade networks, alliances, and shared histories have contributed to a rich tapestry of cultural exchange. The Choctaw people have adopted and adapted elements from other cultures while maintaining the distinctiveness of their own.

The Choctaw Nation actively engages in cultural outreach to share its heritage with the broader community and to foster mutual understanding. Cultural festivals, exhibitions, and educational events provide opportunities for people from different backgrounds to learn about and appreciate Choctaw traditions.

Cultural preservation is not static; it evolves and adapts to changing times and circumstances. Modern technology, such as digital media and the internet, has enabled the Choctaw Nation to reach a global audience and connect with Choctaw members around the world. This technology facilitates the sharing of stories, language resources, and cultural knowledge, ensuring that Choctaw identity remains dynamic and relevant.

In summary, Choctaw identity and cultural expression are integral to the tribe's sense of self and resilience. Through language, storytelling, music, dance, visual arts, and spiritual practices, the Choctaw people celebrate their heritage and pass down their cultural legacy to future generations. These expressions of identity not only preserve the past but also empower the Choctaw Nation to continue thriving and evolving in the modern world. The Choctaw commitment to cultural preservation underscores the tribe's enduring spirit and dedication to its unique heritage.

Chapter 8: Preserving the Legacy: Language, Arts, and Traditions

Language revitalization and preservation programs are at the forefront of efforts to safeguard and revitalize indigenous languages worldwide, and the Choctaw Nation is no exception. The Choctaw people recognize the immense value of their language, Chahta Anumpa, not only as a means of communication but also as a repository of cultural knowledge, identity, and connection to their ancestral heritage.

The Choctaw language, Chahta Anumpa, is a complex and beautiful linguistic tradition with a unique history and grammar. It is a testament to the intellectual and cultural depth of the Choctaw people. However, like many indigenous languages, Chahta Anumpa faced a decline in usage and fluency over the years due to factors such as colonization, forced removal, and the pressure of English dominance.

To combat the decline and ensure the survival of the Choctaw language, the Choctaw Nation has implemented a multifaceted approach to language revitalization and preservation. These programs are not only focused on teaching the language but also on instilling a deep cultural understanding among tribal members.

One of the cornerstones of language revitalization efforts is language immersion programs. These programs create immersive environments where Choctaw children and learners can become fluent speakers. The immersion approach goes beyond traditional language instruction and provides learners with opportunities to engage with the language in everyday contexts. It is a powerful method for fostering language acquisition and cultural connection.

Additionally, the Choctaw Nation has developed written resources, textbooks, and educational materials in the Choctaw language. Schools and educational institutions within the tribe have incorporated language programs to ensure that Choctaw children have the opportunity to learn their native language from a young age.

Language preservation also extends to efforts to document and archive Chahta Anumpa. Linguists, scholars, and community members have worked together to compile dictionaries, grammars, and resources that serve as references for future generations. These resources are invaluable in maintaining the integrity of the language and ensuring its proper usage.

Moreover, language revitalization programs recognize the pivotal role of elders and fluent speakers within the community. Elders possess a wealth of linguistic and cultural knowledge, and they play a crucial role in teaching the language to younger generations through oral tradition. Storytelling, conversations, and family gatherings are occasions where the language is actively used and passed down.

Cultural immersion experiences are another essential component of language revitalization. These experiences offer Choctaw learners the opportunity to engage with cultural activities, traditions, and customs while using the language. Immersion camps, workshops, and cultural events provide a holistic approach to language learning and cultural preservation.

The incorporation of Chahta Anumpa into various aspects of daily life is a fundamental part of language revitalization efforts. Signs, place names, and public announcements are being translated into the Choctaw language, making it a visible and integral part of tribal communities.

Language revitalization is not limited to the younger generation; it extends to adults and learners of all ages. Language classes and courses are offered to tribal members to ensure that everyone has the opportunity to learn and use the language. These classes are designed to cater to various levels of proficiency, from beginners to advanced speakers.

The efforts of the Choctaw Nation also extend beyond its borders. Collaboration with other indigenous nations and language revitalization organizations fosters a network of support and shared resources. The exchange of knowledge and best practices contributes to the success of language revitalization programs not only within the Choctaw Nation but also across indigenous communities.

Language revitalization is not a short-term endeavor; it requires ongoing commitment and dedication. The Choctaw Nation recognizes that the revitalization of Chahta Anumpa is a long-term journey that will span generations. The ultimate goal is to create a sustainable environment where the language is actively spoken, used, and cherished by Choctaw citizens.

In summary, language revitalization and preservation programs are central to the Choctaw Nation's commitment to preserving its cultural heritage and identity. Through immersion programs, educational resources, intergenerational learning, and cultural engagement, the tribe is actively working to ensure that Chahta Anumpa continues to thrive. The Choctaw language is not just a means of communication; it is a source of cultural pride and a connection to the past, present, and future of the Choctaw people. These efforts are a testament to the tribe's determination to pass down its linguistic and cultural legacy to generations yet to come.

Traditional arts, crafts, and storytelling are integral components of the Choctaw cultural heritage, serving as a vibrant tapestry that weaves together the tribe's history, values, and creativity. These expressions of cultural identity have been handed down through generations, preserving the Choctaw way of life and connecting tribal members to their ancestral roots.

Traditional Arts and Crafts:
Choctaw traditional arts and crafts encompass a wide array of artistic expressions, each rooted in the tribe's deep cultural traditions. These art forms not only showcase the artistic

talents of Choctaw artisans but also serve as tangible links to the past.

Beadwork: Beadwork is a cherished Choctaw art form that involves creating intricate patterns and designs using colorful beads. These beadwork creations are often found in regalia, clothing, and accessories, and they reflect the individuality and creativity of the artisan.

Pottery: Choctaw pottery is a testament to the tribe's historical reliance on clay for practical and artistic purposes. Choctaw potters craft both functional and decorative pieces, incorporating traditional designs and techniques passed down through the generations.

Basketry: Basketry is another significant Choctaw craft, with artisans skillfully weaving baskets and containers from natural materials such as rivercane and pine needles. These baskets serve various purposes, from storage to ceremonial use.

Woodworking: Traditional woodworking includes the creation of tools, utensils, and decorative items from wood. Choctaw artisans use their woodworking skills to craft items that are both utilitarian and aesthetically pleasing.

Textile Arts: Choctaw textile arts encompass weaving and textile decoration. Skilled weavers create intricate patterns on looms, producing textiles used in clothing, blankets, and other items. Textile decoration may involve dyeing and painting to add vibrant colors and designs.

Storytelling and Oral Tradition:

Storytelling is a vital aspect of Choctaw cultural expression, with a rich tradition of oral narratives that convey history, wisdom, and moral lessons. Elders and storytellers play a pivotal role in preserving and passing down these stories, ensuring that the tribe's oral tradition endures.

Creation Stories: Choctaw creation stories recount the origins of the Choctaw people and their connection to the land. These narratives explain how the Choctaw came to be and their responsibilities as stewards of their homeland.

Myths and Legends: Myths and legends are a repository of cultural knowledge, offering insights into Choctaw values, beliefs, and the natural world. These stories often feature characters and events that teach important lessons and convey cultural teachings.

Historical Narratives: Historical narratives provide a glimpse into the past, chronicling the experiences of Choctaw ancestors, including their struggles, triumphs, and resilience. These narratives serve as a reminder of the Choctaw people's endurance and adaptability.

Moral and Ethical Stories: Many Choctaw stories convey moral and ethical lessons, guiding tribal members on the path of right conduct, respect for others, and harmony with the natural world.

Storytelling is a dynamic tradition that adapts to contemporary contexts. While traditional narratives continue to be shared, modern Choctaw storytellers also address contemporary issues and challenges facing their community, demonstrating the enduring relevance of this oral tradition.

Cultural Significance:

Traditional arts, crafts, and storytelling hold profound cultural significance within the Choctaw Nation. They serve as conduits for cultural transmission, allowing knowledge and wisdom to be passed from one generation to the next. These cultural expressions also foster a sense of identity and pride among tribal members, reinforcing their connection to their Choctaw heritage.

The creation of traditional arts and crafts is often a communal and intergenerational endeavor. Elders and experienced artisans pass on their skills and knowledge to younger generations, ensuring the continuity of these crafts. This intergenerational transfer of knowledge strengthens family bonds and preserves cultural practices.

Traditional arts and crafts are not static; they evolve and adapt over time while retaining their cultural authenticity. Choctaw artisans may incorporate contemporary materials and techniques into their work, demonstrating the resilience and adaptability of Choctaw cultural expression.

Similarly, storytelling remains a living tradition that responds to the changing needs and aspirations of the Choctaw community. Storytellers use their narratives to address issues such as identity, cultural preservation, and social change, making the tradition relevant in the modern era.

The Choctaw Nation actively promotes these cultural expressions through cultural centers, workshops, and educational programs. These initiatives provide opportunities for tribal members to learn traditional crafts, storytelling techniques, and the Choctaw language. They also create spaces where Choctaw culture can be celebrated and shared with the broader community.

In summary, traditional arts, crafts, and storytelling are the threads that weave the fabric of Choctaw culture, connecting the past, present, and future of the tribe. These expressions of cultural identity serve as a testament to the creativity, resilience, and rich heritage of the Choctaw people. As they continue to evolve and adapt, traditional arts, crafts, and storytelling remain integral to the cultural vitality of the Choctaw Nation.

Cultural centers and celebrations hold a special place within the Choctaw Nation, serving as vibrant hubs of cultural preservation, education, and community unity. These institutions and events play a crucial role in fostering a deep sense of cultural identity, passing down traditions to future generations, and celebrating the rich heritage of the Choctaw people.

Cultural Centers:

Cultural centers within the Choctaw Nation are dynamic spaces that serve as focal points for cultural preservation and education. They are dedicated to showcasing the diverse aspects of Choctaw culture, including language, arts, crafts, history, and traditional knowledge.

Language Revitalization: Many cultural centers offer language programs and resources aimed at revitalizing the Choctaw language, Chahta Anumpa. These programs provide opportunities for tribal members to learn, practice, and speak the language, ensuring its continuity.

Exhibitions and Artifacts: Cultural centers house exhibitions and collections of artifacts that highlight the history and cultural achievements of the Choctaw people. These exhibits provide a window into the past, allowing visitors to explore the tribe's journey, traditions, and contributions.

Arts and Crafts Workshops: Choctaw cultural centers often host arts and crafts workshops where tribal members can learn traditional skills such as beadwork, pottery, basketry, and textile arts. These workshops are led by experienced artisans who pass down their knowledge.

Storytelling and Oral Traditions: Cultural centers serve as venues for storytelling and oral traditions, where elders and storytellers share Choctaw myths, legends, and historical narratives. These storytelling sessions help preserve the tribe's oral tradition.

Educational Programs: Cultural centers offer a wide range of educational programs for tribal members of all ages. These programs encompass cultural awareness, history, language, and traditional practices, empowering individuals to connect with their heritage.

Community Gatherings: Cultural centers host community gatherings, meetings, and events that foster a sense of unity and belonging among tribal members. These spaces provide opportunities for Choctaw citizens to come together and celebrate their shared culture.

Cultural Celebrations:

Cultural celebrations and festivals are vibrant occasions where the Choctaw Nation comes alive with music, dance, food, and communal spirit. These events are deeply rooted in tradition and serve as an expression of cultural pride and resilience.

Powwows: Powwows are among the most iconic cultural celebrations within the Choctaw Nation and among indigenous communities across North America. These gatherings feature competitive dancing, drumming, regalia, and traditional foods. Powwows are a time for Choctaw citizens to reconnect with their cultural roots, showcase their talents, and strengthen community bonds.

Stickball: Stickball, known as "the little brother of war," is a traditional Choctaw sport that holds immense cultural significance. Stickball games are not only athletic competitions but also ceremonies that honor Choctaw traditions. These games are accompanied by songs, rituals, and deep spiritual meaning.

Green Corn Ceremonies: Green Corn Ceremonies are spiritual and cultural events held during the corn harvest season. These ceremonies include purification rituals, feasts, dances, and storytelling. They serve as an opportunity for tribal members to renew their connections to the land and express gratitude for the harvest.

Community Feasts: Choctaw cultural celebrations often include communal feasts where traditional foods and dishes are shared among tribal members. These feasts are a time for families and communities to come together, strengthen bonds, and celebrate their cultural heritage.

Cultural Pageants: Cultural pageants are events that showcase the talent, beauty, and cultural knowledge of Choctaw women. These pageants highlight the role of Choctaw women in preserving and promoting cultural traditions.

Social Dances: Social dances are a form of cultural expression that brings people together to celebrate, share stories, and enjoy music. These dances often have specific meanings and are an essential part of cultural celebrations.

Community Parades: Choctaw cultural celebrations may feature parades that showcase traditional clothing, regalia, and historical reenactments. These parades allow tribal members to share their culture with a broader audience.

Cultural centers and celebrations are not limited to tribal members; they also provide opportunities for the broader community to learn about and appreciate Choctaw culture. These events are often open to the public and serve as a means of promoting cultural awareness and understanding among different communities.

In recent years, technology has played a role in expanding the reach of cultural celebrations. Live streaming, social media, and digital storytelling have allowed Choctaw cultural events to connect with a global audience, raising awareness of the tribe's traditions and contributions.

In summary, cultural centers and celebrations are essential pillars of the Choctaw Nation's efforts to preserve, celebrate, and pass down its cultural heritage. These institutions and events are a testament to the tribe's commitment to maintaining its unique identity, fostering community unity, and sharing its vibrant culture with the world. Through cultural centers and celebrations, the Choctaw people continue to celebrate their resilience, creativity, and enduring connection to their ancestral heritage.

BOOK 3
CHICKASAW HOMELAND
A JOURNEY THROUGH HISTORY

BY A.J. KINGSTON

Chapter 1: The Ancient Roots of the Chickasaw People

The early origins and migration of the Chickasaw people are rooted in a complex history that traces their path from ancestral homelands to their eventual settlement in the southeastern region of the United States. Understanding the journey of the Chickasaw people provides insights into their rich heritage and cultural resilience.

Ancient Roots:

The Chickasaw people are part of the larger Southeastern Woodlands Native American cultural group, which includes several tribes that inhabited the southeastern region of North America. Archaeological evidence suggests that the Chickasaw people have deep roots in the Mississippi Valley, particularly in what is now Mississippi and Tennessee. Their ancestors established a presence in these areas thousands of years ago, developing distinct cultural practices, traditions, and a way of life closely tied to the land and its resources.

Early Migration and Expansion:

The early history of the Chickasaw people involves a series of migrations and movements as they sought to establish themselves in the region. They were originally part of a larger tribal confederacy known as the Choctaw-Chickasaw, but over time, the Chickasaw people emerged as a distinct group with their own language and culture.

As neighboring tribes and nations expanded their territories and populations, the Chickasaw people faced both alliances and conflicts. They engaged in trade networks, forging relationships with other tribes such as the Choctaw, Creek, and Cherokee, which played a significant role in shaping their culture and history. The Chickasaw people also encountered European explorers and traders who ventured into the southeastern United States in the early 16th century.

European Contact and Colonial Period:

European contact with the Chickasaw people began with the arrival of Spanish explorers in the early 16th century. The Chickasaw initially maintained a degree of autonomy and navigated relationships with European powers, including the Spanish, French, and British, through strategic alliances and trade partnerships. The Chickasaw's reputation as formidable warriors also contributed to their ability to negotiate on their terms.

During the colonial period, the Chickasaw people faced challenges from European encroachment and conflicts with other tribes, particularly the Choctaw and Creek. The competition for territory and resources in the Southeastern Woodlands led to tensions and intermittent warfare.

Chickasaw Removal and Resilience:

The Chickasaw people, like many other indigenous nations, experienced the devastating effects of European diseases, such as smallpox, which resulted in population decline. In the early 19th century, the United States government's policy of Indian removal led to the forced relocation of many southeastern tribes, including the Chickasaw.

In 1837, the Chickasaw people were forcibly removed from their ancestral lands and relocated to Indian Territory, which is present-day Oklahoma. This traumatic event, known as the Chickasaw Removal or Trail of Tears, was a harrowing journey marked by hardship and loss.

Despite the challenges and displacement, the Chickasaw people demonstrated remarkable resilience and adaptability in their new homeland. They established a government, rebuilt their communities, and worked to preserve their culture and traditions. Over time, the Chickasaw Nation flourished, embracing education, agriculture, and economic development to secure their future.

Contemporary Chickasaw Nation:

Today, the Chickasaw Nation is a thriving sovereign nation with a vibrant cultural heritage. The Chickasaw people have preserved their language, traditions, and identity through cultural initiatives, language revitalization programs, and educational efforts. The Chickasaw Nation is also known for its commitment to healthcare, education, and economic development, ensuring a prosperous future for its citizens.

In summary, the early origins and migration of the Chickasaw people are a testament to their resilience and adaptability in the face of changing circumstances and challenges. Their journey from ancient roots in the Mississippi Valley to their present-day homeland in Oklahoma reflects a rich history marked by cultural continuity and a deep connection to their ancestral heritage. The Chickasaw people's legacy endures through their commitment to preserving their traditions and passing them on to future generations.

The Chickasaw homeland, located in what is now the southeastern United States, was once home to a vibrant and complex network of indigenous societies and cultures. These societies played a crucial role in shaping the region's history, with each group contributing to the cultural mosaic of the Chickasaw homeland.

1. Chickasaw Nation: The Chickasaw people themselves were the dominant indigenous society in their homeland. They were organized into a matrilineal kinship system and inhabited villages with traditional council houses. Their society was known for its warrior traditions, diplomacy, and trade networks. The Chickasaw were skilled hunters, farmers, and traders, and their society had a rich oral tradition that included myths, legends, and historical narratives.

2. Choctaw: The Choctaw were a neighboring indigenous society to the Chickasaw and shared similar cultural and linguistic roots. They were part of the same Choctaw-Chickasaw confederacy before the Chickasaw became a distinct group. The Choctaw had their own distinct villages and societal organization. They were skilled farmers and hunters, and like the Chickasaw, they had a matrilineal kinship system.

3. Creek: The Creek Nation, also known as the Muscogee Creek, inhabited a region that included parts of Alabama, Georgia, and Florida. They had a complex societal structure, with a central government known as the Creek Confederacy. The Creek were skilled farmers who cultivated maize, beans, and other crops. They were also known for their pottery, basketry, and artwork.

4. Cherokee: To the north of the Chickasaw homeland were the Cherokee people. The Cherokee Nation had a highly developed society with a centralized government, a written language, and a complex religious and political system. They practiced agriculture and were known for their skill in growing crops like corn, beans, and squash.

5. Natchez: The Natchez were a society located in the lower Mississippi Valley, near the Chickasaw homeland. They had a distinctive social structure with a hereditary nobility known as the "Great Sun." The Natchez practiced agriculture, particularly maize cultivation, and had a complex religious system.

6. Yuchi: The Yuchi people inhabited the southeastern United States, including parts of Alabama and Georgia. They had their own language and a unique societal structure. The Yuchi were known for their traditional houses, which were circular and made of wattle and daub.

These indigenous societies had their own languages, traditions, and ways of life, but they often interacted through trade, alliances, and diplomacy. The Chickasaw, in particular, maintained important relationships with neighboring tribes, which influenced their culture and history. Over time, European contact and colonial expansion had a significant impact on these indigenous societies, leading to changes in their ways of life and, in some cases, forced removal from their ancestral lands.

Despite the challenges and disruptions brought about by European colonization, the legacy of these indigenous societies persists in the cultural heritage and traditions of their descendants. Today, the Chickasaw Nation and other indigenous nations continue to celebrate and preserve their rich histories and cultural identities, ensuring that the stories and traditions of these societies are passed down to future generations.

Cultural practices and traditions are the heart and soul of any society, providing a framework for its identity, values, and way of life. Within indigenous cultures like the Chickasaw Nation, these practices and traditions are deeply rooted, serving as a means of preserving the heritage and passing it down through generations.

Oral Traditions and Storytelling:
Oral traditions and storytelling are cornerstones of Chickasaw culture. Elders and storytellers play a pivotal role in the transmission of knowledge, wisdom, and history. Through oral narratives, myths, legends, and historical accounts, the Chickasaw people connect with their past and communicate their values and beliefs.

Myths and Legends: Myths and legends are sacred narratives that explain the origin of the Chickasaw people, their connection to the land, and their relationship with the natural world. These stories often feature legendary figures and events that hold profound spiritual and cultural significance.

Historical Narratives: Historical narratives recount the experiences of Chickasaw ancestors, including their interactions with neighboring tribes and European settlers. These narratives provide insights into the challenges and triumphs of the Chickasaw people throughout their history.

Ceremonial Practices:
Ceremonial practices are an integral part of Chickasaw culture, marking important milestones and events in the lives of tribal members. These ceremonies are often rooted in ancient

traditions and are passed down from one generation to the next.

Green Corn Ceremonies: The Green Corn Ceremony is a central Chickasaw tradition, celebrating the corn harvest season. It involves purification rituals, feasts, dances, and storytelling. The ceremony reinforces the tribe's connection to the land and expresses gratitude for the harvest.

Stickball: Stickball, known as "the little brother of war," is a traditional Chickasaw sport with deep cultural and spiritual significance. Stickball games are not only athletic competitions but also ceremonies that honor Chickasaw traditions. They include songs, rituals, and communal participation.

Stomp Dances: Stomp dances are vibrant, rhythmic celebrations that feature singing, drumming, and communal dancing. These dances often accompany various ceremonies and gatherings within the Chickasaw community.

Artistic Expressions:

Artistic expressions are a testament to the creativity and talent of the Chickasaw people. They encompass a wide range of traditional arts and crafts that reflect the tribe's cultural heritage.

Beadwork: Chickasaw artisans create intricate beadwork designs using colorful beads, often incorporating them into clothing, accessories, and regalia. Beadwork is a cherished art form that reflects individual creativity.

Pottery: Chickasaw potters craft both functional and decorative pottery using traditional techniques and designs. These pieces are not only utilitarian but also artistic expressions of Chickasaw culture.

Basketry: Basketry is another significant Chickasaw craft, with artisans skillfully weaving baskets and containers from natural materials such as rivercane and pine needles. These baskets serve various purposes, from storage to ceremonial use.

Textile Arts: Chickasaw textile arts encompass weaving and textile decoration. Skilled weavers create intricate patterns on looms, producing textiles used in clothing, blankets, and other items. Textile decoration may involve dyeing and painting to add vibrant colors and designs.

Language and Communication:

Language is a vital component of Chickasaw culture. The Chickasaw language, Chahta Anumpa, is an integral part of daily life and cultural expression.

Language Revitalization: Efforts to revitalize the Chickasaw language are ongoing, with language programs, classes, and resources aimed at preserving and teaching the language to future generations. Language revitalization is seen as a crucial way to maintain cultural continuity.

Ceremonial Language: The Chickasaw language is often used in ceremonial practices, reinforcing its significance in cultural and spiritual contexts. Ceremonial language helps preserve traditional knowledge and rituals.

Governance and Leadership:

Chickasaw governance and leadership are deeply tied to cultural practices and traditions. The Chickasaw Nation's political structure reflects its commitment to preserving its heritage.

Tribal Government: The Chickasaw Nation has a modern tribal government that operates within the framework of its traditional values and principles. It is a sovereign nation with its own constitution, leadership, and laws.

Cultural Leadership: Cultural leaders within the Chickasaw Nation play a vital role in preserving and promoting cultural practices and traditions. They work alongside tribal government leaders to ensure the cultural continuity of the Chickasaw people.

Interconnectedness with the Natural World:

A fundamental aspect of Chickasaw culture is the belief in the interconnectedness of all living beings and the natural world.

Stewardship of the Land: Chickasaw traditions emphasize responsible stewardship of the land and its resources. This includes practices that promote sustainability and environmental conservation.

Harmony with Nature: Chickasaw cultural practices and traditions reflect a deep respect for the natural world, promoting harmony with nature and a sustainable way of life.

In summary, cultural practices and traditions are the threads that bind the Chickasaw people to their history, values, and way of life. These practices serve as a bridge between generations, connecting the past to the present and ensuring that the rich heritage of the Chickasaw Nation continues to thrive. Through storytelling, ceremonies, artistic expressions, language, and a deep connection to the land, the Chickasaw people celebrate their culture, foster community unity, and pass down their traditions to future generations.

Chapter 2: Early Encounters and European Contact

The arrival of European explorers in Chickasaw territory marked a significant turning point in the history of the Chickasaw Nation and the southeastern United States. These encounters with European explorers, who ventured into the region seeking new lands, resources, and trade routes, had far-reaching consequences for the Chickasaw people and their way of life.

Early European Contact:
The earliest recorded contact between European explorers and the Chickasaw people occurred in the early 16th century. Spanish explorers, including Hernando de Soto, were among the first Europeans to journey into the Chickasaw homeland. De Soto's expedition, which arrived in the southeastern United States in 1539, aimed to explore and conquer the region. This marked the beginning of a series of interactions between the Chickasaw and European explorers.

De Soto's Encounters: Hernando de Soto's expedition encountered the Chickasaw people during their travels through the southeastern United States. The Chickasaw, known for their warrior traditions and formidable defenses, resisted de Soto's advances. These early encounters were marked by clashes and tensions, as the Chickasaw sought to protect their homeland and sovereignty.

Trade and Alliances:
As European explorers continued to explore the southeastern United States, trade and alliances became key aspects of Chickasaw-European interactions. The Chickasaw people engaged in trade networks, forging relationships with European powers, including the Spanish, French, and British. These alliances were strategic and often revolved around trade in

valuable goods such as fur pelts, deerskins, and other natural resources.

European Alliances: The Chickasaw entered into alliances with European nations, often choosing to align with one European power against another in a bid to safeguard their interests. These alliances sometimes placed the Chickasaw in positions of leverage, allowing them to negotiate trade agreements on their terms.

Trade Networks: The Chickasaw were skilled traders, exchanging their agricultural products, including maize (corn), beans, and other crops, for European goods like metal tools, firearms, and cloth. This trade brought European manufactured items into Chickasaw communities and influenced their material culture.

Impact on Chickasaw Society:

European contact had a profound impact on Chickasaw society, introducing new technologies, crops, and diseases that reshaped their way of life.

Disease and Population Decline: The introduction of European diseases, such as smallpox, had devastating consequences for the Chickasaw people. These diseases, to which they had no immunity, led to a significant decline in their population, as many succumbed to illness.

Material Culture: European trade introduced new materials and technologies to the Chickasaw, altering their material culture. Firearms, metal tools, and European-style clothing became part of Chickasaw life, influencing their daily routines and practices.

Conflict and Adaptation:

As European colonization expanded in the southeastern United States, the Chickasaw people faced challenges and conflicts from encroaching settlers.

Intertribal Conflicts: The Chickasaw were not only in conflict with European settlers but also engaged in intertribal conflicts with neighboring indigenous nations, including the Choctaw and Creek, often fueled by competition for territory and resources.

Resistance and Diplomacy: The Chickasaw people were known for their resistance to European and indigenous adversaries. They employed a combination of military prowess and diplomacy to navigate the changing landscape of southeastern North America.

Forced Relocation and the Chickasaw Nation Today:

In the 19th century, the policy of Indian removal led to the forced relocation of many southeastern tribes, including the Chickasaw.

Chickasaw Removal: In 1837, the Chickasaw people were forcibly removed from their ancestral lands and relocated to Indian Territory, which is present-day Oklahoma. This traumatic event, known as the Chickasaw Removal or Trail of Tears, was a harrowing journey marked by hardship and loss.

Chickasaw Nation Today: Despite the challenges and displacement, the Chickasaw Nation today is a thriving sovereign nation with a vibrant cultural heritage. The Chickasaw people have preserved their language, traditions, and identity through cultural initiatives, language revitalization programs, and educational efforts.

In summary, the arrival of European explorers in Chickasaw territory was a pivotal moment in the history of the Chickasaw people and the southeastern United States. These encounters, marked by trade, alliances, conflict, and adaptation, had a profound and lasting impact on Chickasaw society and shaped the trajectory of their history. Today, the Chickasaw Nation continues to honor its heritage, celebrate its resilience, and ensure that the stories and traditions of its people are passed down to future generations.

Trade and interaction with European settlers played a pivotal role in shaping the history and culture of the Chickasaw Nation and other indigenous tribes in the southeastern United States. These exchanges, often marked by mutual interest and negotiation, had significant implications for both Native American societies and the European settlers who sought to establish a foothold in the New World.

Early Encounters:

The earliest recorded interactions between the Chickasaw people and European settlers occurred in the early 16th century when Spanish explorers, such as Hernando de Soto, embarked on expeditions into the southeastern United States. These explorers sought to explore new lands, find riches, and expand their empires. The Chickasaw homeland, with its fertile lands and valuable resources, was an attractive destination for these early European visitors.

The Chickasaw as Traders:

From the outset, the Chickasaw people were recognized for their prowess as traders. They inhabited a region rich in natural resources, including fertile agricultural lands and an abundance of wildlife. This made them valuable trading partners for European settlers who were eager to acquire items such as deerskins, furs, and agricultural products.

Trade Networks and Alliances:

Trade networks and alliances played a central role in the interactions between the Chickasaw people and European settlers:

European Alliances: The Chickasaw people, like many indigenous tribes, strategically aligned themselves with different European powers, including the Spanish, French, and British. These alliances were often driven by the desire to gain a competitive advantage in trade and protection against rival tribes or European colonial interests.

Trade Routes: Trade routes crisscrossed the southeastern United States, connecting indigenous communities with European trading posts and settlements. The Chickasaw became active participants in these networks, trading not only with European settlers but also with neighboring tribes.

Goods and Commodities: The Chickasaw traded a wide range of goods, including deerskins, furs, hides, agricultural products (such as maize or corn), and manufactured items such as firearms, metal tools, textiles, and glass beads. European settlers, in turn, provided the Chickasaw with European-manufactured goods that enriched their material culture.

Cultural Exchange:

Trade and interaction with European settlers facilitated a significant cultural exchange between the Chickasaw people and the newcomers:

Language and Communication: Language barriers were initially a challenge in communication, but over time, both sides learned to communicate effectively, often relying on a blend of native languages, simplified languages, or non-verbal communication.

Material Culture: European trade introduced new technologies and materials to the Chickasaw, influencing their material culture. Firearms, metal tools, and European-style clothing became integrated into Chickasaw daily life.

Cultural Practices: Cultural practices and traditions also saw adaptations. For instance, the introduction of European-style clothing influenced Chickasaw attire, while the availability of European metal tools affected their methods of hunting and agriculture.

Challenges and Conflict:

While trade and interaction were central to Chickasaw-European relations, these encounters were not without challenges and conflicts:

Disease: European contact brought diseases such as smallpox, measles, and influenza to which the Chickasaw had no immunity. These diseases had devastating effects on Chickasaw populations, leading to significant population declines.

Land Disputes: As European settlers expanded their presence in the region, land disputes and encroachments on Chickasaw territory became increasingly common. These disputes often led to tensions and conflicts.

Intertribal Rivalry: The competition for European trade goods and alliances also fueled intertribal rivalries among indigenous nations, including the Chickasaw, Choctaw, Creek, and Cherokee.

Resilience and Adaptation:

Despite the challenges posed by European contact, the Chickasaw people demonstrated resilience and adaptability:

Diplomacy and Negotiation: The Chickasaw used diplomacy and negotiation to protect their interests and navigate the changing landscape. They formed alliances and maintained diplomatic relations with European powers to secure favorable trade terms.

Survival Strategies: In response to diseases and encroachments, the Chickasaw people adopted various survival strategies. Some groups moved to more remote areas, while others adapted to new economic opportunities.

Cultural Preservation: While adapting to changing circumstances, the Chickasaw people remained committed to preserving their cultural heritage. They continued to pass down their traditions, oral history, and language to future generations.

In summary, trade and interaction with European settlers were integral to the history of the Chickasaw Nation and other indigenous tribes in the southeastern United States. These encounters, characterized by trade networks, alliances, cultural exchange, and challenges, shaped the trajectory of Chickasaw society. Through resilience and adaptation, the Chickasaw people navigated the complexities of European contact while maintaining their cultural identity and traditions. Today, the Chickasaw Nation continues to honor its heritage and celebrate its history as it looks toward the future.

Early diplomatic relations and alliances played a significant role in the history of the Chickasaw Nation, as they sought to navigate the complex landscape of European colonization and interactions with other indigenous tribes. These early diplomatic efforts were critical for safeguarding their interests, securing trade advantages, and maintaining their sovereignty in a rapidly changing world.

Diplomacy with European Powers:

The Chickasaw Nation engaged in diplomacy with various European powers that sought to establish a presence in the southeastern United States:

1. Spanish Diplomacy: The Chickasaw people engaged in diplomacy with the Spanish, who were among the first European powers to explore the region. While early encounters with Hernando de Soto's expedition were marked by conflict, diplomatic relations eventually developed. The Chickasaw strategically formed alliances with the Spanish to gain access to European goods, particularly firearms and metal tools. These alliances allowed them to resist encroachments from other tribes and European rivals.

2. French Relations: The Chickasaw maintained relations with the French, particularly during the period of French colonial expansion in North America. The French, who were active in the Mississippi River Valley, sought to establish friendly relations with indigenous tribes. The Chickasaw engaged in trade with the French, exchanging deerskins and other goods for European items.

3. British Alliances: In the 18th century, the Chickasaw established strong alliances with the British, who sought to consolidate their control over the southeastern United States. These alliances were based on mutual interests, as the Chickasaw traded deerskins and other valuable resources in exchange for British manufactured goods, firearms, and military support. The Chickasaw's military prowess and alliances with the British made them a formidable force in the region.

Intertribal Diplomacy:

Diplomatic relations among indigenous tribes were also a vital aspect of Chickasaw history:

1. Choctaw Relations: The Chickasaw had complex relations with neighboring tribes, including the Choctaw. These relations ranged from trade and alliances to conflicts over territory and resources. Diplomatic efforts were made to navigate these relations, with alliances formed and treaties negotiated at various points in history.

2. Creek Alliances: The Creek Confederacy, a powerful indigenous coalition in the southeastern United States, also engaged in diplomatic interactions with the Chickasaw. These interactions were influenced by shifting alliances and rivalries among tribes in the region.

3. Cherokee Relations: Diplomatic interactions with the Cherokee Nation were shaped by territorial disputes and competition for resources. At times, conflicts arose over land, leading to negotiations and treaties to address these issues.

Maintaining Sovereignty:

Throughout these diplomatic relations and alliances, the Chickasaw Nation remained committed to preserving its sovereignty and territorial integrity:

Treaty-Making: The Chickasaw Nation engaged in treaty-making with European powers, neighboring tribes, and the United States government. These treaties aimed to define boundaries, establish trade relationships, and address issues such as land disputes.

Resisting Encroachments: The Chickasaw people actively resisted encroachments on their ancestral lands. Their military strength and alliances allowed them to defend their territory against both indigenous competitors and European settlers.

Cultural Preservation: While engaging in diplomacy, the Chickasaw people maintained their cultural identity and traditions. Cultural leaders and elders played a crucial role in preserving Chickasaw heritage, including language, storytelling, and ceremonial practices.

Adaptation and Resilience: Diplomatic efforts were just one aspect of the Chickasaw people's adaptability and resilience. They navigated the challenges of European contact while finding ways to protect their interests and maintain their way of life.

In summary, early diplomatic relations and alliances were central to the Chickasaw Nation's history, serving as a means to navigate the complex interactions with European powers and neighboring tribes. These diplomatic efforts allowed the Chickasaw people to secure trade advantages, protect their sovereignty, and adapt to the changing world around them. Through diplomacy and resilience, the Chickasaw Nation upheld its cultural heritage and maintained its presence in the southeastern United States.

Chapter 3: Chickasaw Culture and Traditions

Social structure and governance within the Chickasaw Nation were fundamental aspects of their society, providing order, organization, and leadership. These structures were essential for the Chickasaw people to thrive in their ancestral lands and navigate the challenges posed by European colonization.

Clans and Kinship:

At the heart of Chickasaw social structure were clans and kinship ties. Clans were extended family groups that played a crucial role in Chickasaw identity and organization:

1. Matrilineal Clans: The Chickasaw, like many southeastern tribes, were matrilineal, meaning that clan membership and descent were traced through the mother's line. Each clan had its own unique name, symbol, and responsibilities.

2. Kinship Relationships: Kinship ties were central to Chickasaw society. Members of the same clan were considered relatives, and these relationships formed the basis of social, political, and ceremonial life. Clan members supported each other in various aspects of life, including leadership roles and decision-making.

Leadership and Governance:

Chickasaw governance was a blend of traditional tribal structures and adaptations to changing circumstances:

1. Tribal Chiefs: The Chickasaw Nation was led by tribal chiefs who held positions of authority and responsibility. Chiefs were often selected based on their leadership qualities, wisdom, and ability to represent the interests of their clans and the broader community.

2. Councils: Decision-making in Chickasaw society involved councils, where leaders and representatives from different clans gathered to discuss important matters. These councils played a pivotal role in governance and diplomacy.

3. Clan Mothers: Clan mothers held significant influence within the Chickasaw social structure. They were responsible for selecting and advising tribal chiefs, ensuring the well-being of their clans, and contributing to the overall governance of the nation.

4. Adaptations to European Contact: As European colonization expanded, the Chickasaw adapted their governance structures to meet new challenges. They engaged in diplomacy with European powers, negotiated treaties, and navigated complex political relationships.

Conflict Resolution: Chickasaw governance also included mechanisms for conflict resolution and justice. Disputes were often addressed through tribal councils, and leaders worked to maintain peace within the community.

Religious and Ceremonial Roles:

Chickasaw social structure extended into religious and ceremonial life:

1. Priests and Spiritual Leaders: The Chickasaw had priests and spiritual leaders who played important roles in conducting religious ceremonies, connecting with the spirit world, and guiding the spiritual life of the community.

2. Ceremonial Societies: Ceremonial societies were organized groups within Chickasaw society, each with its own set of responsibilities and rituals. These societies played vital roles in preserving and passing down cultural traditions.

3. Ceremonial Grounds: Chickasaw communities had designated ceremonial grounds where important rituals, dances, and gatherings took place. These grounds served as central hubs for cultural and spiritual activities.

Maintaining Cultural Continuity:

Despite the challenges posed by European contact and the forced removal of the Chickasaw people from their ancestral lands, efforts were made to maintain cultural continuity:

1. Oral Tradition: Chickasaw elders and storytellers played a crucial role in preserving oral traditions, passing down the tribe's history, myths, and legends to future generations.

2. Language Preservation: The Chickasaw language, Chahta Anumpa, was a vital aspect of their cultural identity. Efforts were made to preserve and revitalize the language through language programs and education.

3. Ceremonial Practices: Traditional ceremonial practices, such as the Green Corn Ceremony and stomp dances, were maintained to reinforce Chickasaw cultural identity and spiritual connections.

In summary, the Chickasaw social structure and governance system were integral to the tribe's identity, cohesion, and ability to navigate the challenges of European colonization. Matrilineal clans, tribal chiefs, clan mothers, and councils formed the foundation of their governance. These structures allowed the Chickasaw people to adapt to changing circumstances while preserving their cultural heritage and maintaining a sense of unity and purpose within their community. Today, the Chickasaw Nation continues to honor its social and governance traditions as it celebrates its history and looks toward the future.

Language, oral tradition, and communication were central elements of Chickasaw culture, serving as the means through which knowledge, history, and cultural heritage were passed down from one generation to the next. These aspects played a vital role in defining the Chickasaw identity and preserving their rich heritage.

Chickasaw Language:

The Chickasaw language, known as Chahta Anumpa, was the cornerstone of Chickasaw culture and communication. It was a unique language with its own grammatical structure and vocabulary, reflecting the distinct identity of the Chickasaw people. Key aspects of the Chickasaw language included:

1. Matrilineal Kinship Terms: The matrilineal nature of Chickasaw society was reflected in the language. Kinship terms and clan affiliations were an integral part of Chickasaw identity, and the language provided precise ways to express these relationships.

2. Verbal Aspect: Chickasaw, like many indigenous languages, featured a complex verbal aspect system that conveyed not only the action itself but also aspects such as duration, repetition, and intensity.

3. Cultural Concepts: The Chickasaw language had specific terms and concepts that were essential for expressing cultural ideas and practices. For example, it had words to describe ceremonies, traditional stories, and spiritual concepts.

Oral Tradition:

Oral tradition was a foundational aspect of Chickasaw culture, enabling the transmission of knowledge, history, and stories from one generation to another:

1. Storytelling: Chickasaw elders and storytellers held a revered position in the community. They were responsible for sharing stories, myths, legends, and historical accounts with younger generations. Through storytelling, Chickasaw youth learned about their heritage and cultural values.

2. Anecdotal History: Much of Chickasaw history was passed down in the form of anecdotes and oral narratives. These stories recounted the tribe's experiences, including their interactions with European settlers, other indigenous tribes, and the challenges they faced.

3. Preservation of Wisdom: Elders and community leaders shared their wisdom and life experiences through oral tradition. This included guidance on tribal governance, ethical conduct, and survival in a changing world.

Cultural Significance: Oral tradition was not just a means of communication but also a source of cultural pride and identity. The Chickasaw people took great care in preserving their oral traditions, recognizing their importance in maintaining the essence of Chickasaw culture.

Communication within the Community:

Effective communication within the Chickasaw community was vital for daily life, decision-making, and cooperation:

1. Councils and Gatherings: Tribal councils and community gatherings were forums for communication and decision-making. Leaders and representatives from different clans would come together to discuss matters of importance, resolve conflicts, and plan for the future.

2. Ceremonial Practices: Communication played a crucial role in the context of ceremonial practices. Ceremonial leaders and participants used specific chants, songs, and verbal rituals to connect with the spiritual world and convey their devotion.

3. Social Interaction: Social events and gatherings provided opportunities for Chickasaw people to interact and communicate with one another. These occasions allowed for the exchange of news, stories, and shared experiences.

Adaptation and Continuity:

Despite the challenges posed by European contact and the forced removal of the Chickasaw people from their ancestral lands, efforts were made to adapt and preserve their language and oral traditions:

1. Language Revitalization: In contemporary times, language revitalization programs have been initiated to preserve and teach the Chickasaw language to new generations. These programs aim to ensure the language's survival and continued use within the Chickasaw community.

2. Cultural Revival: Chickasaw cultural initiatives focus on reviving and preserving oral traditions, storytelling, and the transmission of cultural knowledge. These efforts celebrate the importance of oral tradition in maintaining Chickasaw identity.

In summary, language, oral tradition, and communication were the lifeblood of Chickasaw culture, facilitating the transmission of knowledge, history, and cultural values from one generation to another. These elements not only shaped the Chickasaw identity but also played a critical role in preserving their rich cultural heritage in the face of changing circumstances. Today, the Chickasaw Nation continues to honor and celebrate its linguistic and oral traditions as essential components of its cultural legacy.

Religious beliefs, ceremonies, and artistry were deeply intertwined aspects of Chickasaw culture, playing a profound role in their spiritual, social, and artistic expression. These elements were essential in defining the Chickasaw identity and preserving their cultural heritage.

Religious Beliefs:

Chickasaw religious beliefs were rooted in a profound connection to the natural world, the spirit realm, and the ancestral past. Key aspects of Chickasaw religious beliefs included:

1. Animism: Chickasaw spirituality was animistic, meaning that they believed that all living and non-living things possessed spirits or life forces. This included animals, plants, rocks, rivers, and celestial bodies.

2. Ancestral Spirits: Ancestors held a special place in Chickasaw religious beliefs. They were believed to watch over and guide the living, and their spirits were honored through rituals and ceremonies.

3. The Spirit World: The Chickasaw believed in a spirit world that existed alongside the physical world. Shamans and spiritual leaders were responsible for connecting with this spirit realm through rituals and ceremonies.

Ceremonies:

Chickasaw ceremonies were central to their religious and cultural life, serving as opportunities for spiritual connection, community cohesion, and the expression of cultural values. Some notable ceremonies included:

1. Green Corn Ceremony: The Green Corn Ceremony, also known as the Busk, was one of the most important Chickasaw ceremonies. It marked the new year and the ripening of the first corn crop. The ceremony involved communal feasting, purification, dances, and the making of new fire.

2. Stomp Dances: Stomp dances were held on ceremonial grounds and involved rhythmic dancing and chanting. These dances served various purposes, including healing, prayer, and the celebration of community.

3. Spirit Jumps: Spirit jumps were rituals performed by individuals or small groups to seek guidance or healing from the spirit world. Participants would jump over a small fire while praying and singing.

4. Naming Ceremonies: Naming ceremonies were held to bestow names upon infants. Names were chosen based on personal experiences, dreams, or spiritual insights. The naming process was a reflection of the Chickasaw belief in the importance of individual spiritual connections.

Artistry:

Chickasaw artistry was expressed through various forms, including pottery, basketry, textiles, and beadwork. Key aspects of Chickasaw artistry included:

1. Pottery: Chickasaw pottery was known for its intricate designs and craftsmanship. Pieces often featured geometric patterns, animal motifs, and stylized representations of natural elements. Pottery was both functional and decorative.

2. Basketry: Chickasaw basketry was a highly developed art form. Baskets were created for various purposes, including storage, carrying items, and as ceremonial objects. Intricate patterns and designs were woven into the baskets.

3. Textiles: Chickasaw women were skilled in textile arts, weaving clothing and blankets from plant fibers and animal hides. These textiles often featured symbolic designs and patterns.

4. Beadwork: Beadwork was introduced to the Chickasaw people through European contact, and it became an important art form. Chickasaw beadwork featured intricate designs and was used to create clothing, accessories, and decorative items.

Symbolism: Chickasaw art often incorporated symbolism that reflected their cultural beliefs. Symbols representing animals, plants, celestial bodies, and natural elements held spiritual significance.

Adaptation and Continuity:

Despite the challenges posed by European contact and the forced removal of the Chickasaw people from their ancestral lands, efforts were made to adapt and preserve their religious beliefs, ceremonies, and artistry:

1. Cultural Revival: Chickasaw cultural revival efforts have focused on preserving and revitalizing traditional ceremonies, such as the Green Corn Ceremony and stomp dances. These initiatives celebrate the importance of these ceremonies in Chickasaw culture.

2. Artistic Traditions: Chickasaw artists and artisans continue to create pottery, baskets, textiles, and beadwork that draw upon traditional designs and techniques. These art forms serve as a link to the past and a means of artistic expression.

In summary, religious beliefs, ceremonies, and artistry were integral to Chickasaw culture, providing a framework for spiritual connection, cultural expression, and community cohesion. These elements continue to be cherished and celebrated within the Chickasaw Nation as essential components of their cultural heritage and identity.

Chapter 4: The Chickasaw During the Era of Colonization

In colonial times, the Chickasaw Nation faced a myriad of challenges and opportunities as they navigated the complex landscape of European colonization and interaction with neighboring tribes. These historical circumstances profoundly shaped their identity, culture, and future trajectory.

One of the foremost challenges the Chickasaw people encountered during colonial times was the encroachment of European settlers and the competing interests of colonial powers. As European explorers and settlers ventured into the southeastern United States, they brought with them new technologies, diseases, and economic systems that had far-reaching impacts on indigenous societies like the Chickasaw.

The Chickasaw Nation had to contend with the disruptive effects of diseases introduced by Europeans, such as smallpox, which decimated their population. The loss of lives and the disruption of traditional ways of life were significant challenges that the Chickasaw people had to endure.

Additionally, European settlers and colonial powers sought to establish dominance over indigenous lands, leading to conflicts and territorial disputes. The Chickasaw people had to defend their ancestral territory against encroachments by European settlers and rival indigenous tribes.

One of the opportunities that emerged during this period was trade and economic exchange. The Chickasaw people, known for their trading prowess, engaged in commerce with European colonists, exchanging valuable resources like deerskins, furs, and agricultural products for European manufactured goods, such as metal tools, firearms, and cloth.

The Chickasaw's strategic positioning in the southeastern United States allowed them to benefit from their role as intermediaries in the fur trade. They established trade networks with both European colonists and neighboring tribes, facilitating the exchange of goods and forging alliances that could be advantageous in navigating the challenges of the time.

Furthermore, diplomatic relations and alliances with European powers presented opportunities for the Chickasaw Nation. By forming alliances with European nations like the British, the Chickasaw people were able to secure military support and access to valuable resources. These alliances bolstered their defenses and helped them maintain a degree of autonomy in a changing political landscape.

In the realm of culture and identity, the Chickasaw people faced both challenges and opportunities. The introduction of European religious beliefs and practices posed a challenge to traditional Chickasaw spirituality and worldview. Conversion efforts by European missionaries aimed to reshape indigenous belief systems, leading to cultural conflicts and tensions.

Despite these challenges, the Chickasaw people had opportunities to adapt and synthesize elements of European and indigenous cultures. Cultural exchange led to the incorporation of European goods, such as metal tools and clothing, into Chickasaw daily life. This blending of cultures allowed the Chickasaw to maintain their distinct identity while incorporating beneficial aspects of European technology and trade.

One of the defining challenges of colonial times was the forced removal of the Chickasaw people from their ancestral lands. The Indian Removal Act of 1830 and subsequent policies led to the removal of the Chickasaw Nation to Indian Territory in what is now Oklahoma. This traumatic event disrupted communities and traditional ways of life, resulting in significant hardships for the Chickasaw people.

However, the Chickasaw people also saw opportunities in the challenges of removal. In their new homeland, they established a strong and resilient community, adapting to the different environment and economic opportunities presented in Indian Territory. They established successful farms, businesses, and governance structures, showcasing their ability to thrive even in the face of adversity.

In the aftermath of the Civil War, the Chickasaw Nation faced challenges related to the changing political and economic landscape of the United States. Reconstruction policies and the end of chattel slavery brought significant changes to the region. The Chickasaw people had to navigate the complexities of post-war society while preserving their cultural identity.

Economic opportunities arose as the Chickasaw Nation engaged in commerce and trade with the United States. They utilized their natural resources, such as timber and agriculture, to build a stable economy. The establishment of schools and educational initiatives offered opportunities for Chickasaw children to receive formal education and acquire new skills.

The 20th century brought both challenges and opportunities as the Chickasaw Nation sought to adapt to modernity while preserving its cultural heritage. The impact of federal policies, such as the Indian Reorganization Act of 1934, influenced tribal governance and land management. The Chickasaw people faced decisions regarding tribal governance structures and land management policies that would shape their future.

Despite the challenges of the 20th century, the Chickasaw Nation made significant strides in cultural preservation and revitalization. Efforts to teach and revitalize the Chickasaw language, support traditional arts and crafts, and promote cultural celebrations and ceremonies showcased their commitment to preserving their heritage.

In recent decades, the Chickasaw Nation has seized opportunities for economic development, tribal sovereignty, and self-determination. The establishment of tribal businesses, including gaming enterprises, has provided a stable source of revenue for tribal programs and services. These economic opportunities have allowed the Chickasaw Nation to invest in education, healthcare, and cultural preservation.

In summary, colonial times were marked by both challenges and opportunities for the Chickasaw Nation. They faced the encroachment of European settlers, the disruption of traditional ways of life, and the forced removal from their ancestral lands. However, they also engaged in trade, formed alliances, and adapted to new circumstances, showcasing their resilience and adaptability. The Chickasaw people's ability to navigate these challenges and seize opportunities throughout their history has played a pivotal role in shaping their identity and ensuring their continued presence as a vibrant and resilient nation today.

Throughout their history, the Chickasaw Nation has displayed remarkable resilience and employed various strategies to navigate the challenges they faced, both in their ancestral homelands and after their forced removal to Indian Territory. Their ability to adapt and persevere has been central to their survival and ongoing cultural vitality.

In pre-colonial times, the Chickasaw people inhabited the fertile lands of the southeastern United States. They developed a robust agricultural society, cultivating crops such as maize, beans, and squash, and engaging in trade networks that spanned the region. This agricultural base provided them with the resilience to withstand environmental fluctuations and sustain their growing population.

The Chickasaw's strategic location also played a crucial role in their resilience. Situated in the heart of the Southeast, they acted as intermediaries in the fur trade, establishing trade networks with both European settlers and neighboring tribes. This economic engagement allowed them to access essential European goods while maintaining their autonomy and fostering alliances that could be advantageous.

When European colonization encroached upon their territory, the Chickasaw people faced numerous challenges. They confronted diseases brought by Europeans, which decimated their population and disrupted their communities. Despite these hardships, they demonstrated resilience by adapting to new realities.

In the face of territorial disputes and conflicts with European settlers and rival indigenous tribes, the Chickasaw Nation used strategic diplomacy and military prowess to protect their homeland. Their ability to forge alliances with European powers, particularly the British, provided them with critical support in defending their territory.

During the American Revolution, the Chickasaw people made a calculated decision to side with the British, a strategic choice aimed at protecting their interests and homeland. Their participation in the conflict showcased their adaptability and strategic thinking in the midst of changing political dynamics.

One of the most significant challenges the Chickasaw Nation faced was the forced removal from their ancestral lands in the early 19th century. The Indian Removal Act of 1830 and subsequent policies resulted in the displacement of the Chickasaw people to Indian Territory, now Oklahoma. This traumatic event disrupted communities, uprooted families, and tested their resilience.

Despite the adversity of removal, the Chickasaw people displayed remarkable resilience by adapting to their new homeland. They established strong, cohesive communities in Indian Territory, fostering a sense of unity among displaced tribes. Their agricultural expertise allowed them to thrive in the new environment, ensuring their self-sufficiency.

The Chickasaw Nation's resilience was further demonstrated through their successful efforts to rebuild their society and government in Indian Territory. They established a constitutional government, preserving their tribal sovereignty and adapting to the challenges posed by a new political landscape.

Economic opportunities also emerged as the Chickasaw Nation engaged in commerce and trade with the United States. They utilized their natural resources, such as timber and agriculture, to build a stable economy. Education initiatives were implemented, providing opportunities for Chickasaw children to receive formal education and acquire new skills.

The 20th century brought both challenges and opportunities as the Chickasaw Nation sought to adapt to modernity while preserving its cultural heritage. The impact of federal policies, such as the Indian Reorganization Act of 1934, influenced tribal governance and land management. The Chickasaw people faced decisions regarding tribal governance structures and land management policies that would shape their future.

Despite the challenges of the 20th century, the Chickasaw Nation made significant strides in cultural preservation and revitalization.

Efforts to teach and revitalize the Chickasaw language, support traditional arts and crafts, and promote cultural celebrations and ceremonies showcased their commitment to preserving their heritage.

In recent decades, the Chickasaw Nation has seized opportunities for economic development, tribal sovereignty, and self-determination. The establishment of tribal businesses, including gaming enterprises, has provided a stable source of revenue for tribal programs and services. These economic opportunities have allowed the Chickasaw Nation to invest in education, healthcare, and cultural preservation.

In summary, the Chickasaw Nation's history is marked by resilience and strategic adaptability in the face of numerous challenges. From pre-colonial times through forced removal and into the present day, they have displayed an ability to adapt, rebuild, and preserve their cultural heritage. The Chickasaw people's resilience and strategic thinking continue to be central to their ongoing success as a vibrant and sovereign nation.

The evolving Chickasaw identity and leadership have been central to the tribe's history and their ability to navigate changing circumstances. As the Chickasaw Nation faced various challenges and opportunities throughout their history, their identity and leadership structures adapted and developed in response.

Pre-Colonial Identity:

In pre-colonial times, the Chickasaw people were part of a complex and highly organized society in the southeastern United States. Their identity was rooted in their matrilineal kinship system, which determined clan membership and inheritance. Clans were central to Chickasaw social organization, and individuals identified strongly with their clan affiliations.

Leadership in this era was often associated with clan chiefs and elders who held positions of influence within the community. These leaders played vital roles in decision-making, conflict resolution, and maintaining social cohesion.

Colonial Challenges and Adaptations:

The arrival of European colonists in the Southeast brought significant challenges to the Chickasaw people. They faced diseases introduced by Europeans, territorial disputes, and the encroachment of settlers on their lands. These challenges necessitated adaptations in their identity and leadership.

During this period, Chickasaw leaders recognized the need for unity and cooperation in the face of external pressures. They developed diplomatic skills and formed alliances with European powers, particularly the British, as a means of protecting their homeland and interests.

The Chickasaw's strategic alliances with European powers and their reputation as formidable warriors contributed to their identity as a resilient and sovereign nation. These alliances allowed them to maintain their autonomy while adapting to the changing political landscape.

Forced Removal and Resilience:

The forced removal of the Chickasaw people from their ancestral lands in the 1830s was a traumatic event that tested their resilience and leadership. Despite the hardships of removal, Chickasaw leaders and the broader community demonstrated their determination to rebuild in Indian Territory.

Leadership structures in Indian Territory evolved to address the challenges of the new environment. The Chickasaw Nation established a constitutional government, preserving their tribal sovereignty and adapting to the realities of their new home. Leaders worked to establish strong communities, foster self-sufficiency, and provide for the needs of their people.

Cultural Preservation and Identity Revitalization:

In the 20th century, the Chickasaw Nation faced the challenges of cultural preservation and revitalization. Federal policies and changing political dynamics influenced tribal governance and land management, requiring strategic adaptations in leadership.

Efforts to preserve and revitalize Chickasaw culture and language became central to the tribe's identity. Cultural leaders and educators worked to teach and promote the Chickasaw language, traditional arts, and ceremonies. These initiatives played a critical role in preserving their cultural heritage and revitalizing their identity.

Modern Identity and Leadership:

In recent decades, the Chickasaw Nation has embraced economic development and self-determination as central aspects of their identity. The establishment of tribal businesses, including gaming enterprises, has provided a stable source of revenue for tribal programs and services. This economic development has allowed the Chickasaw Nation to invest in education, healthcare, and cultural preservation.

Chickasaw leadership has adapted to the opportunities presented by economic development while maintaining a commitment to tribal sovereignty. Their leaders have navigated complex legal and political landscapes to ensure the tribe's continued success and prosperity.

In summary, the evolving Chickasaw identity and leadership have been shaped by their ability to adapt and respond to changing circumstances throughout their history. From pre-colonial times to the challenges of forced removal and into the modern era, Chickasaw leaders have demonstrated resilience, strategic thinking, and a commitment to preserving their cultural heritage and sovereignty. Their evolving identity and leadership continue to be central to their ongoing success as a vibrant and self-determined nation.

Chapter 5: The Chickasaw Removal and the Long Walk West

The forced removal of the Chickasaw people from their ancestral lands in the southeastern United States in the early 19th century was driven by a combination of factors and forces, both external and internal. These forces played a significant role in the displacement of the Chickasaw Nation to Indian Territory (present-day Oklahoma). Here are the key forces behind the Chickasaw removal:

Territorial Expansionism: Territorial expansionism was a fundamental driver of the Chickasaw removal. As the United States expanded westward in the early 19th century, there was a growing demand for land to accommodate the increasing population and support economic development. The fertile lands occupied by the Chickasaw people were deemed valuable for agriculture and settlement, making them targets for acquisition by the U.S. government.

Federal Policies: Federal policies, particularly the Indian Removal Act of 1830 signed into law by President Andrew Jackson, played a pivotal role in the Chickasaw removal. This policy authorized the forced relocation of indigenous tribes from their ancestral lands to designated Indian Territory west of the Mississippi River. The Act provided the legal framework for the government's actions.

Conflict and Competition: The Chickasaw people found themselves caught in a complex web of conflicts and competition involving European settlers, rival indigenous tribes, and the United States government. Territorial disputes, competition for resources, and tensions with neighboring tribes further escalated the pressure on the Chickasaw Nation to cede their lands.

Economic Interests: Economic interests were a significant factor behind the Chickasaw removal. The fertile lands of the

Chickasaw homelands were highly desirable for agricultural development, particularly cotton cultivation, which was economically lucrative in the 19th century. White settlers and land speculators sought to exploit these economic opportunities, driving the push for removal.

Disease and Population Decline: The introduction of diseases, such as smallpox and measles, by European settlers had devastating consequences for the Chickasaw population. Epidemics swept through their communities, leading to a significant decline in their numbers. This population decline weakened their ability to resist removal and further contributed to their vulnerability.

Military Pressure: The Chickasaw people faced military pressure from both the U.S. government and rival indigenous tribes. Military campaigns and conflicts, such as the Creek War of 1813-1814, created a precarious environment for the Chickasaw Nation. The U.S. government's military presence in the region also exerted pressure on them to comply with removal.

Treaties and Negotiations: The negotiation of treaties with the U.S. government was a factor that facilitated the Chickasaw removal. Treaty negotiations often occurred under duress and were influenced by the unequal power dynamics between the Chickasaw Nation and the federal government. Some Chickasaw leaders reluctantly agreed to cede their lands in exchange for provisions and promises of support in Indian Territory.

Economic and Political Factors: Economic and political factors within the Chickasaw Nation also played a role in the removal. Some Chickasaw leaders believed that relocation to Indian Territory offered economic opportunities and a chance to preserve their sovereignty in the face of mounting pressure. This internal division contributed to the eventual acceptance of removal.

In summary, the forces behind the Chickasaw removal were driven by a combination of territorial expansionism, federal policies, economic interests, disease, military pressure, and negotiations. These forces, both external and internal, converged to displace the Chickasaw people from their ancestral lands, resulting in their relocation to Indian Territory and the profound and enduring impact on their history and identity.

The long and arduous journey westward, commonly known as the Trail of Tears, was a harrowing chapter in the history of indigenous peoples in the United States, including the Cherokee, Choctaw, Chickasaw, Creek, and Seminole Nations. This forced removal, orchestrated by the U.S. government, resulted in the displacement and suffering of thousands of Native Americans. Here, we explore the experiences and challenges faced during this tragic journey:

Forced Relocation: The Trail of Tears, spanning the late 1830s and early 1840s, marked the forced relocation of several indigenous tribes, including the Cherokee, from their ancestral lands in the southeastern United States to designated Indian Territory in present-day Oklahoma. The removal was carried out under the Indian Removal Act of 1830, signed into law by President Andrew Jackson, and subsequent treaties.

Cherokee Removal: The Cherokee Nation experienced one of the most well-documented removals. In 1838, approximately 16,000 Cherokee were forcibly removed from their homes in Georgia, Tennessee, and North Carolina. The journey westward covered approximately 800 miles, characterized by harsh conditions and inadequate provisions.

Choctaw, Chickasaw, Creek, and Seminole Removal: Similarly, the Choctaw, Chickasaw, Creek, and Seminole Nations endured forced removals during this period. Each tribe faced its own set of challenges, including the hardships of long journeys, exposure to the elements, and the loss of homes, possessions, and loved ones.

Conditions During the Journey: The conditions during the journey were deplorable. Native Americans were often subjected to overcrowded and unsanitary conditions in makeshift detention camps. The lack of proper clothing, food, and medical care led to widespread suffering and loss of life. Families were separated, and many individuals succumbed to disease and exposure.

Loss of Lives: The Trail of Tears witnessed a devastating loss of lives. Estimates vary, but it is believed that thousands of Native Americans perished during the removal process. The toll on families and communities was immeasurable, and the trauma endured by survivors left a lasting impact on their descendants.

Impact on Communities: The forced removal not only disrupted the lives of individuals and families but also shattered the social fabric of indigenous communities. Traditional ways of life, cultural practices, and governance structures were disrupted or lost, leading to a profound and enduring impact on these nations.

Resilience and Adaptation: Despite the immense challenges and suffering, indigenous peoples displayed remarkable resilience during the journey westward. They supported each other, upheld their cultural practices, and retained their sense of identity. Many sought to rebuild their communities and preserve their heritage in the new territories.

Legacy and Remembrance: The Trail of Tears is a somber chapter in American history, and its legacy continues to be remembered and commemorated by Native American communities and the broader society. Efforts to honor the memory of those who suffered and to preserve the history and culture of these nations are ongoing.

In summary, the long and arduous journey westward, known as the Trail of Tears, remains a tragic and deeply significant episode in the history of indigenous peoples in the United

States. It serves as a reminder of the resilience of these nations in the face of adversity and their enduring efforts to preserve their cultures and identities despite the hardships they endured.

Survival and adaptation in new territories were paramount concerns for the indigenous nations, including the Cherokee, Choctaw, Chickasaw, Creek, and Seminole, as they grappled with the aftermath of the forced removal from their ancestral lands and the challenges of establishing new homes in Indian Territory, present-day Oklahoma. This period of transition marked a critical phase in the histories of these nations, characterized by the need to rebuild communities, reclaim cultural practices, and adapt to unfamiliar environments.

Following the arduous journeys westward, the indigenous nations arrived in Indian Territory to face the daunting task of starting anew. They encountered landscapes and climates that often differed significantly from their original homelands, necessitating adaptations in agriculture, housing, and daily life.

Agriculture played a central role in the survival and sustenance of these communities. The knowledge and skills that indigenous peoples brought with them from their ancestral lands enabled them to cultivate crops suited to the local environment. Traditional agricultural practices, such as crop rotation and the cultivation of maize, beans, and squash (the "Three Sisters"), were adapted to the fertile soils of Indian Territory.

The transition to new territories also required the construction of new homes and communities. Traditional building methods and materials gave way to the use of local resources. Indigenous peoples utilized timber, earth, and other available materials to construct dwellings, such as log cabins and thatched-roof houses. These structures provided shelter and protection against the elements.

Survival in the unfamiliar environment of Indian Territory demanded resilience and resourcefulness. Indigenous communities adapted to new climates, ecosystems, and wildlife. They learned to identify and utilize local flora and fauna for food, medicine, and tools. Additionally, they developed strategies for hunting and fishing in the region's rivers, forests, and prairies.

Community life underwent transformations as well. Leadership structures evolved to address the needs of the new territories. Tribes established governments and councils to oversee matters of governance and justice. Elected leaders and chiefs played pivotal roles in guiding their nations through the challenges of reconstruction and adaptation.

Education and knowledge-sharing were essential aspects of survival and adaptation. Indigenous communities placed a strong emphasis on the transmission of traditional knowledge to younger generations. Elders and community leaders served as educators, passing down cultural practices, languages, and oral traditions. Schools and educational programs were established to ensure that indigenous children received both a formal education and an understanding of their heritage.

The preservation and revitalization of cultural practices became a central focus. Indigenous nations were determined to retain their distinct identities and heritage in the face of profound change. Efforts to revive traditional ceremonies, dances, and rituals helped rekindle cultural connections and provide a sense of continuity.

Religion and spirituality remained integral to indigenous life. Spiritual leaders and medicine people played vital roles in guiding their communities, offering solace, and providing a spiritual anchor during challenging times. Ceremonies and gatherings continued to be held to honor ancestors, spirits, and the natural world.

Economic adaptation was another key aspect of survival. Indigenous nations explored various economic opportunities, including trade with neighboring tribes and settlers. They engaged in commerce, selling agricultural products, crafts, and other goods. Economic self-sufficiency and trade networks helped sustain their communities and economies.

Language preservation and revitalization efforts were of paramount importance. Language is not only a means of communication but also a repository of cultural knowledge and identity. Indigenous communities worked diligently to ensure the survival and revitalization of their native languages, offering language programs and immersion initiatives.

In the face of adversity, indigenous communities displayed remarkable resilience and adaptability. The forced removal from ancestral lands had not extinguished their spirit or determination. Instead, it fueled a commitment to preserving their cultures and identities in their new surroundings.

Over time, the indigenous nations of Indian Territory, including the Cherokee, Choctaw, Chickasaw, Creek, and Seminole, rebuilt their communities, forged new bonds, and established vibrant cultures in their new homeland. Their experiences of survival and adaptation serve as a testament to the strength of indigenous resilience and the enduring legacy of these nations in the face of profound challenges.

Chapter 6: Rebuilding a Homeland: Chickasaw Nation in Exile

Establishing a new community and governance structure was a pivotal endeavor for the indigenous nations, including the Cherokee, Choctaw, Chickasaw, Creek, and Seminole, as they resettled in Indian Territory after the forced removal from their ancestral lands in the southeastern United States. This phase marked the beginning of a challenging but resilient effort to rebuild their societies, preserve their cultural identities, and adapt to the realities of their new home.

Community Building:

The process of building a new community was complex and multifaceted. Indigenous nations faced the task of selecting suitable locations for settlements within Indian Territory. Factors such as access to water, fertile land for agriculture, and proximity to natural resources were essential considerations. Communities were strategically situated to ensure the well-being of their members.

Housing and Infrastructure:

One of the immediate priorities was constructing housing and essential infrastructure. The traditional dwellings and architecture of the indigenous nations were adapted to the local environment and available resources. Log cabins, thatched-roof houses, and other structures were built to provide shelter and protection for families and communities. The development of infrastructure included the establishment of roads, bridges, and community spaces.

Leadership and Governance:

Governance structures were established to address the needs of the new communities. Elected leaders, chiefs, and councils played crucial roles in guiding their nations through the challenges of reconstruction and adaptation. These leaders were responsible for decision-making, justice, and the overall well-being of their communities. Tribal governments were formed to manage the affairs of the nations.

Legal Frameworks and Treaties:
Tribal governments negotiated treaties and agreements with the U.S. government to define their rights, boundaries, and relationships with neighboring nations. These treaties played a critical role in shaping the legal framework of governance within Indian Territory. They addressed issues such as land ownership, jurisdiction, and trade.

Economic Endeavors:
Economic self-sufficiency and sustainability were key priorities. Indigenous nations explored various economic opportunities to support their communities. Agriculture remained a fundamental means of subsistence, with tribes adapting their traditional farming practices to the local environment. Additionally, indigenous communities engaged in trade with neighboring tribes and settlers, selling agricultural products, crafts, and other goods.

Education and Cultural Preservation:
Education was an essential component of community building and cultural preservation. Indigenous leaders and educators recognized the importance of transmitting cultural knowledge to younger generations. Schools and educational programs were established to provide both formal education and instruction in traditional practices. Elders and community leaders served as educators, passing down languages, cultural practices, and oral traditions.

Cultural Revival:
Cultural preservation and revival efforts were central to the identity and well-being of the indigenous nations. These initiatives included the revival of traditional ceremonies, dances, and rituals that held deep cultural significance. Cultural leaders and practitioners worked tirelessly to ensure the continuity of these practices, fostering a sense of cultural pride and connection.

Spirituality and Religion:
Spirituality remained a cornerstone of indigenous life. Spiritual leaders and medicine people played vital roles in guiding their communities, offering guidance, and providing a spiritual anchor during challenging times. Ceremonies and gatherings continued to be held to honor ancestors, spirits, and the natural world.

Language Revitalization:
Language preservation and revitalization efforts were crucial to maintaining cultural identity. Native languages were not merely means of communication but also repositories of cultural knowledge and heritage. Language programs and immersion initiatives were developed to ensure the survival and revitalization of these languages.

Community Resilience:
Over time, the communities in Indian Territory demonstrated remarkable resilience and adaptability. They faced the challenges of building new lives and governing themselves in unfamiliar lands with determination and a deep commitment to their cultural values and traditions. The resilience of these communities was a testament to their enduring spirit.

In summary, establishing a new community and governance structure in Indian Territory was a complex and challenging process for the indigenous nations, but it was marked by resilience, determination, and a strong commitment to preserving their cultural identities. These communities adapted to their new environments, built vibrant societies, and played a significant role in shaping the history and legacy of their nations in Indian Territory. Their experiences underscore the enduring strength of indigenous cultures and their ability to thrive even in the face of adversity.

The Chickasaw people, like many indigenous nations, faced significant challenges when forcibly removed from their ancestral homelands in the southeastern United States to Indian Territory, present-day Oklahoma, during the 1830s. This period of exile marked a profound transformation in Chickasaw identity and required determined efforts to preserve their rich cultural heritage in the face of displacement, adversity, and the need to adapt to a new environment.

Chickasaw Identity in Exile:
The forced removal had a profound impact on Chickasaw identity. It represented a rupture with their ancestral lands and traditional way of life. In exile, the Chickasaw people grappled with the loss

of their homes, the disruption of their communities, and the challenges of adapting to unfamiliar territory.

Cultural Preservation:

Cultural preservation became a cornerstone of Chickasaw life in exile. The Chickasaw people were determined to maintain their distinct cultural identity and pass it on to future generations. This commitment was evident in various aspects of their daily lives.

Language Revitalization:

Language, a fundamental element of Chickasaw culture, received significant attention. Efforts to preserve and revitalize the Chickasaw language became a priority. Language programs, immersion initiatives, and educational efforts were established to ensure that Chickasaw children and community members could speak, understand, and appreciate their native language.

Traditional Practices and Ceremonies:

The revival of traditional practices and ceremonies played a vital role in cultural preservation. Chickasaw leaders and cultural practitioners worked diligently to ensure the continuity of ceremonies that held deep cultural and spiritual significance. These events provided a sense of continuity and connection to their heritage.

Leadership and Governance:

Chickasaw leadership and governance structures adapted to the realities of exile. Elected leaders and councils played essential roles in guiding the Chickasaw Nation in Indian Territory. These leaders were responsible for decision-making, justice, and the overall well-being of their communities.

Education and Knowledge Transmission:

Education was another critical component of cultural preservation. Chickasaw elders and community leaders served as educators, transmitting cultural knowledge, traditional practices, and oral histories to younger generations. Schools and educational programs were established to ensure that Chickasaw children received a formal education while also learning about their heritage.

Community Resilience:

Despite the challenges, Chickasaw communities displayed remarkable resilience. Families and communities supported each other and drew strength from their shared history and cultural values. This resilience allowed them to adapt to the demands of life in exile and to persevere through difficult times.

Economic Adaptation:

Economic adaptation was another important aspect of life in exile. Chickasaw communities explored various economic opportunities to support themselves. Agriculture remained a vital means of subsistence, with Chickasaw farmers adapting traditional practices to the local environment. Additionally, trade with neighboring tribes and settlers played a role in sustaining their communities and economies.

Spirituality and Religion:

Spirituality remained a central aspect of Chickasaw life. Spiritual leaders and medicine people continued to play vital roles in guiding their communities, offering guidance, and providing a spiritual anchor during challenging times. Ceremonies and gatherings continued to be held to honor ancestors, spirits, and the natural world.

Community Engagement:

Chickasaw communities engaged with neighboring tribes and settlers in Indian Territory. These interactions allowed for cultural exchange and trade, contributing to the resilience and adaptability of Chickasaw communities. Relationships with neighboring tribes offered opportunities for mutual support and cooperation.

Legacy and Remembrance:

The legacy of Chickasaw identity and cultural preservation in exile is a testament to the resilience and determination of the Chickasaw people. The challenges they faced did not diminish their commitment to preserving their cultural heritage. Today, Chickasaw communities continue to celebrate their cultural identity, language, and traditions, ensuring that their rich heritage endures for future generations.

In summary, Chickasaw identity and cultural preservation in exile reflect a profound commitment to maintaining a distinct cultural identity and heritage despite the challenges of forced removal.

The efforts to preserve the Chickasaw language, traditional practices, and ceremonies demonstrate the enduring strength of Chickasaw culture and its importance to the Chickasaw people in both the past and the present.

Economic development and alliances played crucial roles in the survival and adaptation of the Chickasaw people during their exile in Indian Territory, present-day Oklahoma, following the forced removal from their ancestral lands in the southeastern United States during the 1830s. In this challenging environment, Chickasaw communities navigated economic opportunities and forged alliances with neighboring tribes, settlers, and the U.S. government to ensure their well-being and prosperity.

Economic Strategies:

Economic self-sufficiency and sustainability were paramount concerns for the Chickasaw people. To address these concerns, they employed a range of economic strategies tailored to their new environment:

Agriculture: Agriculture remained a foundational means of subsistence for the Chickasaw community. They adapted their traditional farming practices to the local climate and soil conditions of Indian Territory. Crops such as maize, beans, and squash, known as the "Three Sisters," were cultivated alongside other crops to ensure a reliable food supply.

Hunting and Gathering: Chickasaw communities continued to engage in hunting and gathering activities. The region's diverse ecosystems provided opportunities to hunt game, fish in rivers and streams, and gather wild plants for food and medicinal purposes.

Trade and Commerce: Trade networks were established with neighboring tribes and settlers. The Chickasaw people engaged in commerce, selling agricultural products, crafts, and other goods. These economic exchanges contributed to their self-sufficiency and allowed them to acquire items not readily available within their communities.

Alliances and Partnerships:

Alliances and partnerships were critical for the Chickasaw people's economic development and overall well-being in Indian Territory:

Intertribal Alliances: The Chickasaw Nation formed alliances with neighboring tribes, such as the Choctaw and Creek Nations, to promote mutual support and cooperation. These alliances facilitated trade and offered protection against external threats.

U.S. Government Relations: The Chickasaw Nation engaged with the U.S. government in diplomatic relations and treaty negotiations. These interactions often included provisions for trade, land rights, and financial support. Treaty agreements helped establish the legal framework for Chickasaw governance and economic activities in Indian Territory.

Settler Relationships: Relationships with non-indigenous settlers also played a role in economic development. The Chickasaw people interacted with European-American settlers, including traders and merchants, to engage in economic transactions and secure resources. These interactions were guided by negotiated agreements and trade partnerships.

Infrastructure Development:

Infrastructure development was another facet of economic advancement. Chickasaw communities invested in the construction of roads, bridges, and other infrastructure to facilitate trade and commerce within Indian Territory and with neighboring regions.

Education and Skill Building:

Education and skill-building initiatives were essential for economic development. Chickasaw leaders recognized the importance of equipping community members with the skills and knowledge needed for economic success. Educational programs were established to provide training in various trades and crafts.

Cultural Heritage and Economic Ventures:

Cultural heritage played a significant role in economic ventures. The Chickasaw people leveraged their cultural heritage to engage in economic activities such as traditional arts and crafts, which were highly sought after by collectors and buyers.

Legacy and Continuity:

The legacy of economic development and alliances in exile is a testament to the resourcefulness and adaptability of the Chickasaw people. Their ability to navigate economic opportunities, establish partnerships, and sustain their communities in a challenging environment reflects their determination to preserve their cultural identity and secure a prosperous future.

In summary, economic development and alliances were integral to the Chickasaw people's survival and adaptation during their exile in Indian Territory. Through agriculture, trade, partnerships, and infrastructure development, they demonstrated their resilience and ability to thrive in new surroundings. These efforts underscore the enduring legacy of the Chickasaw people and their commitment to maintaining their cultural heritage while pursuing economic prosperity.

Chapter 7: Return to the Homeland: Reclamation and Resurgence

The Chickasaw people's efforts to reclaim their homelands in the southeastern United States represent a poignant chapter in their history, marked by perseverance, diplomacy, and a deep connection to their ancestral lands. Despite their forced removal to Indian Territory in the 1830s, the Chickasaw Nation remained steadfast in its desire to return to its original homeland.

Continued Displacement:
The Chickasaw Nation, like many indigenous tribes, endured the Trail of Tears, a harrowing journey that led to their resettlement in Indian Territory. However, the desire to reclaim their original lands in the southeastern U.S. never waned. The Chickasaw people maintained a deep emotional and cultural connection to their homelands.

Diplomatic Negotiations:
Diplomacy played a central role in the Chickasaw efforts to reclaim their homelands. The Chickasaw Nation engaged in negotiations with the U.S. government to secure a return to their ancestral territories. These negotiations often involved complex discussions about land rights, compensation, and treaty agreements.

Treaty Agreements:
Several treaty agreements between the Chickasaw Nation and the U.S. government addressed the issue of returning to their original lands. These treaties stipulated the conditions under which the Chickasaw people could regain control of portions of their ancestral territories. However, the practical implementation of these provisions often faced challenges and delays.

Resettlement and Restoration:

The Chickasaw people's determination to reclaim their homelands persisted for generations. They established settlements and maintained connections to their southeastern homelands from their new base in Indian Territory. These efforts demonstrated their enduring commitment to the restoration of their ancestral territories.

Long-Term Vision:

The Chickasaw Nation's quest to reclaim their homelands was guided by a long-term vision of cultural and historical preservation. They understood that returning to their original lands was not merely about physical possession but also about revitalizing their cultural heritage and ensuring the continuity of their traditions.

Challenges and Complexities:

The journey to reclaim homelands was fraught with challenges and complexities. Changing political landscapes, competing interests, and shifting policies within the U.S. government created obstacles along the way. The Chickasaw people navigated these challenges with resilience and tenacity.

Cultural Revival and Connection:

Efforts to reclaim homelands were intertwined with cultural revival and connection. The Chickasaw people sought to maintain their distinct identity and preserve their cultural heritage as they worked towards their goal of returning to their ancestral territories.

Legacy and Resilience:

The legacy of the Chickasaw efforts to reclaim their homelands is a testament to their enduring resilience and commitment to their cultural identity. While the complete restoration of their original lands may not have been realized in the manner they envisioned, their determination and advocacy serve as a reminder of the deep connection between indigenous peoples and their ancestral territories.

In summary, the Chickasaw people's efforts to reclaim their homelands underscore the enduring connection between indigenous nations and their ancestral territories. Their pursuit of diplomatic negotiations and treaty agreements, as well as their commitment to cultural revival, demonstrate the Chickasaw Nation's unwavering dedication to their historical and cultural legacy.

Reconnecting with traditional territories has been a significant and deeply meaningful endeavor for indigenous nations worldwide, including the Chickasaw people. For the Chickasaw Nation, the process of reclaiming, preserving, and revitalizing their ancestral lands has been driven by a profound desire to restore their historical and cultural connection to these territories.

Historical Displacement:
The Chickasaw people faced forced removal from their ancestral homelands in the southeastern United States during the 1830s, a traumatic event known as the Trail of Tears. This displacement severed their ties to their traditional territories, but it did not sever their emotional and cultural connections.

The Spiritual and Cultural Significance:
Traditional territories hold immense spiritual and cultural significance for indigenous nations like the Chickasaw. These lands are not merely physical spaces; they are repositories of history, ancestral knowledge, and sacred sites. Reconnecting with these territories is a profound act of cultural preservation and revival.

Efforts to Reclaim Ancestral Lands:
The Chickasaw Nation has undertaken various efforts to reclaim their ancestral lands. These efforts have included negotiations with the U.S. government, legal actions, and advocacy for land restoration. These endeavors reflect the Chickasaw people's enduring commitment to their historical territories.

Cultural and Historical Preservation:
Reconnecting with traditional territories is inseparable from the preservation of Chickasaw culture and history. The lands

themselves are woven into the fabric of Chickasaw identity. Efforts to reclaim these territories often involve cultural revitalization initiatives, language preservation, and the protection of sacred sites.

Land Stewardship and Conservation:

Reconnecting with traditional territories includes a commitment to responsible land stewardship and conservation. Indigenous nations like the Chickasaw understand the importance of maintaining the ecological health of their ancestral lands. This involves sustainable land management practices and conservation efforts.

Cultural Knowledge Transfer:

One of the essential aspects of reconnecting with traditional territories is the transfer of cultural knowledge and traditions to younger generations. Elders and cultural educators play pivotal roles in passing down ancestral knowledge, stories, and practices related to the land.

Partnerships and Collaborations:

The Chickasaw Nation often collaborates with various stakeholders, including government agencies, conservation organizations, and neighboring tribes, to advance their goals of reconnecting with traditional territories. These partnerships facilitate shared efforts in land restoration, cultural preservation, and conservation.

Challenges and Triumphs:

The journey to reconnect with traditional territories is not without its challenges. Legal complexities, resource constraints, and competing interests can present obstacles. However, indigenous nations like the Chickasaw persist in their efforts, celebrating each triumph as a step closer to their ancestral lands.

Cultural Continuity and Legacy:

The Chickasaw people's dedication to reconnecting with traditional territories ensures the continuity of their cultural legacy. It reflects their unwavering commitment to maintaining their distinct identity, revitalizing their traditions, and honoring the sacrifices of their ancestors.

In summary, reconnecting with traditional territories represents a profound and ongoing journey for indigenous nations like the Chickasaw. It is a journey of cultural preservation, historical reclamation, and the reaffirmation of identity. By restoring their connection to their ancestral lands, the Chickasaw people continue to honor their past and shape their future.

The Chickasaw Nation, like many indigenous nations, has experienced a renewed sense of identity and sovereignty in recent decades, marking a significant chapter in their history. This renewal is characterized by efforts to preserve and revitalize Chickasaw culture, language, governance, and self-determination.

Historical Context:

To understand the renewed sense of identity and sovereignty, it's crucial to recognize the historical context. The Chickasaw Nation, like other indigenous tribes, faced centuries of colonization, forced removal, and cultural suppression. These challenges left lasting impacts on Chickasaw identity and sovereignty.

Cultural Revival and Preservation:

Cultural revival and preservation efforts have been central to the Chickasaw Nation's renewed sense of identity. These efforts encompass a range of activities, from language revitalization programs to the celebration of traditional arts, crafts, and ceremonies. Cultural revitalization serves as a powerful tool for connecting with ancestral heritage and reinforcing a distinct Chickasaw identity.

Language Revitalization:

Language is a cornerstone of Chickasaw culture, and its revitalization has been a top priority. Language programs, immersion initiatives, and educational resources have been developed to ensure that the Chickasaw language is passed down to younger generations. Language revitalization not only preserves linguistic heritage but also fosters a deeper cultural connection.

Educational Initiatives:

Education plays a pivotal role in strengthening Chickasaw identity and sovereignty. The Chickasaw Nation has invested in educational initiatives that incorporate Chickasaw history, culture, and language into school curricula. These efforts empower Chickasaw youth to embrace their heritage and become future leaders.

Tribal Governance and Self-Determination:

Sovereignty is fundamental to the Chickasaw Nation's renewed identity. They have worked to assert their sovereignty and self-determination through tribal governance. Elected leaders and tribal councils oversee matters of jurisdiction, law, and governance, reaffirming their autonomy.

Economic Development and Self-Sufficiency:

Economic development initiatives have played a vital role in Chickasaw sovereignty. The Chickasaw Nation has diversified its economic activities, including gaming, agriculture, and retail, to promote self-sufficiency and reduce dependency on external entities. This economic strength has allowed them greater control over their destiny.

Land Reclamation and Stewardship:

Land reclamation efforts are another dimension of Chickasaw sovereignty. Reacquiring and managing land within their ancestral territories not only reconnects them to their heritage but also gives them control over land use and conservation practices.

Collaborative Partnerships:

Collaborative partnerships with neighboring tribes, states, and the federal government have played a significant role in reinforcing Chickasaw sovereignty. These partnerships facilitate mutual understanding, cooperation, and the recognition of Chickasaw rights and self-governance.

Legal Advocacy:
Legal advocacy has been instrumental in asserting Chickasaw sovereignty. The Chickasaw Nation has pursued legal actions and negotiations to protect their interests, advance their rights, and secure their place as a sovereign nation.

Challenges and Resilience:
Challenges persist in the journey toward renewed identity and sovereignty. Historical injustices, contemporary issues, and external pressures continue to affect indigenous communities. However, Chickasaw resilience and determination have allowed them to navigate these challenges.

Cultural Resilience:
Cultural resilience is a testament to the Chickasaw people's ability to endure and flourish. It reflects their commitment to preserving traditions, storytelling, and ceremonies that have been passed down through generations.

Legacy and Future Generations:
The legacy of the Chickasaw Nation's renewed sense of identity and sovereignty is a source of inspiration for future generations. It instills pride in Chickasaw youth, motivating them to carry forward their cultural heritage and uphold the principles of self-determination.

In summary, the Chickasaw Nation's renewed sense of identity and sovereignty is a multifaceted journey encompassing cultural revival, language revitalization, self-determination, and economic development. It reflects their unwavering commitment to preserving their heritage, strengthening their community, and securing a brighter future for generations to come. This renewal serves as a powerful reminder of the enduring strength of indigenous nations in the face of historical adversity.

Chapter 8: The Chickasaw Nation Today: Identity and Prosperity

Modern Chickasaw governance and tribal sovereignty represent a dynamic and evolving framework that underscores the Chickasaw Nation's capacity to shape its own destiny, uphold its cultural heritage, and advance the well-being of its citizens. The journey to modern governance and sovereignty is rooted in a rich historical context but extends to contemporary efforts that reflect the Chickasaw Nation's commitment to self-determination and self-governance.

Historical Foundations:

To appreciate modern Chickasaw governance, it is essential to recognize its historical foundations. Like many indigenous nations, the Chickasaw people developed their own systems of governance long before European contact. These traditional governance structures continue to influence contemporary practices.

Tribal Constitution and Government:

Modern Chickasaw governance is articulated through a tribal constitution that defines the nation's political structure and governing principles. The constitution establishes a three-branch system consisting of the legislative, executive, and judicial branches. This structure ensures a separation of powers and a system of checks and balances.

Elected Leadership:

The Chickasaw Nation holds regular elections to select its leadership, including a governor and lieutenant governor. The Chickasaw Legislature, consisting of elected representatives from each of the nation's 13 districts, shapes and passes legislation. This elected leadership reflects the principles of representative democracy.

Sovereign Decision-Making:

Sovereignty is a foundational principle of modern Chickasaw governance. The Chickasaw Nation asserts its inherent right to self-governance, making decisions on a range of issues, including tribal law, land use, education, healthcare, and economic development. This sovereignty is recognized and respected by the U.S. government.

Self-Determination:

Self-determination is closely tied to sovereignty and underscores the Chickasaw Nation's authority to determine its own path. This includes the development and implementation of policies and initiatives that align with the nation's values and priorities.

Cultural Preservation and Promotion:

Modern Chickasaw governance places a strong emphasis on cultural preservation and promotion. The nation's leaders actively support cultural programs, language revitalization efforts, and initiatives that celebrate Chickasaw heritage. These efforts are integral to maintaining the distinct Chickasaw identity.

Education and Healthcare Services:

The Chickasaw Nation operates its own educational and healthcare systems. This enables the nation to tailor services to the specific needs of its citizens and ensures the provision of quality education and healthcare within Chickasaw communities.

Economic Development and Self-Sufficiency:

Economic development is a key component of modern governance. The Chickasaw Nation has diversified its economic activities, including gaming, agriculture, retail, and more. These endeavors generate revenue that supports tribal programs and services, reducing dependence on external funding.

Nation-Building Initiatives:

Modern Chickasaw governance includes nation-building initiatives aimed at strengthening the nation's infrastructure, promoting civic engagement, and fostering a sense of community and shared responsibility among citizens.

Collaboration and Partnerships:

Collaboration with federal, state, and local governments, as well as with neighboring tribes and organizations, is integral to Chickasaw governance. These collaborations enable the nation to address shared challenges, advance common goals, and promote the interests of Chickasaw citizens.

Challenges and Adaptation:

Modern Chickasaw governance is not without its challenges. The nation continues to navigate complex issues, including healthcare disparities, economic disparities, and the preservation of cultural heritage. However, adaptive and forward-thinking leadership has allowed the Chickasaw Nation to address these challenges effectively.

Legacy and Future Generations:

Modern Chickasaw governance and tribal sovereignty leave a lasting legacy for future generations. It instills a sense of pride and responsibility among Chickasaw youth, motivating them to participate in the governance of their nation and carry forward the traditions and values of their ancestors.

In summary, modern Chickasaw governance and tribal sovereignty exemplify the Chickasaw Nation's capacity to navigate the complex interplay of tradition and contemporary realities. These governance structures empower the nation to chart its own course, protect its cultural heritage, and pursue a prosperous future for its citizens. The Chickasaw journey from historical foundations to contemporary governance reflects a deep commitment to self-determination and the enduring strength of indigenous nations.

Economic success and community growth within the Chickasaw Nation are integral aspects of the tribe's journey towards self-sufficiency, prosperity, and the overall well-being of its citizens. These endeavors are rooted in a commitment to economic development, job creation, and investment in infrastructure, education, and healthcare.

Diversification of Economic Activities:

Economic success within the Chickasaw Nation is marked by a deliberate diversification of economic activities. The tribe has expanded its economic portfolio to include a wide range of ventures, such as gaming, agriculture, manufacturing, and retail. This diversification minimizes reliance on any single industry and enhances financial stability.

Gaming Enterprises:

The Chickasaw Nation's gaming enterprises have played a significant role in generating revenue and employment opportunities. These enterprises include casinos, hotels, and entertainment venues, attracting visitors and contributing to the local economy.

Agricultural Initiatives:

Investment in agriculture is another key aspect of economic success. The Chickasaw Nation has developed agricultural programs that support local food production, job creation, and sustainability. These initiatives also strengthen the nation's food security.

Retail and Business Development:

The tribe's focus on retail and business development has led to the establishment of thriving enterprises, including restaurants, shops, and service providers. These businesses not only contribute to the local economy but also provide valuable employment opportunities.

Job Creation:

Economic success within the Chickasaw Nation has resulted in substantial job creation. A robust job market ensures that Chickasaw citizens have access to meaningful employment opportunities, reducing unemployment rates and enhancing economic stability.

Investment in Infrastructure:

Community growth is closely linked to investments in infrastructure. The Chickasaw Nation has directed resources toward improving transportation, utilities, and public facilities. These investments enhance the overall quality of life for tribal citizens.

Education and Workforce Development:
A skilled and educated workforce is essential for economic success. The Chickasaw Nation has implemented educational programs and workforce development initiatives to empower citizens with the skills needed to participate in the modern job market.

Healthcare Services:
Access to quality healthcare is vital for community growth. The Chickasaw Nation operates healthcare facilities that provide essential medical services to citizens. This ensures that healthcare needs are met, contributing to overall well-being.

Housing and Community Development:
The Chickasaw Nation has also focused on housing and community development, providing affordable housing options and improving living conditions for tribal citizens. This supports community growth and fosters a sense of stability.

Cultural and Educational Initiatives:
Economic success is not solely measured in financial terms but also by the tribe's ability to invest in cultural and educational initiatives. The Chickasaw Nation supports programs that promote Chickasaw language, traditions, and cultural heritage, ensuring that these aspects are passed down to future generations.

Community Engagement and Collaboration:
Community growth is nurtured through community engagement and collaboration. The Chickasaw Nation actively involves its citizens in decision-making processes and collaborates with local communities and governments to address shared challenges and opportunities.

Challenges and Resilience:

Despite economic success, challenges persist. Economic disparities, healthcare disparities, and social issues require ongoing attention and innovative solutions. The Chickasaw Nation's resilience and adaptability are evident in its ability to navigate these challenges.

Legacy and Future Aspirations:

Economic success and community growth leave a lasting legacy for future generations of Chickasaw citizens. They create a foundation upon which the tribe can build a prosperous and culturally vibrant future.

In summary, economic success and community growth within the Chickasaw Nation are multifaceted endeavors that reflect a commitment to self-sufficiency, cultural preservation, and the well-being of tribal citizens. These efforts serve as a testament to the Chickasaw Nation's dedication to building a thriving and resilient community for generations to come.

Chickasaw identity and cultural revival in contemporary times are intricately intertwined, reflecting the tribe's enduring commitment to preserving its unique heritage, traditions, and language while adapting to the challenges and opportunities of the modern world. This resurgence of Chickasaw identity serves as a beacon of cultural strength and resilience, nurturing a sense of belonging and pride among tribal citizens.

Historical Significance:

To appreciate Chickasaw identity and cultural revival in contemporary times, one must consider the historical significance of the Chickasaw people. The Chickasaw Nation, like many other indigenous tribes, boasts a rich history dating back centuries before European contact. This history serves as the foundation upon which contemporary identity is built.

Cultural Preservation Efforts:

Contemporary Chickasaw identity is rooted in cultural preservation efforts that actively safeguard and celebrate Chickasaw traditions. These initiatives encompass a broad spectrum of activities, including language revitalization, traditional arts and crafts, storytelling, dance, and song. The preservation of cultural practices not only honors the tribe's ancestors but also ensures that Chickasaw identity remains vibrant and dynamic.

Language Revitalization:

Language is an integral component of Chickasaw identity. In contemporary times, there is a concerted effort to revitalize the Chickasaw language. Language immersion programs, language classes, and the creation of language resources are essential components of this revival. Language is a powerful vessel for cultural transmission and cohesion, connecting Chickasaw generations across time.

Cultural Centers and Institutions:

Cultural centers and institutions play a pivotal role in Chickasaw identity revival. These centers serve as hubs of cultural activity, education, and celebration. They house artifacts, host cultural events, and provide spaces for Chickasaw citizens to connect with their heritage. Cultural institutions are vital in fostering a sense of belonging and cultural pride.

Intertribal Collaboration:

Chickasaw identity revival is not limited to the Chickasaw Nation alone. Intertribal collaboration and engagement with other indigenous nations enriches Chickasaw identity. Shared cultural events, powwows, and collaborations on cultural preservation projects enable Chickasaw citizens to connect with broader indigenous communities and strengthen their own identity in the process.

Integration with Modern Life:

Chickasaw identity and cultural revival are not isolated from contemporary life. Rather, they are integrated into daily existence. Chickasaw citizens seamlessly weave traditional practices and values into modern activities, demonstrating the adaptability and resilience of their cultural identity.

Education and Cultural Awareness:

Education is a vital component of Chickasaw identity revival. Educational programs and initiatives within the Chickasaw Nation and beyond are designed to promote cultural awareness, ensuring that Chickasaw history and heritage are part of the curriculum in schools, universities, and community programs.

Traditional Arts and Crafts:

Traditional arts and crafts are a tangible expression of Chickasaw identity. Beadwork, pottery, basketry, and other crafts are not only preserved but also celebrated. These artistic endeavors connect Chickasaw citizens with their ancestral skills and aesthetics.

Storytelling and Oral Traditions:

Storytelling and oral traditions are central to Chickasaw identity revival. Elders and cultural bearers pass down stories, legends, and histories that enrich the collective Chickasaw narrative. These oral traditions instill a deep sense of belonging and cultural continuity. Chickasaw identity revival has not been without its challenges. Historical injustices, cultural suppression, and external pressures have posed obstacles. However, the resilience of the Chickasaw people and their determination to preserve their identity have resulted in remarkable triumphs. Chickasaw identity and cultural revival serve as a lasting legacy for future generations. They inspire Chickasaw youth to embrace their heritage, participate in cultural activities, and become stewards of their traditions. The preservation of Chickasaw identity ensures that it remains vibrant and relevant in an ever-changing world. In summary, Chickasaw identity and cultural revival in contemporary times are dynamic and multifaceted endeavors that reflect the Chickasaw Nation's enduring commitment to preserving its cultural heritage. These efforts celebrate the past, honor the present, and inspire a future where Chickasaw identity remains a source of pride, strength, and cultural richness.

BOOK 4
CREEK NATION CHRONICLES
SURVIVING AND THRIVING

BY A.J. KINGSTON

Chapter 1: The Creek People and Their Ancestral Lands

The history of the Creek Nation is deeply rooted in the pre-European societies and homelands that spanned across what is now the southeastern United States. Understanding the complexities of Creek societies before European contact offers valuable insights into the rich cultural tapestry, social structures, and lifeways that existed in the region.

Geographical Diversity:
The Creek Nation's pre-European societies were marked by geographical diversity. Their homelands encompassed a broad swath of territory, primarily in present-day Alabama, Georgia, and Florida. These lands were characterized by a range of ecosystems, from fertile river valleys to dense forests and coastal plains. This geographical diversity influenced the Creek way of life, as different regions offered distinct resources and opportunities.

Muscogee-speaking People:
The Creek Nation is composed of various Muscogee-speaking groups, each with its own distinct dialect and customs. These groups included the Coweta, Alabama, Tallapoosa, Hitchiti, and many others. Despite linguistic variations, these communities shared a common Creek identity and were part of a larger Creek Confederacy.

Clans and Kinship:
Creek societies were organized around clans and kinship systems. Clans played a crucial role in social organization, with individuals belonging to a specific clan based on their lineage. Clan relationships governed various aspects of life, including marriage, leadership roles, and responsibilities within the community.

Agriculture and Subsistence:
Agriculture was a cornerstone of Creek societies. They cultivated crops such as maize (corn), beans, squash, and sunflowers in river valleys and floodplains. These agricultural practices allowed for the development of sedentary villages, as they provided a stable

food source. Creek farmers also employed innovative techniques like mound gardening, which maximized crop yields.

Hunting and Gathering:

In addition to agriculture, Creek communities practiced hunting and gathering. The forests and wilderness areas of their homelands were rich sources of game, including deer, turkey, and small game animals. Gathering wild plants, nuts, and berries supplemented their diets and contributed to their subsistence.

Social and Political Organization:

Creek societies had intricate social and political structures. Each town or village was led by a chief, known as a mico, who was responsible for both political and spiritual leadership. The Creek Confederacy consisted of numerous towns, each with its own mico, and decisions affecting the entire confederacy were made through consensus and council meetings.

Trade Networks:

Creek societies were active participants in extensive trade networks. They engaged in trade with neighboring indigenous nations, such as the Cherokee and Choctaw, exchanging goods like deerskins, furs, pottery, and agricultural products. These trade networks not only facilitated economic exchange but also cultural interaction.

Religious Beliefs and Practices:

Creek religious beliefs were deeply rooted in their natural surroundings. They revered spirits associated with elements of the natural world, including water, animals, and celestial bodies. Rituals and ceremonies were held to seek guidance, healing, and protection from these spirits.

Ceremonial Mounds:

Creek societies constructed ceremonial mounds, which served as religious and ceremonial centers. These mounds, often located near rivers and waterways, were used for various rituals, including mound burials and ceremonies related to the Green Corn Festival, a significant annual event celebrating the harvest.

European Contact and Its Impact:

European contact, particularly with Spanish and English explorers and settlers, had a profound impact on Creek societies. The introduction of firearms, metal tools, and European diseases transformed their way of life and led to increased competition for resources among indigenous nations and European powers.

Warfare and Alliances:

European contact also altered the political landscape of Creek societies. Competition for resources and European alliances led to conflicts and wars among Creek towns and with neighboring tribes. The Creek War of 1813-1814, for example, was a significant conflict influenced by European colonial interests.

In summary, the pre-European Creek societies and homelands were characterized by cultural diversity, social organization, and a deep connection to the land. These societies thrived through agriculture, hunting, and gathering, and their intricate social and political structures paved the way for cooperative governance. The impact of European contact, however, brought both opportunities and challenges that reshaped the Creek way of life and set the stage for complex interactions and conflicts in the centuries to come. Understanding these pre-European Creek societies is essential for appreciating the depth and complexity of Creek history and heritage.

The Creek tribes, clans, and sociopolitical structures were integral components of the Creek Nation's intricate social organization. This complex system played a pivotal role in governing Creek communities and shaping their identity. To delve into the intricacies of Creek tribes, clans, and sociopolitical structures is to explore the multifaceted tapestry of Creek society.

Creek Confederacy:

The Creek Confederacy, also known as the Muscogee Confederacy, was an alliance of several Creek tribes. These tribes included the Coweta, Alabama, Tallapoosa, Hitchiti, and many others. Each of these tribes had its own distinct dialect, traditions, and territories within the broader Creek Nation.

Tribal Towns:

The Creek Confederacy was organized into tribal towns, each led by a mico, or chief. Tribal towns were the fundamental political units of Creek society. These towns had their own governance structures and responsibilities, including the management of local affairs, decision-making, and resource allocation.

Clan System:

The Creek clan system was a foundational aspect of social organization. Clans were extended kinship groups, and Creek individuals were born into a specific clan based on their lineage. Clans played a significant role in regulating social interactions, marriage practices, and political affiliations within Creek communities.

Clan Roles and Responsibilities:

Each Creek clan had distinct roles and responsibilities within the tribe. For example, the Wind Clan was traditionally associated with leadership positions, while the Bear Clan often held warrior roles. Clan affiliations influenced leadership choices and decision-making processes.

Matrilineal Descent:

Creek clans followed a matrilineal descent system, meaning that clan membership was determined through one's mother's lineage. This matrilineal structure influenced the passing down of names, clan affiliations, and cultural traditions.

Sociopolitical Decision-Making:

Sociopolitical decisions within Creek communities were often made through consensus-building processes. Council meetings, where representatives from various tribal towns convened, played a crucial role in reaching decisions that affected the entire Creek Confederacy. Achieving consensus was a valued practice in Creek governance.

Influence of Micos:

Micos, or chiefs, held leadership positions within tribal towns and the Creek Confederacy as a whole. They were responsible for maintaining order, settling disputes, and representing their tribes in intertribal and colonial interactions. The authority of a mico was derived from the support of clan leaders and other influential community members.

Creek Confederacy Council:

The Creek Confederacy Council was a central governing body that oversaw matters affecting the entire confederacy. It consisted of representatives from each tribal town, and decisions were reached through deliberation and consensus. The council played a pivotal role in both internal and external affairs.

Intertribal Relations:

Intertribal relations were crucial to the Creek Confederacy's stability and security. The Creek Nation engaged in diplomatic efforts and alliances with neighboring indigenous nations, such as the Cherokee and Choctaw, to manage territorial disputes, trade, and regional conflicts.

European Contact and Changes:

European contact, particularly with Spanish, English, and later American settlers, brought significant changes to Creek sociopolitical structures. The introduction of firearms, trade networks, and the spread of European diseases reshaped the balance of power and relationships among tribes.

Impact of Colonization:

Colonization exerted pressure on Creek tribes, often pitting them against each other in conflicts over resources and alliances with European powers. The Creek War of 1813-1814, for instance, was a culmination of these tensions and the influence of external forces.

In summary, the Creek tribes, clans, and sociopolitical structures constituted a multifaceted system that governed Creek communities and shaped their collective identity. This intricate organization, deeply rooted in clan affiliations and tribal towns, facilitated decision-making, social order, and intertribal relations. The Creek Confederacy, with its council and micos, played a central role in managing internal and external affairs. However, the impact of European contact and colonization brought both opportunities and challenges that reshaped the sociopolitical landscape of Creek society. Understanding these structures is essential for comprehending the complexities of Creek history and culture.

Environmental adaptations and subsistence practices were essential components of the Creek Nation's way of life, allowing them to thrive in the diverse ecosystems of the southeastern

United States. These adaptations reflected the deep connection between Creek communities and their natural surroundings, influencing their livelihoods, diets, and cultural practices.

Diverse Ecosystems:

The Creek Nation's homelands covered a range of ecosystems, including fertile river valleys, dense forests, coastal plains, and upland regions. This geographical diversity influenced their environmental adaptations and subsistence practices.

Agriculture:

Agriculture played a crucial role in Creek subsistence. Creek farmers cultivated a variety of crops, including maize (corn), beans, squash, sunflowers, and other vegetables. They practiced agriculture in river valleys and floodplains, where fertile soils allowed for successful crop cultivation. Mound gardening, a technique that involved creating raised garden beds, was utilized to optimize crop yields.

Hunting and Gathering:

Hunting and gathering complemented agricultural practices. The Creek people were skilled hunters who pursued game such as deer, turkey, rabbits, and small mammals in the dense forests of their homelands. Gathering wild plants, nuts, berries, and other edibles from their natural surroundings supplemented their diets and provided valuable nutritional diversity.

Fishing:

Fishing was another important subsistence activity for the Creek Nation. The numerous rivers and waterways within their homelands offered abundant fish and shellfish resources. Creeks used various fishing techniques, including traps, nets, and hook and line fishing, to secure a reliable source of protein.

Seasonal Mobility:

Creek communities practiced seasonal mobility to take advantage of different resources available throughout the year. They moved between upland and riverine areas based on the seasons, allowing them to maximize food resources and adapt to changing environmental conditions.

Preservation Techniques:

To ensure a stable food supply during times of scarcity, the Creek people employed preservation techniques. They dried and smoked meats and fish, as well as stored surplus crops in communal granaries. These practices helped them sustain their communities during challenging periods.

Use of Natural Resources:

Creek communities utilized natural resources wisely. They made use of the abundant hardwood forests for constructing homes, crafting tools, and creating intricate baskets. Clay from local sources was used for pottery and other ceramics. Animal hides were processed for clothing and other essential items.

Cultural Significance of Agriculture:

Agriculture held cultural significance within Creek communities. The Green Corn Festival, or Busk, marked the harvest season and was a time of communal celebration, purification, and renewal. It symbolized the connection between Creek spirituality and agricultural cycles.

Environmental Stewardship:

The Creek people practiced environmental stewardship and sustainability. They recognized the importance of maintaining the balance of natural ecosystems and preserving resources for future generations. These principles were embedded in their cultural values and practices.

Adaptation to European Introduction:

European contact introduced new crops, livestock, and agricultural practices to the Creek Nation. While some of these innovations were integrated into Creek agriculture, others disrupted traditional subsistence patterns and led to changes in land use and food production.

In summary, environmental adaptations and subsistence practices were fundamental to the Creek Nation's ability to thrive in their diverse homelands. Their sustainable practices, agricultural traditions, and resource management reflected a deep connection to the land and its bounty. These adaptations allowed Creek communities to not only survive but also maintain a rich cultural heritage that celebrated their relationship with the natural world.

Chapter 2: Early Encounters and the Impact of Colonization

The arrival of European explorers and colonists had a profound impact on the indigenous peoples of North America, including the Creek Nation. This period of contact and colonization marked a significant turning point in the history and trajectory of Creek societies.

Early European Explorers:
European exploration of the southeastern region of North America, where the Creek Nation resided, began in the early 16th century. Spanish explorers, such as Hernando de Soto in the mid-1500s, were among the first to make contact with indigenous peoples in the Creek homelands. These explorers sought to establish dominance and secure territory for their respective European powers.

Trade and Exchange:
European explorers introduced new goods and technologies to the Creek people through trade and exchange. Items such as metal tools, firearms, cloth, and European goods became part of the trade networks, altering Creek material culture and subsistence practices.

Impact on Sociopolitical Structures:
The presence of European colonists and their attempts to establish footholds in the southeastern region of North America had a transformative impact on the sociopolitical structures of Creek societies. Interactions with Europeans led to shifts in power dynamics, alliances, and intertribal relations.

Deerskin Trade:
One of the most significant economic interactions between Creek people and European colonists was the deerskin trade. Creek hunters and trappers supplied deerskins to European markets, which were in high demand for use in making clothing and leather goods. This trade not only provided valuable resources but also altered traditional hunting and gathering practices.

Alliances and Conflicts:

European powers, including Spain, France, and England, vied for control of Creek territories. Creek communities sometimes formed alliances with European nations to protect their interests or engage in conflicts against rival indigenous nations. The geopolitical landscape was marked by complex relationships and shifting allegiances.

Creek Adaptations and Strategies:
The Creek people adapted to the challenges and opportunities presented by European contact. Some Creek communities established trade relationships and diplomatic ties with European settlers, while others resisted encroachment and maintained their independence.

Disease and Population Decline:
The arrival of European colonists also brought devastating diseases to which indigenous populations had little immunity. Diseases such as smallpox, measles, and influenza had catastrophic effects on Creek communities, leading to population decline and social disruptions.

Creek Wars and Conflicts:
Tensions between European settlers and indigenous nations, including the Creek, sometimes erupted into conflicts and wars. The Creek War of 1813-1814, for example, saw Creek communities divided, with some siding with the United States and others with British forces. This war had significant consequences for Creek sovereignty and land.

Land Cessions and Removal:
The encroachment of European settlers and the United States government's policies of westward expansion resulted in land cessions and forced removals of Creek communities from their ancestral territories. The Creek Removal, often referred to as the Trail of Tears, was a tragic event that displaced many Creek people from their homelands.

In summary, the arrival of European explorers and colonists dramatically altered the course of Creek history. It brought about changes in material culture, sociopolitical structures, and intertribal relations. While interactions with Europeans provided access to new technologies and goods, they also brought diseases, conflicts, and land loss that had profound and enduring effects on Creek societies. The legacy of European contact and colonization continues to shape the history and identity of the Creek Nation and other indigenous peoples in the southeastern United States.

The beginnings of trade and cultural exchange between the Creek Nation and European settlers marked a significant chapter in the history of both Creek societies and European colonization in the southeastern United States. These interactions were complex and multifaceted, influencing the material culture, economies, and social dynamics of Creek communities.

Early Trade Relations:

Trade relations between Creek communities and European settlers began with the arrival of Spanish explorers in the 16th century. The Creek people engaged in trade with Spanish colonists, exchanging goods and resources. The deerskin trade, in particular, became a significant economic activity, with Creek hunters providing deerskins for European markets.

Deerskin Trade:

The deerskin trade was a central aspect of Creek-European interactions. Creek hunters and trappers supplied deerskins to European markets, where they were highly sought after for making clothing, leather goods, and other items. This trade provided the Creek people with access to European manufactured goods, such as metal tools, firearms, cloth, and glass beads.

Impact on Material Culture:

The introduction of European goods had a transformative impact on Creek material culture. Metal tools replaced traditional stone implements, making tasks such as farming and construction more efficient. European textiles influenced clothing styles, while glass beads became popular for adornment and trade.

Cultural Exchange:

Trade relations also facilitated cultural exchange between Creek communities and European settlers. This exchange extended beyond material goods to include the sharing of knowledge, customs, and languages. Both Creek and European cultures were enriched through these interactions.

Alliances and Diplomacy:

Trade relations often went hand in hand with alliances and diplomacy. Creek communities sometimes formed alliances with European powers, such as the English or Spanish, to protect their interests or engage in conflicts against rival indigenous nations. These alliances had political implications for both Creek societies and European colonial powers.

Intertribal Relations:

Creek trade networks extended to interactions with neighboring indigenous nations. Trade routes and networks connected Creek communities to the Choctaw, Cherokee, and other indigenous groups. These intertribal relations were not only economic but also cultural, fostering the exchange of ideas, traditions, and technologies.

Impact of Disease:

One of the unintended consequences of trade and cultural exchange was the introduction of diseases to which indigenous populations had little immunity. Diseases such as smallpox and measles had devastating effects on Creek communities, leading to population decline and social disruptions.

Changing Economies:

The deerskin trade and the exchange of other goods brought changes to Creek economies. Creek communities increasingly relied on hunting and trapping to meet European demands for deerskins, altering traditional subsistence practices and resource management.

Shifts in Power:

Trade relations and alliances with European settlers also influenced power dynamics within Creek societies. Some communities benefited economically and politically from these interactions, while others faced challenges and competition for resources.

In summary, the beginnings of trade and cultural exchange between the Creek Nation and European settlers were multifaceted and shaped the course of history for both groups. These interactions had profound effects on Creek material culture, economies, and sociopolitical structures. They also fostered intertribal relations and contributed to the complex tapestry of indigenous and European interactions in the southeastern United States. The legacy of these early exchanges continues to influence the history and identity of the Creek Nation and the broader history of indigenous-European relations in North America.

Changes in Creek life and society were inevitable as a result of the profound impact of European colonization, trade, and cultural exchange in the southeastern United States. These changes reshaped Creek communities, their way of life, and their sociopolitical structures in significant ways.

Shifts in Economic Practices:
One of the most noticeable changes in Creek life was the shift in economic practices. The introduction of the deerskin trade and the demand for deerskins in European markets transformed Creek economies. Creek hunters and trappers began to focus more on supplying deerskins for trade, altering traditional subsistence patterns.

Dependency on European Goods:
As trade with Europeans increased, Creek communities became increasingly dependent on European manufactured goods. Metal tools replaced traditional stone implements, and European textiles influenced clothing styles. Glass beads became popular for adornment and trade. This dependency on European goods had profound implications for Creek material culture.

Agriculture and Foodways:
Agriculture remained an essential aspect of Creek life, but it was influenced by European practices. Creek farmers adopted new crops introduced by Europeans, such as corn, beans, and squash. These crops became staples in Creek diets, supplementing traditional foods gathered from the forests and waters.

Shifts in Sociopolitical Structures:
European contact and colonization led to shifts in Creek sociopolitical structures. The Creek Confederacy, composed of tribal towns with their own chiefs, experienced changes as some chiefs aligned with European powers for trade and protection. This altered power dynamics within Creek society.

Alliances and Conflicts:

Creek communities engaged in alliances and conflicts with European settlers and other indigenous nations. The Creek Wars of the late 18th and early 19th centuries, for example, saw divisions among Creek communities, with some siding with the United States and others with British forces. These conflicts had far-reaching consequences for Creek sovereignty and land.

European Diseases and Population Decline:

European contact brought diseases such as smallpox, measles, and influenza to which indigenous populations had little immunity. These diseases caused widespread illness and death among Creek communities, resulting in significant population decline and social disruptions.

Land Loss and Forced Removal:

One of the most devastating changes was the loss of Creek lands due to European encroachment and U.S. government policies of westward expansion. The Creek Removal, often referred to as the Trail of Tears, forcibly displaced many Creek people from their ancestral territories, leading to hardship and suffering.

Cultural Exchange and Adaptation:

Despite the challenges and disruptions, Creek communities engaged in cultural exchange with European settlers. This exchange included the sharing of knowledge, customs, and languages. Both Creek and European cultures were enriched through these interactions. While changes were significant, many Creek communities managed to preserve elements of their traditional practices, languages, and cultural heritage. Ceremonies, storytelling, and traditional arts and crafts continued to be important aspects of Creek life.

In summary, changes in Creek life and society were a complex result of European contact and colonization. These changes encompassed economic shifts, alterations in sociopolitical structures, and cultural exchange. The enduring legacy of these changes continues to influence the history and identity of the Creek Nation and serves as a testament to the resilience of Creek communities in the face of profound challenges and transformations.

Chapter 3: Creek Culture and the Mound Builders

The Creek Nation, also known as the Muscogee (Creek) Nation, boasts a rich and diverse cultural heritage that has been shaped by centuries of history, traditions, and resilience. This cultural heritage encompasses various aspects of Creek life, including language, art, music, dance, storytelling, and spirituality.

Language:
The Creek people have a unique language, known as the Creek or Muscogee language. It is a member of the Muskogean language family and is characterized by its complex verb conjugation system. Efforts to preserve and revitalize the Creek language are ongoing, with language immersion programs and educational initiatives playing a crucial role in sustaining this vital aspect of Creek culture.

Oral Traditions and Storytelling:
Oral traditions are at the heart of Creek culture. Elders and storytellers pass down knowledge, myths, legends, and history through storytelling. These narratives often include tales of cultural heroes, animals, and the natural world, conveying important moral and cultural lessons.

Art and Crafts:
Creek artists have a long history of creating intricate and beautiful artwork. Traditional Creek art includes pottery, basketry, beadwork, and carving. Each of these art forms has deep cultural and spiritual significance, often featuring symbols and designs that reflect Creek cosmology and mythology.

Music and Dance:
Music and dance play an integral role in Creek cultural expression. Creek music includes traditional songs, chants, and flute music. Social dances like the stomp dance, also known as the "Creek square dance," are important communal events that celebrate Creek identity and traditions.

Spirituality and Religion:
Creek spirituality is deeply connected to the natural world. Ceremonies and rituals, often held in sacred places within Creek

territory, honor the spirits, ancestors, and the Creator. The Green Corn Ceremony, or Busk, is one of the most significant Creek ceremonies, symbolizing renewal, purification, and the connection between agriculture and spirituality.

Traditional Clothing:

Traditional Creek clothing reflects the culture's historical roots and practical needs. Creek attire includes items such as deerskin clothing, moccasins, and headdresses. These garments were both functional and symbolic, often featuring intricate beadwork and designs.

Ceremonies and Rituals:

Creek ceremonies and rituals are central to Creek cultural life. In addition to the Green Corn Ceremony, other ceremonies mark important life events, such as birth, puberty, marriage, and death. These rituals maintain a strong connection to Creek spirituality and traditions.

Creek Clan System:

The Creek Nation has a complex clan system, which is an integral part of their cultural identity. Clans are organized around kinship and provide a sense of belonging and identity. Each clan has its own distinct animal or natural symbol, and clan affiliations play a role in marriage, leadership, and social dynamics.

Community and Communal Values:

Community values and the importance of communal well-being are deeply embedded in Creek culture. Cooperation, reciprocity, and mutual support are foundational principles that guide interactions within Creek communities.

Resilience and Cultural Preservation:

Despite the challenges posed by European contact, colonization, and forced removal, the Creek Nation has shown remarkable resilience in preserving and revitalizing its cultural heritage. Efforts to maintain traditional practices, language, and ceremonies continue to be a priority within Creek communities.

In summary, the cultural heritage of the Creek Nation is a testament to the strength and resilience of this indigenous people. It reflects their deep connection to the land, spirituality, and a rich history of traditions passed down through generations. Today, the

Creek Nation's commitment to cultural preservation and revitalization ensures that their unique heritage will continue to thrive and be celebrated for generations to come.

Creek art, ceremonies, and spiritual beliefs are integral components of Creek culture, reflecting the deep connection between the Creek people and their ancestral lands, spirituality, and communal traditions. These aspects of Creek heritage are rich and diverse, encompassing a wide range of artistic expressions, sacred rituals, and profound beliefs.

Creek Art:

Pottery: Creek pottery is renowned for its intricate designs and craftsmanship. Traditional Creek pottery is often coil-built and may feature symbols and motifs inspired by nature, animals, and spiritual themes. It is both functional and decorative.

Basketry: Creek basketry is another esteemed art form. Creek basket weavers create baskets with various shapes and sizes, often using river cane and sweetgrass. These baskets serve utilitarian purposes and are also significant cultural artifacts.

Beadwork: Beadwork is a skill passed down through generations among Creek artisans. Beadwork is used to adorn clothing, accessories, and ceremonial regalia. Traditional Creek beadwork often incorporates geometric designs and vibrant colors.

Carving: Creek carvers create intricate designs on wood, stone, and other materials. The carvings may depict animals, symbols, and mythological figures. Creek carving is an important form of artistic expression and storytelling.

Creek Ceremonies:

Green Corn Ceremony (Busk): The Green Corn Ceremony is one of the most significant Creek ceremonies. It marks the new agricultural year and symbolizes renewal and purification. Participants fast, dance, and engage in communal rituals during this multi-day event.

Stomp Dance: The stomp dance, also known as the "Creek square dance," is a social dance that brings the community together. It involves rhythmic drumming, singing, and intricate footwork. The stomp dance celebrates Creek cultural identity and fosters a sense of unity.

Ceremonies of Passage: Creek culture includes various ceremonies to mark significant life events, such as birth, puberty, marriage, and death. These ceremonies involve rituals, prayers, and communal gatherings to honor and support individuals in their life transitions.

Sweat Lodge Ceremony: The sweat lodge ceremony is a purification ritual that involves participants entering a small, enclosed structure heated with hot stones. It is a sacred and spiritual practice aimed at cleansing the mind, body, and spirit.

Spiritual Beliefs:

Animism: Creek spirituality is rooted in animism, which is the belief that all living and non-living things possess a spirit or essence. The Creek people maintain a profound connection to the natural world and view it as imbued with spiritual significance.

Sacred Landscapes: The Creek Nation has sacred landscapes, including rivers, mountains, and forests, where they conduct ceremonies and rituals. These places are believed to hold a powerful spiritual presence and are central to Creek cosmology.

Clan System: The Creek Clan system is an essential aspect of spiritual beliefs and social organization. Each clan has its own totemic animal or natural symbol, and members of the same clan share a kinship and spiritual connection.

Ancestral Veneration: The Creek people hold deep reverence for their ancestors. Ancestral spirits are believed to guide and protect the living. Offerings and rituals are conducted to honor and communicate with ancestors.

Harmony with Nature: Creek spiritual beliefs emphasize living in harmony with the natural world. Practices such as conservation, sustainable resource management, and respecting the balance of nature are fundamental to Creek spirituality.

In summary, Creek art, ceremonies, and spiritual beliefs are intertwined and central to the cultural identity of the Creek Nation. They reflect a deep reverence for the natural world, a strong sense of community, and a commitment to preserving ancestral traditions. These cultural expressions and beliefs continue to thrive and play a vital role in Creek life and heritage today.

The legacy of the Mound Builders in Creek lands is a testament to the rich and complex history of the Creek Nation and the indigenous peoples of the southeastern United States. The Mound Builders were a prehistoric civilization that inhabited the region long before the Creek people and other indigenous nations arrived. Their enduring legacy can be seen in the archaeological remains of earthen mounds and the cultural influence they left behind.

Archaeological Wonders:

Cahokia Mounds: Although located in what is now Illinois, Cahokia Mounds is one of the most famous and significant mound sites built by the Mississippian culture, which is often associated with the Mound Builders. While it is not within Creek lands, it serves as a symbol of the remarkable engineering and architectural achievements of ancient indigenous civilizations in the Southeast.

Etowah Mounds: Etowah Mounds, located in present-day Georgia, is one of the most well-preserved mound sites associated with the Creek culture. The site includes several earthen mounds, a plaza, and a ceremonial complex. These mounds offer valuable insights into the social and religious practices of the Creek people.

Cultural Influence:

Spiritual and Ceremonial Significance: The Mound Builders' mounds held profound spiritual and ceremonial significance. These mounds were often used for religious rituals, burial sites, and as platforms for important ceremonies. The Creek people inherited and continued some of these traditions, incorporating mound sites into their own spiritual practices.

Trade and Exchange: The Mound Builders' complex societies engaged in extensive trade networks that stretched across the southeastern United States. This trade introduced valuable resources, ideas, and technologies to the region, influencing the Creek people and other indigenous nations.

Agriculture and Foodways: The Mound Builders were skilled agriculturalists, cultivating crops such as maize (corn), beans, and squash. These agricultural practices had a lasting impact on the foodways of the Creek people and other indigenous groups, contributing to the development of their agricultural traditions.

Cultural Continuity and Adaptation:
While the Mound Builders' civilization eventually declined and disappeared, their legacy lived on through the Creek people and other indigenous nations. The Creek people adapted and incorporated aspects of Mound Builder traditions into their own cultural practices. Mound sites continued to hold spiritual significance for the Creek, and their use persisted through time.

Archaeological Research:
Modern archaeological research has provided valuable insights into the Mound Builders' history and their influence on Creek lands. Ongoing excavations and studies of mound sites contribute to our understanding of the interconnectedness of indigenous cultures in the Southeast.

In summary, the legacy of the Mound Builders in Creek lands is a testament to the enduring cultural and historical connections among indigenous peoples in the Southeastern United States. The Mound Builders' achievements in architecture, spirituality, and agriculture left a lasting impact on the Creek people and other indigenous nations, shaping their cultural identity and practices for generations to come. Today, the preservation and study of these ancient mound sites continue to honor the legacy of the Mound Builders and the rich heritage of the Creek Nation.

Chapter 4: The Creek War and Removal

The Creek War, also known as the Red Stick War, was a conflict that took place from 1813 to 1814 in the southeastern United States, primarily involving the Creek Nation and the United States. Several complex factors contributed to the outbreak of this war:

Tensions within the Creek Nation: The Creek Nation was divided into two main factions at the time of the war—the Red Sticks and the White Sticks. The Red Sticks were a militant faction that advocated for the preservation of traditional Creek culture and opposed American encroachment. The White Sticks were more open to accommodation with the United States. Internal divisions and disputes over land and culture created a volatile atmosphere within the Creek Nation.

Land Cessions and Treaty Violations: The United States had been pressuring the Creek Nation to cede land through a series of treaties. These land cessions resulted in the loss of significant Creek territories. Many Creeks felt that their leaders were being coerced into signing these treaties and that their land was being unjustly taken from them. Treaty violations and disputes over land ownership further fueled tensions.

Religious and Cultural Factors: The Red Sticks, who were associated with the Creek spiritual and cultural revival movement, sought to maintain traditional Creek religious practices and resist the influence of European-American culture. They believed that the adoption of Euro-American practices threatened the Creek way of life. This cultural and religious revival contributed to the factionalism within the Creek Nation.

External Influences: The Creek War did not occur in isolation. It was part of a broader context of conflict in the southeastern United States, including the War of 1812 between the United States and Great Britain. The Red Sticks received support and inspiration from British agents and traders, who saw the conflict as an opportunity to weaken the United States.

Leadership and Militancy: Prominent Red Stick leaders, such as William Weatherford (Red Eagle), rallied their followers to resist

American encroachment. The Red Sticks engaged in acts of violence against American settlers and forts. This militant stance escalated the conflict and made a negotiated settlement more challenging.

Government Response: The United States responded to the violence by deploying military forces to the Creek territory. General Andrew Jackson played a significant role in the American response to the Creek War. The conflict with the Creeks was also intertwined with the broader goals of American expansion and dominance in the Southeast.

Battle of Burnt Corn Creek: An early skirmish at Burnt Corn Creek in July 1813 between American forces and Red Stick warriors further escalated tensions. While not a decisive battle, it demonstrated the growing hostilities between the two sides.

The Creek War eventually culminated in several key battles, including the Battle of Horseshoe Bend in March 1814, where General Andrew Jackson defeated the Red Sticks. The Treaty of Fort Jackson, signed in August 1814, forced the Creek Nation to cede a significant portion of its land to the United States, further altering the geopolitical landscape of the southeastern United States.

The Creek War had lasting consequences for the Creek Nation, as it marked the beginning of a period of forced removal and dispossession of their ancestral lands. It also contributed to the broader narrative of conflicts between indigenous nations and American expansion during the early 19th century.

The Creek War of 1813-1814, also known as the Red Stick War, and its aftermath had significant and lasting impacts on both the Creek Nation and the broader history of the southeastern United States. The war itself was marked by violence, upheaval, and profound changes, while its consequences continued to shape the region for years to come. Here's an overview of the Creek War and its aftermath:

The Creek War (1813-1814):

Warfare and Battles: The Creek War was characterized by a series of battles and skirmishes between the Red Stick faction of the

Creek Nation and American forces. Notable conflicts included the Battle of Burnt Corn Creek, the Fort Mims Massacre, and the decisive Battle of Horseshoe Bend.

Role of Andrew Jackson: General Andrew Jackson played a prominent role in the conflict, leading American forces in several key engagements. His victory at the Battle of Horseshoe Bend in March 1814 marked a turning point in the war.

Treaty of Fort Jackson: Following their defeat at Horseshoe Bend, the Creek Nation was forced to sign the Treaty of Fort Jackson in August 1814. This treaty resulted in the cession of a significant portion of Creek land to the United States, including much of present-day Alabama and southern Georgia.

Aftermath of the Creek War:

Creek Displacement: The Treaty of Fort Jackson and subsequent treaties led to the forced removal of Creek communities from their ancestral lands. This displacement, which continued over the years, was part of the broader pattern of indigenous removal in the Southeast.

Cherokee Adaptation: Some Creek refugees sought refuge among the Cherokee Nation in the southern Appalachians, leading to cultural exchanges and interactions between the two nations. This migration had a lasting impact on the Cherokee people.

Cherokee Removal: The Creek War and its aftermath contributed to the overall climate of indigenous removal, culminating in the Cherokee Trail of Tears in the 1830s, when the Cherokee Nation was forcibly removed from their homeland.

Changing Creek Society: The Creek Nation underwent significant changes in the wake of the war. The divisions between Red Sticks and White Sticks persisted, and the loss of land disrupted traditional Creek ways of life. The Creek people faced the challenges of rebuilding and adapting to a new reality.

Impact on Southeastern History: The Creek War and other conflicts in the region, such as the War of 1812, marked a period of turbulence and transformation in the Southeastern United States. The war contributed to the broader story of American expansion, indigenous dispossession, and the redrawing of territorial boundaries.

Historical Memory: The Creek War remains a significant part of the historical memory of the Creek Nation and the southeastern United States. It is remembered for its impact on Creek culture, land, and sovereignty.

In summary, the Creek War and its aftermath were pivotal events in the history of the Creek Nation and the southeastern United States. The war itself resulted in the loss of Creek lands and marked the beginning of a period of forced removal, while its consequences reverberated throughout the region, shaping the destinies of indigenous nations and settler communities alike.

The Trail of Tears is a harrowing chapter in American history, marked by the forced removal of indigenous nations from their ancestral lands. Among the nations affected, the Creek people experienced their own tragic journey along this arduous path, one that brought immense suffering and loss but also demonstrated remarkable resilience and determination.

The Creek Nation, comprised of various clans and communities, had inhabited the Southeastern United States for centuries, cultivating a rich and diverse cultural heritage deeply rooted in their ancestral lands. However, the encroachment of European-American settlers and the policies of the United States government would ultimately disrupt their way of life and lead to the Creek's forced removal.

The Creek Removal:

In the early 19th century, the United States government sought to acquire more land for agricultural expansion and economic development. This desire for land led to the negotiation of a series of treaties that pressured the Creek Nation into ceding vast portions of their territory.

One of the most significant of these treaties was the Treaty of Fort Jackson in 1814, following the Creek War. This treaty, which followed the Creek's defeat at the Battle of Horseshoe Bend, resulted in the loss of a significant portion of Creek land. However, the most devastating blow came in 1830 with the passage of the Indian Removal Act, which provided the legal framework for the forced removal of indigenous nations, including the Creek.

Under the provisions of the Indian Removal Act, the Creek Nation was required to cede the remainder of their lands in exchange for land west of the Mississippi River. In 1832, Creek leaders reluctantly signed the Treaty of Cusseta, which paved the way for their removal from their ancestral homeland.

The Tragic Journey:

The Creek people, like other indigenous nations facing removal, were forced to undertake a perilous journey westward. The removal process, often referred to as the Trail of Tears, was characterized by unimaginable hardship and suffering.

Creek families were forcibly uprooted from their homes, often with little time to prepare or gather their belongings. They were herded into stockades and detention camps, where living conditions were deplorable, and disease spread rapidly. Families were separated, and many died from exposure, disease, and malnutrition during the internment.

The actual journey along the Trail of Tears was a grueling ordeal. Creek people were marched hundreds of miles on foot, enduring harsh weather conditions, inadequate clothing, and limited food supplies. They faced the constant threat of violence and exploitation at the hands of military escorts and settlers.

The Journey's Toll:

The toll of the Creek removal was staggering. Thousands of Creek individuals perished during the journey, succumbing to disease, starvation, and exposure. Families were torn apart, and entire communities were forever disrupted. The Creek Nation, once a cohesive and thriving culture, was dispersed and fractured.

The resilience of the Creek people, however, shone brightly even in the face of such adversity. Despite the immense suffering they endured, Creek survivors sought to rebuild their lives in the unfamiliar territory of Indian Territory (present-day Oklahoma). They established new communities and worked to preserve their cultural heritage and traditions.

Resilience and Rebuilding:

In Indian Territory, Creek communities faced the formidable task of adapting to their new environment. They engaged in agriculture, established towns, and developed governance structures to maintain their cohesion and identity. Many Creek leaders, such as Opothleyahola, played key roles in helping their people navigate these challenging times.

Efforts to preserve Creek culture and traditions remained at the forefront of their priorities. The Creek language, customs, and ceremonies were passed down to new generations, ensuring that their heritage would endure. Creek artisans continued to create pottery, baskets, beadwork, and other crafts that reflected their cultural identity.

Creek Identity and Legacy:

Today, the Creek Nation thrives as a federally recognized tribe with a vibrant culture and a strong sense of identity. The legacy of the Trail of Tears remains an integral part of their history, a testament to their endurance and determination in the face of unimaginable hardship.

The Creek people have made significant contributions to the cultural mosaic of the United States. Their artistry, agricultural practices, and traditional knowledge continue to enrich not only their own communities but also the broader society.

In remembering the tragic Trail of Tears and the Creek removal, we acknowledge the profound injustices suffered by indigenous nations during this dark period in American history. It is a somber reminder of the importance of acknowledging and addressing the historical trauma experienced by indigenous communities while celebrating their resilience and ongoing contributions to the nation.

Chapter 5: Life in Exile: The Creek Nation's Struggles

The Creek people's exile and displacement from their ancestral lands in the southeastern United States, commonly referred to as the Trail of Tears, was a profound and traumatic experience that brought with it a multitude of challenges and hardships. This forced removal, orchestrated by the United States government in the early 19th century, had lasting consequences that reverberated through Creek society and history.

Loss of Homeland and Culture: The most immediate and profound challenge for the Creek people was the loss of their homeland. Generations of Creek families had cultivated a deep connection to their ancestral lands, which were intricately woven into their cultural and spiritual identity. The forced removal disrupted their way of life and severed the bonds they had with their traditional territories.

Displacement and Destitution: The physical displacement of Creek families from their homes was a devastating experience. Many were stripped of their possessions and forced to leave behind cherished belongings and irreplaceable family heirlooms. This displacement often left them destitute, with few resources to rebuild their lives in unfamiliar territory.

Hardship and Suffering on the Journey: The journey along the Trail of Tears itself was marked by immense hardship and suffering. Creek people were forced to travel hundreds of miles on foot, often in harsh weather conditions. They faced hunger, exposure, and disease, resulting in a significant loss of life along the way. Families were torn apart, and the emotional toll was immeasurable.

Health and Well-Being: The unsanitary and overcrowded conditions in internment camps and detention facilities contributed to the spread of diseases, further decimating the Creek population. Diseases like cholera, smallpox, and dysentery took a heavy toll on those already weakened by the journey, leading to high mortality rates.

Families and Communities Disrupted: The Creek removal led to the fragmentation of families and communities. Many families were separated, and the cohesion of Creek communities was disrupted. The bonds that had held Creek clans and towns together for generations were strained, and the sense of unity and belonging was deeply challenged.

Adapting to New Territories: Upon reaching their designated lands in Indian Territory (present-day Oklahoma), Creek survivors faced the daunting task of adapting to a new environment. This required not only establishing new homes and communities but also adapting agricultural practices to a different climate and landscape.

Governance and Leadership: The Creek Nation had to navigate the challenges of rebuilding governance structures and leadership in a new territory. Leaders like Opothleyahola played crucial roles in helping the Creek people reestablish a sense of order and cohesion.

Preservation of Culture: Despite the immense challenges they faced, Creek individuals and communities were determined to preserve their cultural heritage. They made concerted efforts to maintain their language, customs, and traditional knowledge. Ceremonies and rituals remained integral to their identity, helping to connect them to their roots.

Resilience and Rebuilding: Perhaps the most remarkable aspect of the Creek experience was their resilience and ability to rebuild their lives. Despite the immense suffering and loss, Creek communities endured and adapted to their new circumstances. They created new homes, schools, and institutions, ensuring that their cultural legacy would continue.

Legacy and Contributions: Today, the Creek Nation thrives as a vibrant and culturally rich community. Their legacy is one of survival and resilience, but it is also one of contributions to the broader American society. Creek art, agriculture, and traditions have left an indelible mark on the cultural fabric of the United States.

In reflecting on the challenges of Creek exile and displacement, it is essential to recognize the profound injustices suffered by the

Creek people and other indigenous nations during this dark chapter in American history. Their endurance and determination in the face of overwhelming adversity serve as a testament to the strength of the human spirit. The Creek experience is a somber reminder of the importance of acknowledging the historical trauma experienced by indigenous communities while celebrating their resilience and ongoing contributions to the nation.

The Creek people's forced removal from their ancestral lands and their subsequent settlement in Indian Territory (present-day Oklahoma) marked a period of immense cultural upheaval and adaptation. In the face of these profound challenges, Creek communities displayed remarkable resilience and employed various survival strategies to navigate their new circumstances while striving to preserve their cultural heritage.

1. Agricultural Innovations: Agriculture had been central to Creek society in the Southeastern United States, and it continued to be vital in their new homeland. However, the climate and soil conditions in Indian Territory were different from those in the Southeast. Creek farmers adapted by experimenting with new crops and agricultural techniques suited to the region. They cultivated crops like corn, beans, and squash, as well as introduced crops like peaches and apples.

2. Rebuilding Communities: Creek communities sought to rebuild a sense of cohesion and structure in their new territories. Towns and villages were established, mirroring the social organization and town square layouts of their ancestral lands. These towns provided a sense of continuity and familiarity amidst the upheaval.

3. Leadership and Governance: Creek leadership played a crucial role in guiding their people through the challenges of relocation. Leaders like Opothleyahola and others helped to reestablish governance structures and maintain order within the community. This leadership was instrumental in providing stability during a period of great uncertainty.

4. Language Preservation: The Creek language, an integral part of their cultural identity, remained a priority. Efforts were made to ensure the transmission of Creek language and oral traditions to younger generations. Elders played a vital role in passing down knowledge and stories, preserving linguistic and cultural ties.

5. Traditional Arts and Crafts: Creek artisans continued to create traditional pottery, baskets, beadwork, and other crafts. These artistic traditions not only served as a means of cultural expression but also as a source of income for many Creek families.

6. Ceremonial Practices: Despite the challenges of displacement, Creek ceremonial practices remained an essential part of their identity. Stomp dances, Green Corn ceremonies, and other rituals continued to be performed, fostering a sense of community and connection to their cultural roots.

7. Adaptation to New Environment: Creek people had to adapt to the different environment of Indian Territory, which included the learning of new plant and animal species and adjusting to the prairie landscape. They also developed methods for managing the region's frequent wildfires, which were a feature of the Plains ecosystem.

8. Cultural Exchange: The Creek people encountered other indigenous nations in Indian Territory, including the Cherokee and Choctaw. This interaction resulted in cultural exchanges, as different nations shared knowledge and traditions. These interactions contributed to the rich tapestry of cultural diversity in the region.

9. Resilience in the Face of Hardship: The challenges faced by Creek communities were immense, including disease, malnutrition, and economic hardship. Yet, their resilience and determination allowed them to persevere. Many Creek families supported one another during times of crisis, emphasizing the importance of community bonds.

10. Education and Institutions: Creek communities recognized the importance of education for future generations. Schools were established, providing formal education alongside the transmission of traditional knowledge. These institutions played a crucial role in preparing Creek youth for the challenges of a rapidly changing world.

11. Intergenerational Continuity: The Creek people placed a strong emphasis on passing down cultural knowledge from one generation to the next. Elders played a central role in this process, ensuring that the traditions, stories, and values of the Creek Nation were carried forward.

In reflecting on the cultural adaptations and survival strategies of the Creek people, it is evident that their resilience and determination allowed them to persevere in the face of immense challenges. While the forced removal had a profound impact on Creek society, it did not erase their cultural identity. Instead, Creek communities found ways to adapt, rebuild, and preserve their heritage, leaving a lasting legacy of strength and cultural richness in the heart of Indian Territory. Their story is a testament to the enduring spirit of indigenous peoples and their ability to thrive in the face of adversity.

The Creek people's exile and displacement from their ancestral lands in the southeastern United States brought about a profound disruption to their communities and way of life. However, this period of exile also showcased the remarkable resilience and the enduring strength of Creek community bonds. Despite the immense challenges they faced, Creek families and clans found ways to support one another and rebuild their sense of community, which became a source of resilience during a time of great adversity.

1. Collective Suffering and Shared Hardships: As Creek families were uprooted from their homes and communities, they shared a collective experience of suffering and hardship. This shared experience fostered a sense of solidarity among Creek people, as they understood that they were all facing the same trials and tribulations along the arduous journey westward.

2. Families as the Bedrock of Community: The concept of family held a central place in Creek society. Extended families, known as clans, formed the basis of Creek communities. These clans provided not only emotional support but also practical assistance in times of need. Families often banded together to share resources, care for the elderly and the young, and provide a sense of continuity in the face of displacement.

3. Cultural Traditions and Ceremonies: Creek ceremonial practices, such as the Stomp Dance and Green Corn ceremonies, played a crucial role in maintaining a sense of community and cultural continuity. These gatherings provided opportunities for Creek people to come together, express their cultural identity, and find strength in their shared traditions.

4. Leadership and Guidance: Creek leaders emerged as vital figures during this challenging period. Individuals like Opothleyahola and other Creek leaders provided guidance and reassurance to their communities. Their leadership was instrumental in maintaining order, making decisions for the collective good, and offering hope for the future.

5. Mutual Support in Times of Crisis: The hardships encountered along the Trail of Tears were numerous, from disease outbreaks to food shortages. Creek families and clans often supported one another during these crises, sharing whatever resources they had to ensure that all members of the community could endure the challenges.

6. Elders as Keepers of Wisdom: Creek elders held a revered position within the community, serving as the keepers of wisdom and cultural knowledge. During the displacement, elders played a crucial role in passing down oral traditions, stories, and the Creek language to younger generations. Their presence provided a link to the past and a source of guidance for the future.

7. Creating New Communities: In Indian Territory, Creek families worked together to establish new communities. These towns and villages were designed to mirror the social organization of Creek towns in the Southeast. By recreating familiar structures, Creek people sought to rebuild their sense of community and continuity.

8. Collective Decision-Making: The importance of consensus and collective decision-making within Creek society remained intact during the displacement. Creek leaders often convened councils and meetings to discuss important matters, seeking input and agreement from the community. This participatory approach helped maintain a sense of unity and shared purpose.

9. Preserving Cultural Identity: Despite the challenges of exile, Creek communities were resolute in preserving their cultural identity. They continued to speak the Creek language, practice traditional crafts, and pass down stories and songs. This commitment to cultural preservation reinforced their sense of community and cultural resilience.

10. Educational Initiatives: Recognizing the importance of education for the future, Creek communities established schools and institutions to ensure that younger generations received both formal education and cultural teachings. These efforts aimed to equip Creek youth with the knowledge and skills needed to navigate a rapidly changing world.

In reflecting on the community bonds and resilience of the Creek people during their exile, it is evident that their shared experiences of suffering and hardship fostered a profound sense of unity and mutual support. Despite the forced removal and the disruption of their way of life, Creek communities found strength in one another, their cultural traditions, and their commitment to preserving their identity. The enduring bonds that held Creek families and clans together served as a source of resilience, enabling them to persevere through the most challenging of times and rebuild their communities in a new homeland.

Chapter 6: Rebuilding on New Ground: The Creek's Resilience

The Creek people's forced removal from their ancestral lands in the southeastern United States to Indian Territory (present-day Oklahoma) marked a period of profound disruption and transformation. As they settled in their new homeland, Creek communities faced the formidable task of establishing new communities and adapting to a different environment. During this process, leadership played a critical role in guiding the Creek people through the challenges of rebuilding their lives and maintaining a sense of cohesion.

1. Town Planning and Layout: One of the first tasks in establishing new communities in Indian Territory was town planning and layout. Creek towns were designed to mirror the social organization and layout of their ancestral towns in the Southeast. The creation of familiar town squares and communal spaces helped provide a sense of continuity and belonging.

2. Rebuilding Homes and Infrastructure: Creek families faced the daunting task of rebuilding their homes and infrastructure in a new environment. Using available materials, they constructed homes, communal buildings, and other essential structures. This process required adaptability as they adjusted to the different building materials and techniques suited to the Plains region.

3. Agricultural Adaptations: Agriculture had been central to Creek society, and adapting their agricultural practices to the different climate and soil conditions of Indian Territory was essential for survival. Creek farmers experimented with new crops and farming techniques suited to the region, such as growing corn, beans, and squash in the fertile river valleys.

4. Leadership in Governance: Creek leaders played a vital role in guiding their communities through the challenges of relocation. While the Creek Nation had experienced significant disruptions, leaders like Opothleyahola and others emerged to reestablish governance structures and maintain order within the community. Their leadership helped provide stability during a period of great uncertainty.

5. Clans and Extended Families: The Creek social structure was based on extended families, known as clans. These clans formed the bedrock of Creek communities. Leaders within each clan played important roles in decision-making, ensuring that the collective needs of the community were met and that resources were distributed equitably.

6. Cultural Traditions and Ceremonies: Creek ceremonial practices, including the Stomp Dance and Green Corn ceremonies, continued to be important in establishing a sense of community and cultural continuity. These gatherings provided opportunities for Creek people to come together, express their cultural identity, and find strength in shared traditions.

7. Education and Institutions: Recognizing the importance of education for future generations, Creek communities established schools and institutions. These institutions aimed to provide formal education alongside the transmission of traditional knowledge. They played a crucial role in preparing Creek youth for the challenges of a rapidly changing world.

8. Community Decision-Making: Creek communities continued to emphasize consensus and collective decision-making. Leaders often convened councils and meetings to discuss important matters, seeking input and agreement from the community. This participatory approach helped maintain a sense of unity and shared purpose.

9. Resilience and Adaptability: The challenges of exile and relocation tested the resilience and adaptability of Creek communities. Their ability to adapt to new circumstances, maintain cultural continuity, and rebuild their lives in unfamiliar territory showcased their enduring strength and determination.

10. Intergenerational Continuity: Creek families placed a strong emphasis on passing down cultural knowledge from one generation to the next. Elders played a central role in this process, ensuring that the traditions, stories, and values of the Creek Nation were carried forward to younger generations.

In reflecting on the establishment of new communities and leadership among the Creek people during their exile, it is evident that their resilience and adaptability allowed them to persevere in the face of immense challenges. Despite the forced removal and the disruption of their way of life, Creek communities found ways to rebuild, maintain their cultural identity, and create a sense of belonging in their new homeland. The enduring bonds of leadership, extended families, and cultural traditions served as cornerstones for the Creek people as they faced the uncertainties of the future.

The Creek people's forced removal from their ancestral lands to Indian Territory marked a period of immense cultural upheaval and challenges. Despite these difficulties, Creek communities were resolute in their commitment to preserving their cultural heritage and renewing their sense of identity. Cultural preservation and identity renewal became central to their efforts as they sought to maintain their unique traditions, language, and way of life.

1. Language Preservation: The Creek language, a fundamental component of their cultural identity, was a top priority for preservation. Efforts were made to ensure that the Creek language was passed down to younger generations. Elders played a pivotal role in teaching the language and oral traditions, ensuring its continued use within the community.

2. Oral Traditions and Storytelling: Creek communities placed a strong emphasis on the preservation of oral traditions, including stories, legends, and historical accounts. These narratives served as a repository of cultural knowledge and were a means of passing down important lessons, values, and a sense of identity from one generation to the next.

3. Cultural Practices and Ceremonies: Despite the challenges of displacement, Creek ceremonial practices remained an essential part of their identity. The Stomp Dance, Green Corn ceremonies, and other rituals continued to be performed, providing a sense of community and connection to their cultural roots. These ceremonies were opportunities to renew cultural bonds and celebrate their heritage.

4. Traditional Arts and Crafts: Creek artisans continued to create traditional pottery, baskets, beadwork, and other crafts. These artistic traditions not only served as a means of cultural expression but also as a source of income for many Creek families. Artistry was a way to connect with their heritage while adapting to new economic realities.

5. Intertribal Exchange: In Indian Territory, Creek communities encountered other indigenous nations, including the Cherokee and Choctaw. This interaction resulted in cultural exchanges, as different nations shared knowledge, traditions, and artistic techniques. These interactions enriched Creek culture and added to the diversity of their cultural tapestry.

6. Adaptation and Innovation: Creek communities demonstrated adaptability and innovation in response to their new environment. While preserving traditional practices, they also incorporated elements of their new surroundings, such as learning about local flora and fauna and adopting new farming methods suited to the Plains region.

7. Leadership in Cultural Preservation: Creek leaders played a critical role in cultural preservation efforts. They recognized the importance of maintaining Creek identity and heritage and often provided support and guidance for initiatives aimed at preserving cultural traditions.

8. Educational Initiatives: Educational institutions within Creek communities played a dual role in preserving culture and preparing youth for the future. They not only taught academic subjects but also incorporated cultural teachings to ensure that Creek youth had a well-rounded education that included their cultural heritage.

9. Intergenerational Transmission: Elders within Creek communities played a crucial role in transmitting cultural knowledge to younger generations. Their wisdom and experiences were highly valued, and efforts were made to create opportunities for intergenerational sharing of traditions, stories, and skills.

10. Cultural Centers and Museums: Over time, Creek communities established cultural centers and museums dedicated to preserving and showcasing their heritage. These institutions became important hubs for cultural renewal, education, and the exhibition of Creek art, artifacts, and history.

In summary, the Creek people's commitment to cultural preservation and identity renewal during their exile and resettlement in Indian Territory reflects their resilience, determination, and deep connection to their heritage. Despite the challenges they faced, Creek communities found ways to adapt to their new environment while safeguarding their cultural traditions, language, and identity. Their efforts not only preserved their unique heritage but also contributed to the rich tapestry of indigenous cultures in the United States. The story of the Creek people serves as a testament to the enduring strength of indigenous communities and their ability to renew their cultural identities in the face of adversity.

The journey of the Creek people in the 19th century, marked by forced removal and resettlement in Indian Territory, severed their ties to their ancestral lands in the southeastern United States. Despite the immense challenges they faced during this period, Creek communities never lost their deep connection to their traditional territories. Over time, efforts were made to reconnect with these lands, reestablishing a spiritual and cultural bond with the places that held their history, memories, and identity.

For the Creek people, their traditional territories held profound significance. These lands were not merely geographic locations; they were repositories of their history, culture, and collective memory. The creeks, rivers, forests, and rolling hills were interwoven with the stories of their ancestors, the traditions of their people, and the natural resources that sustained their communities.

Rekindling Spiritual Connections: As Creek communities settled in Indian Territory, many Creeks felt a longing to rekindle their spiritual connections with their ancestral lands. The landscapes of their traditional territories were imbued with spiritual meaning, and these places held a special role in their religious beliefs and ceremonies. Efforts were made to replicate these ceremonies in their new homeland, with the hope of maintaining a connection to the spiritual essence of their original territories.

Returning to Ceremonial Grounds: Creek ceremonial grounds, where important rituals and gatherings took place, held a unique place in their cultural and spiritual practices. Over time, Creek communities made journeys back to their ancestral ceremonial grounds in the Southeast. These visits allowed them to reconnect with the physical and spiritual aspects of these sacred places, reinforcing their ties to their cultural heritage.

Maintaining Oral Traditions: The Creek people continued to pass down oral traditions that recounted the history and significance of their traditional territories. Stories of ancestral villages, hunting grounds, and sacred sites were shared from one generation to the next. These narratives kept the memory of their lands alive and ensured that younger generations understood the importance of these places.

Revisiting Ancestral Villages: Some Creek families and communities undertook pilgrimages to visit the sites of their ancestral villages in the Southeast. These visits were often emotional and deeply meaningful, allowing them to stand on the same ground where their forebears had lived and thrived. The experience of being in these places helped reaffirm their connection to their roots.

Cultural Revival and Renewal: The Creek people's commitment to cultural revival included efforts to reconnect with their traditional territories. Language revitalization programs, art, music, and dance all played a role in preserving and celebrating their cultural identity. These cultural expressions often drew inspiration from the natural world and landscapes of their ancestral lands.

Ecological Awareness: Creek communities in Indian Territory developed a deep understanding of their new environment, but they also maintained an ecological awareness of their traditional territories in the Southeast. The plants, animals, and ecosystems of their homelands held cultural, practical, and spiritual significance. This knowledge was passed down as part of their cultural heritage.

Land Reclamation Efforts: In some cases, Creek communities explored opportunities to reclaim or purchase parcels of their ancestral lands. These efforts aimed to reestablish a physical connection to their traditional territories and, in some instances, allowed for the development of cultural and educational centers that celebrated Creek history and heritage.

Intertribal Collaboration: Creek communities in Indian Territory often engaged in intertribal collaboration with neighboring nations, such as the Cherokee and Choctaw. These interactions provided opportunities for cultural exchange and learning about the diverse landscapes and histories of the region.

Tribal Sovereignty and Land Management: Tribal sovereignty became a key aspect of efforts to reconnect with traditional territories. The Creek Nation, like other indigenous nations, sought to assert control over its lands and resources, enabling them to make decisions that aligned with their cultural values and preservation efforts.

In summary, the Creek people's journey to reconnect with their traditional territories represents a powerful testament to their enduring cultural resilience and spiritual connection to the land. Despite the forced removal and the challenges of adapting to a new homeland, Creek communities maintained a deep bond with the landscapes of their ancestors. Their efforts to revisit ancestral sites, uphold oral traditions, and preserve ecological knowledge helped keep their connection to their traditional territories alive. These efforts reflect the profound importance of land and place in indigenous cultures and the resilience of Creek communities in maintaining their cultural identity through the generations.

Chapter 7: Creek Nation Today: Governance and Identity

In the present day, the Creek Nation, officially known as the Muscogee (Creek) Nation, stands as a sovereign indigenous nation with its own government, constitution, and institutions. The journey from the forced removal and resettlement in the 19th century to the contemporary era has seen the Creek Nation assert its tribal sovereignty and rebuild its government structures to serve the needs of its citizens and preserve its cultural heritage.

1. Tribal Government: The Creek Nation operates under a constitutional government, which was established in 1979 and revised in 2007. The government consists of an elected principal chief, second chief, and a National Council composed of representatives from various districts within the Creek Nation's jurisdiction. These leaders are responsible for making decisions on behalf of the nation and upholding tribal sovereignty.

2. Tribal Constitution: The Creek Nation's constitution outlines the framework of its government and delineates the powers and responsibilities of its branches. It ensures the protection of tribal sovereignty and the rights of tribal citizens. Amendments to the constitution can be proposed and voted upon by the National Council.

3. Legal Jurisdiction: The Creek Nation exercises legal jurisdiction over its territory, including civil and criminal matters. Tribal courts play a critical role in administering justice and upholding the rule of law within the nation. This legal system is an integral part of the Creek Nation's sovereignty.

4. Cultural Preservation: The Creek Nation places a strong emphasis on cultural preservation and revitalization. Cultural centers and museums showcase Creek art, history, and traditions. Language revitalization efforts aim to preserve the Creek language and ensure its transmission to younger generations.

5. Education: The Creek Nation operates its own education system, including schools and programs that incorporate Creek culture and history into the curriculum. These institutions not only provide academic education but also promote cultural awareness among Creek youth.

6. Healthcare: The Creek Nation operates healthcare facilities and services for its citizens, addressing the healthcare needs of the community. This includes clinics, hospitals, and programs focused on wellness and public health.

7. Economic Development: The Creek Nation engages in economic development initiatives, including businesses, industries, and partnerships that generate revenue and create employment opportunities. These enterprises help support the tribal government and provide resources for essential services.

8. Environmental Stewardship: The Creek Nation is committed to environmental stewardship, including conservation efforts and sustainable practices that protect the natural resources within its territory. This reflects the nation's respect for the land and its cultural significance.

9. Intergovernmental Relations: The Creek Nation engages in government-to-government relations with federal, state, and local governments. These relationships are essential for addressing issues of mutual concern, protecting tribal sovereignty, and advocating for the interests of Creek citizens.

10. Citizenship and Identity: The Creek Nation maintains citizenship criteria that define who is considered a tribal citizen. This recognition of tribal citizenship is an important aspect of cultural identity and tribal sovereignty.

11. Self-Determination: The Creek Nation's government and leadership prioritize self-determination, allowing the nation to make decisions that best serve its citizens and promote its cultural values. This principle is central to the exercise of tribal sovereignty.

12. Economic Self-Sufficiency: Economic self-sufficiency is a goal of the Creek Nation. By developing a diverse economic base and managing its resources, the nation strives to reduce dependency on external entities and strengthen its ability to provide for its citizens.

13. Challenges and Aspirations: Like many indigenous nations, the Creek Nation faces various challenges, including socioeconomic disparities and healthcare disparities. However, the nation remains resilient and committed to addressing these challenges while preserving its cultural heritage and ensuring a prosperous future for its citizens.

In summary, the Creek Nation's journey from the Trail of Tears to the present day is marked by its unwavering commitment to tribal sovereignty, cultural preservation, and self-determination. The modern Creek government, with its elected leaders and institutions, continues to work diligently to uphold these principles, provide for its citizens, and safeguard the cultural heritage of the Muscogee (Creek) Nation.

The 21st century has witnessed a remarkable resurgence of cultural identity and revival among the Creek people, officially known as the Muscogee (Creek) Nation. Despite the challenges of the past, including the forced removal from their ancestral lands, Creek communities have demonstrated a strong commitment to preserving and revitalizing their cultural heritage. This resurgence encompasses various aspects of Creek identity, from language and traditional arts to spirituality and community bonds.

1. Language Revitalization: Language preservation and revitalization efforts have been at the forefront of Creek cultural revival. The Creek language, known as Maskoke, is central to their identity. Language immersion programs, language classes, and cultural camps have been established to ensure that younger generations can speak, read, and write in Creek.

2. Cultural Centers and Museums: Cultural centers and museums within the Muscogee (Creek) Nation play a pivotal role in preserving and showcasing Creek history, art, and traditions. These institutions provide educational resources and cultural exhibits that celebrate the rich heritage of the Creek people.

3. Traditional Arts and Crafts: The resurgence of traditional Creek arts and crafts has been a source of cultural pride and economic empowerment. Creek artisans continue to create pottery, basketry, beadwork, and textiles that reflect their cultural traditions. These crafts serve as a means of cultural expression and contribute to the local economy.

4. Spiritual Revival: Creek spirituality and religious practices have experienced a resurgence, with traditional ceremonies like the Stomp Dance and Green Corn ceremonies being performed and celebrated. These rituals not only strengthen the spiritual bonds within the community but also connect Creek people to their ancestral practices.

5. Oral Traditions: The preservation of oral traditions remains a vital aspect of Creek cultural identity. Elders pass down stories, legends, and historical accounts that recount the history, wisdom, and values of the Creek people. These narratives continue to serve as a source of cultural knowledge and identity.

6. Community Bonds: The Creek sense of community and kinship has been revitalized through cultural gatherings, festivals, and events. These gatherings provide opportunities for Creek citizens to come together, celebrate their shared heritage, and strengthen their community bonds.

7. Cultural Education: Educational institutions within the Muscogee (Creek) Nation prioritize cultural education. Creek youth are exposed to their cultural heritage through curricula that include Creek language instruction, traditional storytelling, and lessons on Creek history and customs.

8. Intertribal Collaboration: Creek communities engage in intertribal collaborations with neighboring nations, fostering cultural exchanges and learning from the diverse indigenous cultures of the region. These interactions enrich Creek culture and deepen their connection to the broader indigenous community.

9. Advocacy for Cultural Preservation: The Muscogee (Creek) Nation actively advocates for policies and initiatives that support cultural preservation. This includes efforts to protect sacred sites, traditional lands, and cultural practices.

10. Technological Resources: The use of modern technology, such as websites, social media, and digital archives, has enabled Creek communities to share their culture and history with a global audience. These platforms serve as valuable tools for education and cultural dissemination.

11. Cultural Reclamation: Creek communities have made efforts to reclaim and repatriate cultural artifacts, sacred objects, and ancestral remains. These initiatives contribute to the restoration of cultural practices and the strengthening of cultural identity.

In summary, the 21st century has seen a vibrant resurgence of Creek cultural identity and revival. Through language revitalization, the preservation of traditional arts, and the celebration of spiritual practices, the Muscogee (Creek) Nation has reaffirmed its commitment to preserving its cultural heritage. This cultural revival not only ensures the continuity of Creek traditions but also fosters a strong sense of pride, resilience, and community among Creek citizens. As the Creek people navigate the challenges and opportunities of the modern world, their cultural revival stands as a testament to the enduring strength of indigenous cultures and their determination to preserve their identity for future generations. In the 21st century, the Muscogee (Creek) Nation, like many indigenous nations, faces a complex landscape of challenges and opportunities. As a sovereign nation with a rich cultural heritage and a vibrant community, the Creek Nation is actively addressing these issues while pursuing a path towards a more prosperous and sustainable future.

Historical Legacy and Healing: One of the primary challenges the Creek Nation faces today is dealing with the historical legacy of colonization, forced removal, and the Trail of Tears. Healing from the trauma of these events remains an ongoing process, and the Creek people continue to work towards reconciliation and understanding.

Cultural Preservation: While there has been a significant revival of Creek culture, the ongoing preservation of language, traditions, and ceremonies remains a challenge. Ensuring that younger generations continue to embrace their cultural heritage and identity requires sustained effort and resources.

Economic Development: The Creek Nation has made strides in economic development, including establishing businesses and industries. However, economic disparities persist, and many Creek citizens face financial challenges. The nation seeks opportunities to create more jobs and generate revenue for essential services.

Education: Providing quality education that incorporates Creek culture and history is a priority for the Creek Nation. Challenges include improving educational outcomes, reducing disparities in educational achievement, and addressing the needs of students with diverse learning styles.

Healthcare: Access to healthcare services and addressing health disparities are critical challenges. The Creek Nation is working to ensure that its citizens receive quality healthcare, especially in rural areas where healthcare infrastructure can be limited.

Environmental Stewardship: Balancing economic development with environmental conservation is an ongoing challenge. The Creek Nation places a strong emphasis on protecting its natural resources and addressing environmental issues, such as land conservation and water quality.

Sovereignty and Jurisdiction: Protecting tribal sovereignty and jurisdictional rights is a constant endeavor. The Creek Nation works to maintain its authority over its territory, legal systems, and governance while navigating complex intergovernmental relations.

Land and Resource Management: Effective land and resource management are essential for the Creek Nation's economic sustainability. Ensuring responsible land use, land reclamation, and resource protection are ongoing priorities.

Tribal Governance: Maintaining a stable and effective tribal government is crucial. The Creek Nation seeks to address issues of governance, including transparency, accountability, and citizen engagement, to ensure that the government serves the needs of its citizens.

Cultural Awareness: Promoting cultural awareness and understanding among non-indigenous communities is a challenge but also an opportunity. The Creek Nation works to foster positive relationships and partnerships with neighboring communities while educating them about Creek history and culture.

Intertribal Collaboration: Collaborating with other indigenous nations in the region offers opportunities for sharing resources, knowledge, and solutions to common challenges. The Creek Nation actively engages in intertribal cooperation and seeks to strengthen these relationships.

Technological Advancements: Embracing technology and digital resources presents opportunities for the Creek Nation to enhance communication, education, and economic development. Leveraging modern tools can help bridge gaps and increase access to services.

Youth Engagement: Encouraging the involvement of Creek youth in cultural activities, leadership roles, and decision-making processes is essential for the nation's future. Fostering a sense of pride and responsibility among younger generations is a priority.

Community Resilience: Creek communities have a strong tradition of resilience. Leveraging this resilience to address contemporary challenges and opportunities is key to the nation's continued success.

Tribal Identity and Pride: Maintaining a strong sense of tribal identity and pride among Creek citizens is a fundamental goal. Celebrating cultural achievements, preserving traditions, and acknowledging the strength of the Creek people contribute to a sense of unity and purpose. In summary, the Creek Nation faces a wide range of challenges in the 21st century, stemming from historical legacies, socioeconomic disparities, and the need to protect cultural heritage. However, these challenges are met with resilience, determination, and a commitment to addressing them for the benefit of present and future generations. The Creek Nation also embraces opportunities for economic development, cultural revitalization, and intertribal collaboration as it navigates the complexities of the modern world while honoring its rich history and traditions.

Chapter 8: From Survival to Success: Economic Development and Cultural Preservation

The economic progress and diversification of the Muscogee (Creek) Nation have been central to its journey towards self-sufficiency, sustainability, and prosperity in the 21st century. This progress reflects the Creek Nation's commitment to improving the quality of life for its citizens, preserving its cultural heritage, and strengthening its sovereignty.

1. Tribal Enterprises: The Creek Nation has established a diverse portfolio of tribal enterprises, including businesses in various sectors such as gaming, hospitality, retail, and manufacturing. These enterprises generate revenue that supports essential services, infrastructure development, and community programs.

2. Employment Opportunities: The tribal enterprises and economic development initiatives have created employment opportunities for Creek citizens and residents of the nation's territory. Job creation enhances the economic well-being of the community and reduces unemployment rates.

3. Economic Diversification: Recognizing the importance of economic diversification, the Creek Nation has expanded its economic ventures beyond gaming and hospitality. Investments in agriculture, renewable energy, real estate, and technology have contributed to a more diversified and resilient economy.

4. Small Business Support: The Creek Nation provides support and resources for small businesses within its jurisdiction. This includes business development programs, financial assistance, and technical assistance to help entrepreneurs succeed.

5. Tourism: Tourism plays a significant role in the Creek Nation's economic progress. Cultural centers, museums, and heritage sites attract visitors interested in Creek history and culture, contributing to the local economy.

6. Infrastructure Development: The revenue generated from tribal enterprises has been reinvested in infrastructure development projects, including road improvements, public facilities, and housing initiatives. These investments enhance the quality of life for Creek citizens.

7. Healthcare Services: Economic progress has enabled the Creek Nation to expand and improve healthcare services for its citizens. Healthcare facilities, clinics, and programs are critical for addressing the healthcare needs of the community.

8. Education Initiatives: The Creek Nation has invested in education initiatives that not only improve educational outcomes but also prepare Creek youth for careers in various fields. Scholarships, educational programs, and partnerships with educational institutions contribute to workforce development.

9. Cultural Preservation: Economic development is intertwined with cultural preservation. Revenue generated from tribal enterprises supports cultural centers, language revitalization efforts, and programs that celebrate Creek traditions. This ensures that cultural heritage remains a priority.

10. Environmental Stewardship: The Creek Nation's economic progress includes responsible environmental practices. Sustainable land management, conservation efforts, and renewable energy projects align with the nation's commitment to environmental stewardship.

11. Financial Stability: Achieving financial stability is a cornerstone of the Creek Nation's economic progress. Prudent fiscal management and diversification of revenue sources contribute to a stable economic foundation.

12. Sovereignty and Self-Sufficiency: Economic progress is a key component of tribal sovereignty and self-sufficiency. The Creek Nation's ability to generate revenue and provide for its citizens reduces dependence on external entities and enhances its capacity to make decisions that benefit the community.

13. Economic Partnerships: The Creek Nation actively engages in economic partnerships and collaborations with other tribes, neighboring communities, and non-indigenous entities. These partnerships contribute to economic growth and regional development.

14. Economic Planning: Strategic economic planning guides the Creek Nation's economic progress. Long-term planning, financial forecasting, and investment strategies are essential for sustainable economic development.

In summary, the economic progress and diversification of the Muscogee (Creek) Nation are integral to its efforts to build a better future for its citizens. By fostering economic development, creating job opportunities, and investing in essential services and cultural preservation, the Creek Nation demonstrates its commitment to self-determination, sovereignty, and the well-being of its community. This economic progress not only strengthens the Creek Nation's resilience but also ensures a brighter and more prosperous future for generations to come.

Cultural preservation and education are central to the Muscogee (Creek) Nation's efforts to ensure the continuity of its rich heritage and traditions. Through a variety of initiatives, the Creek Nation has been proactive in safeguarding its cultural identity and passing it on to future generations.

1. Language Revitalization Programs: The Creek Nation has implemented comprehensive language revitalization programs to preserve and promote the Creek language, known as Maskoke. These programs include language immersion schools, language classes for all age groups, and the development of language teaching materials.

2. Cultural Centers and Museums: The Creek Nation has established cultural centers and museums that serve as repositories of tribal history, art, and artifacts. These institutions offer educational exhibits, workshops, and cultural events that educate both Creek citizens and the broader community about Creek traditions.

3. Heritage Sites and Preservation: The Creek Nation actively works to preserve and protect its heritage sites, including sacred grounds and historical landmarks. These sites are maintained to ensure their cultural significance is preserved and accessible for educational purposes.

4. Cultural Workshops and Seminars: Cultural workshops and seminars are regularly organized by the Creek Nation to provide hands-on experiences and in-depth knowledge about traditional practices, crafts, and ceremonies. These events engage both Creek citizens and interested individuals from outside the tribe.

5. Traditional Arts and Crafts Programs: Initiatives that support traditional Creek arts and crafts play a crucial role in cultural preservation. These programs provide training and resources to artisans, ensuring that traditional skills are passed down and practiced.

6. Storytelling and Oral Tradition: The Creek Nation recognizes the importance of oral tradition and storytelling as vehicles for cultural transmission. Storytelling events and workshops bring elders and youth together to share stories, legends, and historical accounts.

7. Cultural Awareness Campaigns: The Creek Nation conducts cultural awareness campaigns aimed at fostering understanding and respect among non-indigenous communities. These campaigns often involve educational materials, cultural events, and outreach programs.

8. Tribal Schools and Education Initiatives: Tribal schools within the Creek Nation's jurisdiction prioritize cultural education. Creek history, language, and traditions are integrated into the curriculum to ensure that students are well-grounded in their cultural heritage.

9. Community Cultural Events: Regular community cultural events, such as powwows, stomp dances, and Green Corn ceremonies, celebrate Creek traditions and provide opportunities for citizens to participate in cultural practices.

10. Intertribal Collaborations: The Creek Nation actively collaborates with other indigenous nations to share cultural knowledge and resources. These collaborations foster a broader understanding of indigenous cultures and strengthen intertribal bonds.

11. Cultural Competitions: The Creek Nation organizes cultural competitions that encourage citizens to showcase their talents in traditional arts, crafts, dance, and music. These competitions serve as platforms for cultural expression and excellence.

12. Language Immersion Camps: Language immersion camps offer intensive language learning experiences in a culturally immersive environment. Creek youth have the opportunity to engage with fluent speakers and practice the language.

13. Cultural Mentorship Programs: Mentorship programs connect Creek elders and cultural experts with younger generations. These programs facilitate the transfer of traditional knowledge and skills from one generation to the next.

14. Digital Resources: The Creek Nation leverages modern technology to create digital resources, such as websites, apps, and online archives, that provide access to cultural materials, language lessons, and historical records.

In summary, the Muscogee (Creek) Nation's initiatives for cultural preservation and education reflect its commitment to maintaining a strong sense of cultural identity and passing on its traditions to future generations. These efforts encompass language revitalization, cultural centers, educational programs, and collaborations that ensure the vitality and continuity of Creek culture. By embracing both traditional and contemporary methods, the Creek Nation is actively working to preserve its cultural heritage in the face of modern challenges.

The Muscogee (Creek) Nation's legacy is a testament to the resilience, strength, and enduring cultural heritage of its people. Throughout its history, the Creek Nation has faced numerous challenges and triumphs, shaping its legacy into what it is today. Here, we explore the ongoing legacy of the Creek Nation, encompassing its historical significance, cultural contributions, and its continued pursuit of sovereignty and self-determination.

Historical Significance:

The Creek Nation holds a unique place in American history. Its role in early interactions with European settlers, its participation in conflicts like the Creek War and the American Civil War, and its forced removal on the Trail of Tears are significant chapters in the nation's history. The Creek Nation's history is a testament to its endurance in the face of adversity and its commitment to maintaining its cultural identity.

Cultural Contributions:

The Creek Nation has made enduring contributions to the cultural tapestry of the United States. Its language, Maskoke (Creek), is a vital part of its heritage, and efforts to revitalize and preserve it continue to bear fruit. Creek art, including pottery, basketry, and beadwork, showcases the artistic talents of its people. Traditional dances and music, such as the stomp dance, reflect the nation's rich cultural traditions. These cultural contributions enrich not only Creek society but also the broader world of indigenous cultures.

Sovereignty and Self-Determination:
The Creek Nation's pursuit of sovereignty and self-determination remains a cornerstone of its legacy. The nation's governance structure, its legal system, and its ability to make decisions that impact its citizens are all manifestations of its sovereignty. The Creek Nation actively engages in legal and political endeavors to protect its rights, jurisdiction, and territorial integrity.

Trail of Tears Remembrance:
The Creek Nation's commemoration of the Trail of Tears serves as a poignant reminder of the nation's historical trauma and its commitment to honoring the memory of those who suffered during the forced removal. Annual events, educational programs, and cultural activities related to the Trail of Tears ensure that this significant chapter in Creek history is never forgotten.

Community Resilience:
Creek communities have a long history of resilience and adaptability. Despite the challenges of history, including forced relocations and the disruption of traditional lifeways, Creek citizens continue to thrive, preserving their cultural identity and passing it on to future generations.

Cultural Revival and Education:
The Creek Nation's commitment to cultural revival and education is a vital aspect of its ongoing legacy. Through language revitalization programs, cultural centers, museums, and educational initiatives, the Creek Nation ensures that its cultural heritage remains vibrant and accessible to all, fostering a strong sense of identity among its citizens.

Intertribal Cooperation:
The Creek Nation actively engages in intertribal cooperation and collaboration, recognizing the strength and solidarity that come

from working with other indigenous nations. These partnerships strengthen the broader indigenous community and contribute to shared efforts in cultural preservation, legal advocacy, and resource management.

Economic Progress:

The Creek Nation's economic progress and diversification have created opportunities for its citizens and contributed to the nation's self-sufficiency. Investments in tribal enterprises, infrastructure, and job creation have improved the quality of life for Creek citizens and residents.

Environmental Stewardship:

The Creek Nation's commitment to environmental stewardship reflects its respect for the land and natural resources. Initiatives aimed at land conservation, responsible land use, and renewable energy contribute to a sustainable future.

In summary, the ongoing legacy of the Muscogee (Creek) Nation encompasses its historical significance, cultural contributions, pursuit of sovereignty, and commitment to cultural preservation and education. The Creek Nation's resilience, strength, and cultural vitality continue to shape its legacy, ensuring that its rich heritage endures for generations to come.

BOOK 5
SEMINOLE NATION SAGA
ADAPTATION AND SURVIVAL

BY A.J. KINGSTON

Chapter 1: Origins and Traditions of the Seminole People

The Seminole people have a rich history that is deeply intertwined with the lands they have inhabited for centuries. The origins of the Seminole Nation and their ancestral lands are essential aspects of their cultural identity and historical legacy.

Origins and Migration:

The origins of the Seminole people are complex and rooted in a fusion of various indigenous groups. It is believed that the Seminole Nation emerged as a distinct entity in the southeastern United States during the late 18th century. They are often referred to as one of the Five Civilized Tribes due to their adoption of some European customs and agricultural practices.

Ancestral Lands:

The ancestral lands of the Seminole people encompassed a vast territory in the southeastern United States, primarily in present-day Florida, Georgia, Alabama, and parts of South Carolina. These lands were characterized by diverse ecosystems, including swamps, forests, and fertile plains, which provided abundant resources for the Seminole way of life.

Adaptation to the Environment:

The Seminole people were skilled hunters, gatherers, and farmers. They cultivated crops such as maize, beans, and squash, and their agricultural practices contributed to their self-sufficiency. The abundant wildlife and waterways in their ancestral lands allowed them to engage in hunting, fishing, and gathering.

Cultural Traditions:

The Seminole people had rich cultural traditions that included distinctive clothing, crafts, and ceremonies. They are known for their intricate patchwork clothing and baskets, which are highly regarded for their craftsmanship and artistry. Seminole ceremonies, such as the Green Corn Dance, were essential cultural expressions.

Encounters with Europeans:

The arrival of European explorers and settlers in the Southeast had a profound impact on the Seminole people and their ancestral lands. Early interactions included trade, but as European settlement expanded, conflicts arose over land and resources. The Seminole Wars, which spanned from the early 19th century to the mid-19th century, marked a significant chapter in their history as they resisted forced removal from their lands.

Trail of Tears:

The Seminole Nation experienced its own Trail of Tears, although it was not as widely recognized as the Cherokee Trail of Tears. During the mid-1800s, the U.S. government attempted to forcibly relocate Seminole people from Florida to Indian Territory (present-day Oklahoma). The Seminole Wars were part of the resistance to this removal, and many Seminoles endured immense hardships and losses during their journey westward.

Survival and Resurgence:

Despite the challenges of removal and conflict, the Seminole people persevered. They adapted to new environments, maintained their cultural practices, and preserved their distinct identity. Seminole communities in Oklahoma and Florida continue to thrive and contribute to the cultural mosaic of their respective regions.

Cultural Revival:

Efforts to revive and preserve Seminole culture have been ongoing. Cultural centers, museums, and educational programs in both Oklahoma and Florida play a crucial role in transmitting traditions to younger generations. The Seminole language, Creek (Mvskoke), is also being revitalized to ensure its survival.

Contemporary Seminole Identity:

Today, the Seminole Nation is composed of two main federally recognized tribes: the Seminole Tribe of Florida and the Seminole Nation of Oklahoma. These tribes maintain their distinct identities, governance structures, and cultural practices while adapting to the challenges and opportunities of the 21st century.

In summary, the Seminole people's origins and ancestral lands are integral to their identity and history. Their ability to adapt, survive, and maintain their cultural traditions in the face of adversity reflects their resilience and enduring legacy.

Indigenous traditions and lifeways encompass a diverse array of practices, beliefs, and customs that have been passed down through generations within indigenous communities around the world. These traditions are deeply rooted in the relationship between indigenous peoples and their ancestral lands, and they often emphasize cultural, spiritual, and environmental interconnectedness. Here, we explore some key aspects of indigenous traditions and lifeways:

1. Connection to Ancestral Lands: Indigenous traditions are closely tied to the specific landscapes and ecosystems where indigenous communities have resided for centuries. Land is not merely a resource; it is considered sacred and central to cultural identity. Many indigenous belief systems involve a spiritual connection to the land and its natural elements.

2. Oral Traditions: Oral traditions play a significant role in indigenous cultures. Stories, myths, legends, and histories are passed down orally from one generation to the next. These narratives often contain valuable teachings about ethics, morality, and the relationship between humans and the natural world.

3. Respect for Nature: Indigenous traditions commonly emphasize a profound respect for the environment and all living beings. This respect is rooted in the belief that humans are caretakers of the Earth and must live in harmony with the natural world. Practices like sustainable hunting, fishing, and farming are guided by this principle.

4. Traditional Ecological Knowledge (TEK): Indigenous communities possess vast stores of traditional ecological knowledge, which are based on centuries of observation and interaction with their environments. TEK informs sustainable resource management, weather prediction, and understanding local ecosystems.

5. Spiritual Beliefs and Ceremonies: Indigenous spirituality is often inseparable from daily life. Ceremonies, rituals, and practices are performed to honor the spirits, seek guidance, and maintain balance in the community. These ceremonies can vary widely among different indigenous groups.

6. Communal Living: Indigenous lifeways frequently prioritize communal living and interdependence. Families and communities work together in various aspects of life, from subsistence activities to decision-making processes.

7. Cultural Arts and Crafts: Indigenous communities have a rich tradition of arts and crafts, including pottery, beadwork, basketry, textiles, and carvings. These artistic expressions often carry cultural and spiritual significance.

8. Traditional Medicine: Many indigenous cultures have their own systems of traditional medicine, which may involve the use of plants, herbs, and spiritual practices for healing. These systems are often holistic, addressing physical, mental, and spiritual well-being.

9. Elders and Traditional Knowledge Keepers: Elders and traditional knowledge keepers are highly respected within indigenous communities. They play a crucial role in passing on cultural knowledge, stories, and traditions to younger generations.

10. Land Stewardship and Conservation: Indigenous communities are often at the forefront of environmental conservation efforts. They advocate for land rights, protect sacred sites, and promote sustainable resource management to preserve their ancestral lands.

11. Cultural Revival: In many indigenous communities, there is an ongoing effort to revitalize and preserve traditional languages, practices, and ceremonies. Cultural centers, language immersion programs, and educational initiatives are essential in this regard.

12. Challenges and Resilience: Indigenous traditions and lifeways have faced numerous challenges, including colonization, forced assimilation, and land dispossession. Despite these challenges, many indigenous communities have demonstrated resilience and continue to uphold their cultural heritage.

In summary, indigenous traditions and lifeways are rich, diverse, and deeply intertwined with the values and beliefs of indigenous peoples. These traditions serve as a source of cultural pride, resilience, and a means of maintaining a strong connection to ancestral lands and heritage. They also offer valuable insights into sustainable living and harmonious coexistence with the natural world, which hold relevance for addressing contemporary environmental challenges.

Seminole cultural practices and traditions are deeply rooted in the rich history and unique identity of the Seminole Nation. These practices have evolved over centuries and reflect the Seminole people's close relationship with their ancestral lands, their cultural resilience, and their enduring commitment to preserving their heritage. In this exploration, we delve into the diverse cultural practices and traditions of the Seminole Nation.

Oral Traditions and Storytelling: At the heart of Seminole culture is the tradition of oral storytelling. Elders and storytellers pass down myths, legends, and historical narratives to younger generations. These stories convey essential teachings about morality, community values, and the interconnectedness of all living beings.

Language Revitalization: The Seminole language, Creek (Mvskoke), is a vital component of their cultural identity. Efforts to revitalize and preserve the language are ongoing, with language immersion programs and educational initiatives playing a crucial role in ensuring its survival.

Seminole Clothing and Textiles: Seminole clothing is renowned for its vibrant colors and intricate patchwork designs. Traditional clothing includes dresses, blouses, and skirts for women and shirts, pants, and turbans for men. These garments are adorned with vibrant beadwork and exquisite patchwork, reflecting Seminole craftsmanship and artistry.

Basketry and Weaving: Seminole basketry is a revered craft known for its intricate patterns and durability. Women in Seminole communities are skilled weavers, creating baskets and other woven items used for both functional and ceremonial purposes.

Ceremonial Practices: Ceremonies play a significant role in Seminole culture. The Green Corn Dance, also known as the Busk, is one of the most important ceremonial events. It is held annually to mark the new year, renew spiritual connections, and celebrate the harvest.

Medicine and Healing Practices: Traditional Seminole medicine blends herbal remedies with spiritual healing practices. Medicine people, often referred to as medicine men or women, use their knowledge of the natural world to diagnose and treat illnesses. Healing rituals may involve songs, dances, and the use of specific herbs.

Stomp Dance: The Seminole Stomp Dance is a communal dance and musical tradition that brings together participants in a circle. The rhythmic drumming, singing, and synchronized movements are not only a form of cultural expression but also a means of connecting with the spirit world.

Fishing and Hunting: Seminole communities have a deep connection to their natural environment, and fishing and hunting are integral to their way of life. Fishing in swamps, rivers, and coastal waters, as well as hunting game like deer and alligator, provides sustenance and is intertwined with cultural traditions.

Canoe Making: Traditional Seminole canoes are crafted from cypress logs and are used for transportation and fishing. The art of canoe making is passed down through generations, and these canoes remain an important symbol of Seminole culture.

Seminole Patchwork: Seminole patchwork, also known as strip or band patchwork, is a distinctive form of textile art. It involves sewing together narrow strips of fabric to create intricate geometric designs. This art form is often seen in clothing, accessories, and home decor items.

Spiritual Beliefs: Seminole spiritual beliefs are deeply rooted in the concept of interconnectedness with the natural world and the spiritual realm. Many ceremonies and rituals are conducted to maintain harmony with the spirits and to seek guidance and protection.

Cultural Centers and Museums: Seminole cultural centers and museums in Oklahoma and Florida serve as important repositories of cultural artifacts, historical documents, and educational resources. These institutions play a vital role in preserving and sharing Seminole culture with both tribal members and the broader public.

Challenges and Resilience: While Seminole cultural practices and traditions have endured over the centuries, they have also faced challenges, including the impacts of colonization and forced removal. Nevertheless, the Seminole Nation has demonstrated remarkable resilience in preserving its cultural heritage and adapting to changing circumstances.

In summary, Seminole cultural practices and traditions are a testament to the Seminole people's enduring commitment to their cultural identity and their deep connection to their ancestral lands. These traditions encompass a wide range of artistic, spiritual, and practical aspects of daily life, and they continue to play a vital role in shaping the cultural landscape of the Seminole Nation. Efforts to revitalize and preserve these traditions ensure that they will thrive for generations to come.

Chapter 2: Early Encounters with Europeans and Africans

European exploration during the Age of Discovery, which spanned from the late 15th century to the early 17th century, had profound and far-reaching impacts on the indigenous peoples and regions it encountered. As European explorers ventured into new lands, they brought about significant changes, both intended and unintended. Here, we delve into the multifaceted impact of European exploration on indigenous cultures and the broader world.

1. Cultural Exchange: European exploration facilitated cultural exchange between indigenous societies and Europeans. This exchange included the sharing of foods, languages, technologies, and religious beliefs. Indigenous people often adopted European tools and goods, such as metal implements and firearms, which transformed their ways of life.

2. Disruption of Traditional Societies: The arrival of Europeans often disrupted traditional indigenous societies. The introduction of new diseases, such as smallpox and measles, for which indigenous populations had no immunity, resulted in devastating epidemics that decimated their numbers. Additionally, competition for resources and alliances with European powers led to conflicts among indigenous groups.

3. Economic Transformations: European exploration brought about economic transformations in indigenous communities. The fur trade, for example, became a significant economic activity, with indigenous peoples trading furs for European goods. However, this trade also led to the overhunting of certain animal populations and changes in the balance of power among indigenous groups.

4. Land Dispossession: European colonization often resulted in land dispossession and displacement of indigenous peoples. As European powers claimed territory, indigenous communities were forcibly removed from their ancestral lands or coerced into signing treaties that ceded their territories. Land loss had enduring and profound impacts on indigenous cultures and livelihoods.

5. Religious Conversion: European explorers and missionaries introduced Christianity to indigenous populations, leading to religious conversions. Indigenous people sometimes adopted Christianity, either voluntarily or under pressure, and incorporated elements of Christian religious practice into their existing belief systems.

6. Cultural Exchange: European exploration facilitated cultural exchange between indigenous societies and Europeans. This exchange included the sharing of foods, languages, technologies, and religious beliefs. Indigenous people often adopted European tools and goods, such as metal implements and firearms, which transformed their ways of life.

7. Impact on Indigenous Languages: The contact between indigenous languages and European languages led to linguistic changes and the emergence of pidgin languages or creoles. While some indigenous languages have been preserved, many others have become endangered or extinct due to linguistic assimilation.

8. Environmental Impact: European exploration had significant environmental impacts, as settlers cleared land for agriculture, introduced non-native species, and exploited natural resources. These changes often disrupted ecosystems and altered indigenous subsistence patterns.

9. Knowledge Exchange: Indigenous knowledge, particularly in areas such as agriculture, medicine, and navigation, influenced European explorers. Indigenous peoples' understanding of local ecosystems, plants, and traditional navigation techniques proved valuable to Europeans in adapting to new environments.

10. Legacy of Colonization: The legacy of European exploration and colonization continues to shape the lives of indigenous peoples today. Many indigenous communities continue to grapple with the consequences of dispossession, loss of cultural heritage, and socio-economic disparities.

In summary, European exploration had complex and multifaceted impacts on indigenous societies. While it brought about cultural exchange and innovations, it also led to displacement, disease, and disruption of traditional ways of life. Understanding these impacts is essential for recognizing the historical challenges faced by indigenous communities and the ongoing efforts to preserve their cultures and address the legacies of colonization.

The Seminole Nation, a Native American tribe primarily located in the southeastern United States, has a unique cultural heritage that reflects the influences of various cultural groups, including indigenous, African, and European. The complex history of the Seminole people has shaped their society in diverse ways, with each influence contributing to the rich tapestry of Seminole culture. Here, we explore the African and European influences on Seminole society:

African Influences:

African Presence: African influences on Seminole society stem from the presence of enslaved Africans who escaped from plantations and sought refuge with the Seminole people. These escaped slaves, known as Black Seminoles or maroons, formed their communities within Seminole villages.

Cultural Exchange: The interaction between African Americans and Seminoles resulted in a cultural exchange. Elements of African culture, such as music, dance, and religious practices, were integrated into Seminole life. For example, the Seminole stomp dance exhibits African rhythmic patterns and call-and-response singing.

Seminole Language and Creole: The linguistic exchange between African Americans and Seminoles gave rise to a creole language known as "Seminole Negro," which blended Seminole and African linguistic elements. This language was spoken by the Black Seminoles and reflected their unique cultural identity.

European Influences:

Trade and Material Culture: European exploration and trade brought European goods and technologies to Seminole communities. Items such as metal tools, firearms, cloth, and glass beads became integrated into Seminole material culture, influencing their daily lives and craftsmanship.

Agricultural Practices: European agricultural practices and crops, such as maize (corn), beans, and squash, were introduced to Seminole agriculture. These crops complemented the Seminoles' existing agricultural practices and contributed to their food security.

Religion and Christianity: European missionaries played a role in introducing Christianity to Seminole communities. While some Seminoles adopted elements of Christianity, their spiritual beliefs remained intertwined with indigenous and African spiritual practices.

Political Alliances: European colonial powers, including the Spanish, British, and later the United States, sought alliances with the Seminoles. These alliances often had significant political and social consequences for Seminole society, including changes in territorial boundaries and leadership.

Land Dispossession and Conflicts: European colonization efforts led to land dispossession and conflicts with Seminole communities. The Seminole Wars, in particular, were driven by European and American expansionist goals, resulting in significant challenges for Seminole society.

Education and Acculturation: European-American efforts to assimilate indigenous peoples into Euro-American culture, including through boarding schools and forced acculturation, had lasting impacts on Seminole communities. These efforts often aimed to suppress indigenous languages and traditions.

Legal and Political Systems: European legal and political systems, including treaties and land agreements, had a profound impact on the sovereignty and territorial integrity of the Seminole Nation. These interactions continue to influence Seminole political dynamics.

In summary, African and European influences on Seminole society have contributed to the complex and multifaceted cultural identity of the Seminole people. These influences are intertwined with their indigenous heritage, resulting in a unique blend of traditions, languages, and practices. Understanding these influences is essential for appreciating the rich cultural heritage of the Seminole Nation and their ongoing efforts to preserve their traditions and identity in the face of historical challenges.

The initial interactions between European explorers and indigenous peoples in the Americas were marked by curiosity, mutual misunderstanding, and the forging of alliances that would shape the course of history. These encounters, which occurred during the Age of Exploration, were often characterized by cultural exchanges, diplomacy, and the search for mutually beneficial relationships. In this exploration, we delve into the dynamics of these initial interactions and alliances:

Curiosity and Discovery: When European explorers, including Christopher Columbus, arrived in the Americas in the late 15th century, they encountered indigenous societies that were entirely new to them. The explorers were driven by curiosity and a desire to discover new lands, resources, and trade routes.

Language Barriers: Language differences posed a significant challenge during initial interactions. Indigenous peoples spoke a multitude of languages and dialects, making communication difficult. However, explorers often relied on interpreters, some of whom were indigenous individuals with knowledge of multiple languages.

Cultural Exchange: Initial interactions led to a cultural exchange between Europeans and indigenous peoples. Europeans introduced new crops, animals, and technologies, while indigenous societies shared their knowledge of local resources, herbal medicine, and survival skills.

Diplomacy and Alliances: Many explorers sought to establish peaceful and mutually beneficial alliances with indigenous groups. These alliances were often motivated by the desire for trade, protection, or strategic advantages. Indigenous leaders, recognizing the potential benefits of European alliances, entered into diplomatic negotiations.

Trade Networks: The establishment of trade networks was a significant outcome of initial interactions. Europeans brought goods such as metal tools, textiles, and firearms, which were highly sought after by indigenous communities. In exchange, indigenous peoples provided resources like furs, food, and local products.

Cultural Misunderstandings: Cultural misunderstandings were common during these interactions. Misinterpretations of gestures, rituals, and customs could lead to tensions or conflicts.

Additionally, differing worldviews and spiritual beliefs often clashed, contributing to misunderstandings.

Impact of Diseases: One of the most devastating consequences of initial interactions was the introduction of diseases, such as smallpox and measles, by Europeans. Indigenous populations lacked immunity to these diseases, leading to catastrophic epidemics that decimated communities.

Religious Conversion: Some European explorers, particularly missionaries, sought to convert indigenous peoples to Christianity. These efforts resulted in religious syncretism, as indigenous beliefs and practices often blended with Christian elements.

Territorial Claims: As explorers claimed lands on behalf of their home countries, disputes over territorial boundaries arose. These disputes eventually led to conflicts, such as the colonization of the Americas by European powers and the displacement of indigenous peoples.

Long-Term Consequences: The alliances and conflicts forged during initial interactions had long-term consequences for indigenous peoples. Land dispossession, forced labor, and the disruption of traditional societies were among the enduring effects of European colonization.

In summary, the initial interactions and alliances between European explorers and indigenous peoples in the Americas were marked by complex dynamics that shaped the course of history. These encounters, while often characterized by curiosity and diplomacy, also brought about profound changes, including cultural exchanges, trade networks, and, unfortunately, devastating epidemics and conflicts. Understanding these dynamics is crucial for appreciating the complexity of the historical relationships between indigenous peoples and European explorers.

Chapter 3: The Unique Culture of the Seminole Nation

The Seminole Nation, a Native American tribe primarily located in the southeastern United States, has a unique social structure and system of governance that reflect their rich cultural heritage and history. Understanding the Seminole social structure and governance is essential for appreciating their traditional way of life and the challenges they have faced throughout their history. Here, we delve into the key aspects of Seminole social structure and governance:

1. Clan-Based Society: The Seminole people traditionally organized themselves into clans, which played a central role in their social structure. Clans were matrilineal, meaning descent and membership were traced through the mother's line. Each clan had its own distinct identity and responsibilities within the community.

2. Clan Roles and Responsibilities: Clans in Seminole society had specific roles and responsibilities. For example, some clans were responsible for leadership and decision-making, while others were associated with hunting, gathering, or agricultural activities. These roles were interconnected and ensured the well-being of the entire community.

3. Council of Chiefs: The Seminole Nation had a council of chiefs who were selected from the various clans. These chiefs were responsible for making important decisions, resolving disputes, and representing their clans and communities. The council of chiefs played a crucial role in the governance of the Seminole Nation.

4. Matrilineal Descent: Seminole society followed a matrilineal descent system, where lineage and clan membership were passed down through the mother's side of the family. This matrilineal system influenced social structure, inheritance, and kinship ties.

5. Kinship Networks: Kinship was highly valued in Seminole society. Extended families and kinship networks provided support and cooperation in daily life, including hunting, farming, and childcare. These networks reinforced social bonds and community cohesion.

6. Village Communities: Seminole communities were often organized into villages, with each village having its own leadership structure and council of chiefs. Village communities were self-sufficient and relied on a combination of hunting, fishing, farming, and gathering for their subsistence.

7. Oral Tradition and Storytelling: The Seminole people maintained their cultural heritage through oral tradition and storytelling. Elders passed down knowledge, history, and traditions through storytelling, ensuring that their cultural heritage continued to thrive.

8. Adaptability and Resilience: Seminole society displayed adaptability and resilience throughout their history. They successfully resisted forced removal from their ancestral lands during the Seminole Wars and adapted to changing circumstances while preserving their cultural identity.

9. Contemporary Governance: Today, the Seminole Nation operates under a modern governance structure. They have tribal councils and elected leaders who work to address the needs of their communities, promote cultural preservation, and engage in economic development initiatives.

10. Challenges and Preservation: Despite the challenges posed by historical events such as forced removal and cultural assimilation efforts, the Seminole Nation continues to preserve their cultural heritage and traditions. Cultural preservation efforts include language revitalization, arts and crafts, and educational programs.

In summary, the Seminole social structure and governance system reflect the rich and resilient culture of this Native American tribe. Their matrilineal clan-based society, council of chiefs, and emphasis on kinship and community cooperation have been essential in preserving their cultural identity and adapting to changing circumstances. Today, the Seminole Nation continues to thrive while working to preserve their traditions and pass them down to future generations.

Language, communication, and storytelling are integral components of Seminole culture, playing a significant role in preserving their heritage, passing down traditions, and fostering community cohesion. The Seminole people, a Native American tribe primarily located in the southeastern United States, have a rich linguistic tradition that reflects their unique cultural identity. Here, we explore the importance of language, communication, and storytelling in Seminole culture:

1. Language Diversity: Seminole culture is characterized by linguistic diversity. The Seminole Nation historically consisted of several linguistic groups, each with its own language and dialects. Creek (Muskogee) and Mikasuki are among the prominent languages spoken by the Seminole people.

2. Creek and Mikasuki Languages: Creek and Mikasuki are the two major languages spoken by the Seminole people. Creek is a Muskogean language, while Mikasuki belongs to the Hitchiti-Mikasuki language family. These languages are central to Seminole identity and are actively preserved through language revitalization efforts.

3. Importance of Language Preservation: The Seminole Nation places great importance on preserving their native languages. Language preservation initiatives, including language immersion programs, classes, and documentation, are undertaken to ensure that future generations continue to speak and understand Creek and Mikasuki.

4. Oral Tradition: Oral tradition is a cornerstone of Seminole culture. Elders and storytellers within the community pass down knowledge, history, and traditions through spoken word. Stories, songs, and narratives are transmitted orally from one generation to the next.

5. Storytelling as Education: Seminole storytelling serves as a form of education, teaching community members about their history, cultural practices, and the natural world. Stories often convey moral lessons and provide guidance on how to live in harmony with the land and each other.

6. Cultural Identity: Language and storytelling are essential in maintaining Seminole cultural identity. They help reinforce a sense of belonging and connection to their heritage, even in the face of external challenges and influences.

7. Language as a Cultural Marker: The Seminole language serves as a cultural marker that distinguishes them from other tribes and cultures. It encapsulates their worldview, values, and unique perspective on the world.

8. Role of Elders: Elders hold a revered position within Seminole communities. They are the custodians of traditional knowledge and the oral history of the tribe. They play a vital role in passing down linguistic and cultural knowledge to younger generations.

9. Preservation Through Technology: In addition to traditional oral transmission, modern technology has also been harnessed to preserve Seminole languages. Audio recordings, written materials, and digital resources are used to document and teach the languages.

10. Cultural Revival and Adaptation: Seminole language and storytelling are not static; they continue to evolve and adapt to contemporary circumstances. While preserving their traditions, Seminole communities also embrace new technologies and methods to ensure the survival of their cultural heritage.

In summary, language, communication, and storytelling are essential aspects of Seminole culture, serving as the glue that binds the community together and connects them to their rich cultural heritage. Through language preservation efforts and the continuation of oral traditions, the Seminole people ensure that their unique identity and traditions are passed down to future generations, fostering resilience and cultural continuity.

The Seminole people, a Native American tribe with a rich cultural heritage, have deeply rooted spiritual beliefs, intricate ceremonial practices, and a unique tradition of artistry. These elements are interwoven into the fabric of Seminole culture, shaping their worldview, rituals, and creative expressions. In this exploration, we delve into the significance of spiritual beliefs, ceremonies, and artistry in Seminole culture.

Spiritual Beliefs and Worldview:

At the core of Seminole culture are spiritual beliefs that guide their understanding of the world and their place within it. These beliefs are deeply tied to their natural surroundings and emphasize a harmonious relationship with the land and all living beings.

1. Animism and Connection to Nature: Seminole spirituality is characterized by animism, the belief that everything in the natural world possesses a spirit or essence. This worldview fosters a profound connection to nature and a sense of reciprocity with the environment.

2. Balance and Harmony: Central to Seminole spiritual beliefs is the idea of balance and harmony. They believe that maintaining equilibrium in their interactions with the natural world, spirits, and other humans is essential for well-being and prosperity.

3. Ancestral Reverence: The Seminole people hold deep reverence for their ancestors, believing that their spirits continue to influence and protect the living. Ancestral guidance is sought during important decisions and ceremonies.

Ceremonial Practices:

Ceremonial practices play a vital role in Seminole culture, serving as occasions for spiritual expression, community bonding, and the preservation of traditions. These ceremonies are marked by intricate rituals and symbolism.

1. Green Corn Ceremony (Busk): The Green Corn Ceremony, known as the Busk, is one of the most significant Seminole ceremonies. It marks the new year and the ripening of corn, a staple crop. Participants engage in purification rituals, communal feasts, dances, and the making of new commitments.

2. Stomp Dance: The Stomp Dance is a lively and rhythmic communal dance that is an integral part of Seminole culture. It is performed during various ceremonies, symbolizing unity and the connection between the human and spirit worlds.

3. Medicine Rituals: Seminole medicine rituals involve healing practices, often led by medicine people or healers. These rituals seek to restore balance and health by addressing physical, emotional, and spiritual ailments.

4. Fire Ceremonies: Fire is considered sacred in Seminole culture, and fire ceremonies are performed to purify and protect. The lighting of a ceremonial fire is a solemn and meaningful act.

Artistry and Creative Expressions:

Seminole artistry is characterized by intricate craftsmanship, vibrant colors, and symbolism that reflect their cultural values and spiritual beliefs. Artistic expressions encompass a wide range of mediums and serve both functional and symbolic purposes.

1. Clothing and Regalia: Seminole clothing and regalia are adorned with colorful patchwork and beadwork. The distinctive Seminole patchwork, featuring bold geometric patterns, is a hallmark of their artistic tradition.

2. Basketry: Seminole basketry is renowned for its intricacy and beauty. Baskets are not only functional but also hold spiritual significance, often used in ceremonies and as gifts.

3. Beadwork and Jewelry: Beadwork is a prominent art form among the Seminole people. They create intricate beadwork patterns on clothing, jewelry, and accessories, each design carrying unique meanings and stories.

4. Storytelling through Art: Seminole art often tells stories of their history, mythology, and spiritual beliefs. These visual narratives are a means of passing down cultural knowledge to future generations.

5. Canoe Carving: Canoes, an essential mode of transportation in Seminole culture, are often elaborately carved and decorated. The intricate designs on canoes reflect the connection between the Seminole people and the waterways.

6. Contemporary Artistry: While preserving traditional artistic practices, contemporary Seminole artists also embrace innovation and incorporate their cultural heritage into modern forms of art, such as painting and sculpture.

In summary, spiritual beliefs, ceremonial practices, and artistry are integral components of Seminole culture, reflecting the profound connection between the Seminole people and their environment. These elements are not only a testament to their rich heritage but also serve as a source of resilience, cultural continuity, and a means of conveying their worldview to future generations. Seminole culture stands as a vibrant tapestry of spirituality, tradition, and creative expression.

Chapter 4: Seminole Resistance and the Seminole Wars

The Seminole people, a Native American tribe primarily located in the southeastern United States, are renowned for their fierce resistance against encroachments on their land and sovereignty. Over the centuries, multiple factors contributed to the Seminole resistance, shaping their history and struggles. Here, we delve into the key factors that led to Seminole resistance:

1. Cultural Cohesion and Identity: The Seminole Nation possessed a strong sense of cultural identity and cohesion. Their matrilineal clan-based society, distinct languages (Creek and Mikasuki), and unique customs created a shared sense of belonging, fostering unity and determination in the face of external pressures.

2. Land Disputes and Encroachment: One of the primary drivers of Seminole resistance was the continual encroachment on their ancestral lands. European settlers and, later, the United States government sought to acquire Seminole territory for agriculture, leading to conflicts over land ownership and usage.

3. Influence of Seminole Wars: The Seminole Wars, a series of conflicts fought between the Seminole people and the United States, were instrumental in shaping their resistance. These wars, including the First Seminole War (1817-1818), the Second Seminole War (1835-1842), and the Third Seminole War (1855-1858), were characterized by Seminole resilience and determination to defend their homeland.

4. Leadership and Strategy: The Seminole people had skilled leaders who devised effective strategies to resist encroachments and removal efforts. Leaders like Osceola and Micanopy emerged as influential figures who rallied their communities in defense of their land and way of life.

5. Adaptability and Guerrilla Warfare: Seminole resistance tactics included guerrilla warfare, which allowed them to effectively combat larger U.S. forces. Their knowledge of the local terrain, hit-and-run tactics, and ability to navigate the challenging Florida swamps gave them an advantage.

6. Cultural Preservation and Spiritual Resistance: Seminole cultural preservation efforts played a vital role in their resistance. Ceremonies, storytelling, and the preservation of their languages served as a means of resistance by maintaining their cultural identity despite external pressures.

7. Collaboration with African Americans: Seminole communities often collaborated with escaped African American slaves, known as Black Seminoles or Maroons. These alliances were rooted in a shared desire for freedom and resistance against enslavement and displacement.

8. International Diplomacy: The Seminole people engaged in international diplomacy to garner support for their cause. They sought alliances with other Indigenous nations and even explored the possibility of receiving assistance from foreign governments, including Great Britain and Spain.

9. Economic Independence: Seminole communities sought economic independence by engaging in activities such as trade, agriculture, and hunting. These economic pursuits allowed them to maintain their self-sufficiency and resist dependency on external authorities.

10. Determination to Remain on Ancestral Lands: Above all, the Seminole people were determined to remain on their ancestral lands and protect their way of life. Their unwavering commitment to this goal fueled their resistance against removal policies and resettlement.

Despite facing formidable challenges and the eventual forced removal of some Seminole communities, their resistance efforts left a lasting legacy of resilience and cultural preservation. Today, the Seminole Nation thrives, maintaining its cultural traditions, sovereignty, and a deep connection to its ancestral lands, while continuing to honor the legacy of those who resisted against overwhelming odds.

The Seminole Wars, a series of conflicts between the Seminole people and the United States government, were marked by dynamic leadership on both sides. These wars, spanning a period from the early 19th century to the mid-19th century, were fueled by land disputes, encroachments on Seminole territory, and the

U.S. government's efforts to remove the Seminole people from their ancestral lands. Here, we delve into the Seminole Wars and the leadership that shaped these pivotal events:

1. First Seminole War (1817-1818):

U.S. Leadership: Andrew Jackson, then a general in the U.S. Army, played a prominent role in the First Seminole War. He led American forces into Florida and captured several Seminole towns. Jackson's aggressive pursuit of Seminole resistance set the stage for subsequent conflicts.

Seminole Leadership: Osceola, a charismatic Seminole leader, emerged during the First Seminole War. His fierce determination and leadership abilities made him a symbol of Seminole resistance. Osceola's defiance and refusal to accept the Treaty of Fort Moultrie in 1823 foreshadowed further conflicts.

2. Second Seminole War (1835-1842):

U.S. Leadership: General Winfield Scott and later General Thomas Jesup led U.S. forces during the Second Seminole War. Jesup's strategies included capturing Seminole leaders and offering terms for surrender. However, the war proved to be protracted and challenging for U.S. forces.

Seminole Leadership: Osceola continued to be a prominent figure during the Second Seminole War, leading Seminole resistance. Other leaders, such as Micanopy and Alligator, also played key roles. The Seminole use of guerrilla tactics, knowledge of the Florida terrain, and alliances with escaped slaves contributed to their resilience.

3. Third Seminole War (1855-1858):

U.S. Leadership: The U.S. government remained committed to removing the Seminole people from Florida during the Third Seminole War. Several U.S. military commanders were involved, including Colonel Gustavus Loomis and Colonel William S. Harney.

Seminole Leadership: By this time, many Seminole leaders from earlier conflicts had been captured or had perished. However, the spirit of resistance endured among the Seminole people. Leaders like Billy Bowlegs and Sam Jones continued to resist relocation, and their efforts prolonged the conflict.

Leadership Traits and Legacy:

Seminole leaders displayed resilience, adaptability, and a deep commitment to protecting their land and culture. Their ability to adapt to changing circumstances and employ guerrilla warfare tactics posed significant challenges to U.S. forces.

The Seminole Wars left a lasting legacy of Seminole resistance and cultural preservation. Despite the eventual removal of some Seminole communities, their commitment to their homeland and cultural traditions endured.

Cultural Preservation and Resistance:

Throughout the Seminole Wars, Seminole leaders and communities emphasized the importance of cultural preservation. Ceremonies, storytelling, and language played key roles in maintaining their cultural identity and resisting assimilation.

In summary, the Seminole Wars were complex and protracted conflicts characterized by dynamic leadership on both sides. While U.S. leaders sought to remove the Seminole people from their ancestral lands, Seminole leaders like Osceola and later leaders demonstrated resilience and determination in defense of their homeland and cultural heritage. The legacy of Seminole resistance and cultural preservation endures as a testament to their enduring spirit and commitment to their way of life.

The Seminole people, having endured the tumultuous Seminole Wars and the forced removal from their ancestral lands, faced a multitude of challenges as they sought to rebuild their communities and preserve their cultural heritage. The period following the wars was marked by both resilience and adversity as the Seminole people grappled with the aftermath of conflict, the loss of their homelands, and the challenges of survival in unfamiliar territories.

1. Forced Removal and Displacement: The aftermath of the Seminole Wars was characterized by the forced removal of many Seminole people from Florida to Indian Territory in present-day Oklahoma. The removal process, often referred to as the "Trail of Tears," was marked by hardship, loss of life, and the wrenching separation of families and communities.

2. Rebuilding Communities in New Territories: Upon arriving in Indian Territory, the Seminole people faced the daunting task of establishing new communities. They had to adapt to unfamiliar landscapes, climates, and resources, which presented significant challenges to their traditional way of life.

3. Preservation of Cultural Traditions: Despite the hardships of displacement, Seminole communities were determined to preserve their cultural traditions. Ceremonies, storytelling, and the passing down of oral history played a crucial role in maintaining their cultural identity in their new surroundings.

4. Resilience and Adaptation: Seminole resilience was evident in their ability to adapt to the conditions of Indian Territory. They embraced new agricultural practices, such as farming and cattle raising, to sustain their communities in the West.

5. Integration with Other Indigenous Peoples: In Indian Territory, Seminole communities interacted with other Indigenous nations, leading to cultural exchanges and the sharing of knowledge. These interactions contributed to the cultural diversity and resilience of the Seminole people.

6. Challenges to Tribal Governance: The establishment of tribal governments in Indian Territory posed challenges as Seminole leaders grappled with new forms of governance. Decisions about land distribution, resource management, and community development were complex and often contentious.

7. Economic Struggles and Land Issues: Economic challenges arose as Seminole communities sought self-sufficiency. Land allotment policies, such as the Dawes Act, had a profound impact on land ownership and resource allocation, further complicating economic development.

8. Adaptation of Traditional Practices: Seminole communities adapted their traditional practices to the realities of life in Indian Territory. This included modifications to housing, clothing, and food preparation, reflecting the influence of their new environment.

9. Challenges to Language Revitalization: While efforts were made to preserve the Seminole language, the use of English became increasingly prevalent, particularly among younger generations. This posed challenges to language revitalization efforts.

10. Legal Battles and Land Reclamation: Throughout the late 19th and early 20th centuries, Seminole communities engaged in legal battles to reclaim land lost during the removal process. These efforts were often protracted and required persistence.

11. Cultural Renaissance in the 20th Century: The 20th century witnessed a cultural renaissance among the Seminole people. They revitalized traditional arts, crafts, and ceremonies, and embraced innovative approaches to preserving their heritage.

12. Sovereignty and Tribal Identity: Seminole sovereignty and tribal identity remained at the forefront of their struggles. The Seminole Nation and the Seminole Tribe of Florida asserted their sovereignty and engaged in efforts to protect their rights and interests.

In summary, the period following the Seminole Wars was marked by a complex interplay of challenges, survival, and adaptation. Despite the profound hardships of forced removal, the Seminole people demonstrated remarkable resilience in rebuilding their communities and preserving their cultural heritage. Their ability to adapt to new circumstances and maintain their unique identity speaks to their enduring spirit and determination to overcome adversity. Today, the Seminole Nation and the Seminole Tribe of Florida continue to thrive, embodying the legacy of their ancestors who faced the challenges of the aftermath of conflict with unwavering resolve.

Chapter 5: The Seminole Trail of Tears and Life in Unfamiliar Lands

The Seminole Trail of Tears was a harrowing and tragic chapter in the history of the Seminole people, characterized by their forced removal from their ancestral lands in Florida to Indian Territory in present-day Oklahoma. This traumatic event was driven by a combination of political, economic, and social forces that ultimately culminated in the expulsion of the Seminole Nation from their homeland. Here, we explore the multifaceted forces that played a pivotal role in the Seminole Trail of Tears:

1. Territorial Expansionism: One of the primary forces behind the Seminole Trail of Tears was the United States' relentless pursuit of territorial expansion. As the U.S. population grew and the demand for fertile lands increased, there was immense pressure to acquire the lands inhabited by Native American nations, including the Seminole.

2. Land Disputes and Treaties: Land disputes between the Seminole people and the United States were a recurring issue. The U.S. government sought to secure Seminole lands through a series of treaties, including the Treaty of Paynes Landing (1832) and the Treaty of Fort Gibson (1833). These treaties aimed to force the Seminole to relinquish their territory and relocate westward.

3. Economic Interests: Economic considerations played a significant role in the Seminole Trail of Tears. Seminole lands were coveted for their agricultural potential, particularly for cotton cultivation, which was a lucrative cash crop in the 19th century. The desire for economic gain drove the push for Seminole removal.

4. Slavery and Black Seminoles: The presence of Black Seminoles, who were formerly enslaved African Americans living in Seminole communities, added complexity to the issue of Seminole removal. The U.S. government sought to recapture escaped slaves living among the Seminole, further escalating tensions and contributing to the removal policy.

5. Military Conflicts: The Seminole Wars, particularly the Second Seminole War (1835-1842), were instrumental in setting the stage for the Trail of Tears. These wars were marked by Seminole resistance and conflicts with U.S. forces, exacerbating the U.S. government's determination to remove the Seminole people.

6. Political Pressures: Political pressures at the federal level, including pressure from influential politicians and interest groups, played a role in advocating for the removal of the Seminole and other Indigenous nations. Prominent figures like President Andrew Jackson supported the removal policy.

7. Displacement and Loss of Homeland: The Seminole Trail of Tears was fundamentally driven by the U.S. government's intent to displace the Seminole people from their ancestral lands and relocate them to a distant and unfamiliar territory in the West. The removal policy led to the loss of their homeland, resulting in profound cultural and social upheaval.

8. Resistance and Resilience: Despite the overwhelming forces aligned against them, the Seminole people displayed remarkable resilience and resistance throughout the removal process. Leaders like Osceola and Micanopy symbolized this spirit of defiance, and Seminole communities engaged in protracted resistance efforts.

9. Trauma and Loss: The Seminole Trail of Tears inflicted profound trauma and loss on the Seminole Nation. Families were torn apart, and many Seminole people lost their lives during the arduous journey westward.

In summary, the Seminole Trail of Tears was the result of a complex interplay of political, economic, social, and military forces that drove the U.S. government's policy of Indigenous removal. This tragic event left a lasting scar on the Seminole people and their cultural heritage. Despite the challenges they faced, the Seminole Nation has persevered and thrived, preserving their unique identity and continuing to honor the memory of those who endured the Trail of Tears.

The forced removal of Native American nations from their ancestral lands to unfamiliar territories in the West, often referred to as the "Trail of Tears," was a dark and traumatic chapter in American history. This arduous journey had a profound impact on the Indigenous peoples involved, including the Cherokee, Choctaw, Chickasaw, Creek, and Seminole Nations. In this narrative, we explore the difficult and harrowing experiences faced by these nations as they embarked on the challenging journey westward.

1. Displacement and Loss of Homeland: The journey westward was marked by the forced displacement of entire communities from their ancestral lands. For the Cherokee, Choctaw, Chickasaw, Creek, and Seminole Nations, this meant leaving behind the places they had called home for generations, including sacred sites and burial grounds.

2. Emotional and Psychological Toll: The emotional and psychological toll of the journey was immense. Families were torn apart, and communities were shattered as they were forced to leave behind loved ones and familiar surroundings. The trauma of this separation would linger for generations.

3. Harsh Environmental Conditions: The journey was fraught with harsh environmental conditions, especially for those traveling on foot. Native American people faced extreme weather, including bitter cold and sweltering heat, as they traversed challenging terrain. Exposure to the elements took a toll on their health.

4. Lack of Adequate Supplies: Many of the Indigenous peoples who were removed lacked adequate supplies for the journey. Food, clothing, and shelter were often in short supply, leading to hunger and suffering along the way.

5. Disease and Illness: The close quarters in which people were forced to travel facilitated the spread of diseases. Outbreaks of illnesses like cholera, dysentery, and smallpox were devastating, further adding to the death toll.

6. Loss of Life: The journey westward resulted in a significant loss of life. Thousands of Native Americans, including elders, women, children, and infants, perished due to the grueling conditions, disease, and exhaustion.

7. Forced Marches and Camps: Forced marches, often under the watch of U.S. military escorts, were a common feature of the journey. These marches were relentless, with little regard for the well-being of those being removed. Camps along the way provided only temporary respite from the hardships.

8. Cultural Disruption: The forced removal disrupted Indigenous cultures and ways of life. Traditional practices, languages, and customs were eroded during the journey and in the unfamiliar territories where they were resettled.

9. Survival and Resilience: Despite the immense challenges they faced, many Native American individuals and communities displayed remarkable resilience and determination to survive. Leaders emerged who provided support and guidance during this trying time.

10. Arrival in Unfamiliar Territories: Upon reaching their destination in Indian Territory (present-day Oklahoma), the challenges did not end. Indigenous nations had to contend with the task of establishing new communities and adapting to a different environment.

11. Ongoing Impact: The Trail of Tears had a long-lasting impact on the Cherokee, Choctaw, Chickasaw, Creek, and Seminole Nations. It shaped their histories, identities, and relationships with the U.S. government.

12. Cultural Memory and Healing: Today, the memory of the Trail of Tears is preserved as a testament to the strength and resilience of Indigenous peoples. Healing and cultural revitalization efforts continue as communities work to reclaim and celebrate their heritage.

In summary, the journey westward for the Cherokee, Choctaw, Chickasaw, Creek, and Seminole Nations was a grueling and tragic ordeal that left an indelible mark on their histories. It was a test of their endurance, strength, and resilience in the face of immense hardship and loss. The memory of the Trail of Tears serves as a solemn reminder of the profound impact of forced removal on Native American communities and the ongoing importance of acknowledging and honoring their experiences.

The forced removal of Native American nations from their ancestral lands to unfamiliar territories in the West, often referred to as the "Trail of Tears," marked a devastating chapter in American history. However, despite the immense challenges and hardships they faced during the journey, the Indigenous peoples, including the Cherokee, Choctaw, Chickasaw, Creek, and Seminole Nations, demonstrated remarkable resilience and adaptability upon arriving in their new territories. This narrative explores the survival and adaptation of these communities as they navigated the unfamiliar landscapes and worked to rebuild their lives.

1. Establishing New Communities: Upon arrival in their new territories, the displaced Indigenous communities faced the daunting task of establishing new settlements. They had to identify suitable locations for villages, build shelters, and create the infrastructure necessary for daily life.

2. Agricultural Adaptations: For many Indigenous nations, agriculture was a fundamental part of their traditional way of life. In their new territories, they had to adapt their agricultural practices to the local climate and soil conditions. They experimented with new crops and farming techniques to ensure food security.

3. Hunting and Gathering: In addition to agriculture, hunting and gathering remained important means of subsistence. Indigenous peoples adapted their hunting and gathering practices to the fauna and flora of their new environments. They learned to identify and utilize local resources for sustenance.

4. Interactions with Other Indigenous Nations: The new territories were often inhabited by other Indigenous nations. Interaction with these neighboring communities was essential for trade, alliances, and mutual support. These interactions shaped cultural exchange and adaptation.

5. Cultural Preservation and Adaptation: Indigenous communities faced the challenge of preserving their cultural traditions while adapting to new circumstances. This required finding ways to maintain languages, ceremonies, and customs amidst the changes brought about by removal and resettlement.

6. Governance and Leadership: The establishment of new governments and leadership structures was crucial for the stability and well-being of Indigenous communities in their new territories. Chiefs and leaders emerged to guide their people through these challenging times.

7. Resilience in the Face of Hardships: Despite the hardships and losses endured during the journey, Indigenous communities displayed immense resilience. Their determination to survive and preserve their identities fueled their efforts to adapt to the new realities they faced.

8. Efforts to Rebuild and Thrive: Indigenous nations were not content with mere survival; they aspired to thrive in their new environments. They engaged in trade, cultivated relationships with neighboring tribes, and sought economic opportunities to improve their quality of life.

9. Education and Cultural Revival: Education played a pivotal role in both survival and cultural revival. Indigenous communities established schools and cultural programs to pass down their traditions to younger generations and ensure the continuity of their cultures.

10. Modern Challenges and Successes: Today, many of the descendants of the Cherokee, Choctaw, Chickasaw, Creek, and Seminole Nations continue to live in their respective territories in Oklahoma. These communities have faced modern challenges, but they have also achieved significant successes in areas such as tribal governance, education, and economic development.

11. Resilient Communities: The survival and adaptation of Indigenous communities in their new territories stand as a testament to their resilience. They have persevered through centuries of adversity, demonstrating their strength and commitment to their cultures and traditions.

In summary, the forced removal of Indigenous peoples from their ancestral lands was a traumatic and devastating experience, but it did not extinguish their spirit. The survival and adaptation of the Cherokee, Choctaw, Chickasaw, Creek, and Seminole Nations in their new territories showcase their enduring resilience and their ability to overcome immense challenges. Their stories serve as a testament to the indomitable spirit of Indigenous communities in the face of adversity.

Chapter 6: Seminole Diaspora and the Struggle for Identity

The Seminole people, like many other Indigenous nations, experienced a forced removal from their ancestral lands to unfamiliar territories in the West during a tragic episode known as the "Trail of Tears." Upon their arrival in these new lands, the Seminole communities faced numerous challenges and had to adapt to a drastically different environment. This narrative explores the life of Seminole communities in exile and their efforts to rebuild and thrive in their new territories.

1. Establishing New Communities: Upon arriving in Indian Territory (present-day Oklahoma), the Seminole people had to establish new communities. They selected locations for villages, constructed shelters, and developed the infrastructure necessary for daily life.

2. Agricultural Adaptations: Agriculture was a fundamental part of Seminole society, and adapting their farming practices to the new environment was essential. They had to learn which crops thrived in the local soil and climate and develop new farming techniques accordingly.

3. Hunting and Gathering: In addition to agriculture, hunting and gathering remained important means of subsistence for the Seminole people. They adapted their hunting and gathering practices to the fauna and flora of their new territories.

4. Interactions with Neighboring Tribes: The Seminole people were not alone in their new territories; other Indigenous nations also resided there. Interactions with these neighboring tribes were crucial for trade, alliances, and mutual support. Cultural exchange occurred as they adapted to their new surroundings.

5. Preservation of Cultural Traditions: Preserving their cultural traditions was a priority for the Seminole people. Despite the challenges of removal and resettlement, they worked diligently to maintain their languages, ceremonies, and customs.

6. Emergence of Leadership and Governance: Leadership and governance structures were established to ensure the well-being and stability of Seminole communities in exile. Chiefs and leaders emerged to guide their people during this challenging period.

7. Resilience in the Face of Hardships: Despite the hardships endured during the Trail of Tears, Seminole communities displayed remarkable resilience. Their determination to survive and preserve their cultural identity fueled their efforts to adapt to their new environment.

8. Rebuilding and Thriving: The Seminole people aspired not only to survive but also to thrive in their new territories. They engaged in trade, formed alliances with neighboring tribes, and sought economic opportunities to improve their quality of life.

9. Education and Cultural Revival: Education played a vital role in both survival and cultural revival. Seminole communities established schools and cultural programs to pass down their traditions to younger generations and ensure the continuity of their cultures.

10. Modern Challenges and Successes: Today, many descendants of the Seminole Nation continue to reside in their territories in Oklahoma. These communities have faced modern challenges but have also achieved significant successes in areas such as tribal governance, education, and economic development.

11. Resilient Communities: The Seminole people's ability to survive and adapt in their new lands serves as a testament to their resilience. They have persevered through centuries of adversity, demonstrating their strength and commitment to their cultures and traditions.

In summary, the Seminole communities' life in exile was marked by immense challenges, but it also showcased their resilience and adaptability. Despite the trauma of removal, they were able to establish new communities, adapt their traditional practices, and preserve their cultural identity. Their story is a testament to the enduring spirit of Indigenous peoples in the face of adversity and change.

The Seminole people have a rich and diverse cultural heritage that spans centuries. This unique culture has faced numerous challenges throughout history, particularly during the forced removal and resettlement of the Seminole Nation. Despite these challenges, Seminole communities have demonstrated a remarkable commitment to preserving and revitalizing their cultural traditions. This narrative explores the ongoing struggle to preserve Seminole culture.

1. Cultural Diversity: Seminole culture is characterized by its diversity, with a blend of Indigenous, African, and European influences. This cultural richness is evident in their language, art, music, and religious practices.

2. Oral Traditions and Storytelling: One of the fundamental ways Seminole culture is preserved is through oral traditions and storytelling. Elders and community members pass down stories, myths, and histories, ensuring that important knowledge and cultural narratives are preserved for future generations.

3. Language Revitalization: Language is a cornerstone of any culture, and Seminole languages are no exception. Efforts have been made to revitalize and preserve the Seminole languages, ensuring that they continue to be spoken and understood within the community.

4. Ceremonies and Rituals: Seminole ceremonies and rituals play a crucial role in cultural preservation. These events celebrate important milestones, religious beliefs, and community bonds. They provide an opportunity for younger generations to learn and participate in traditional practices.

5. Art and Craftsmanship: Seminole art, including beadwork, basketry, and clothing, is an integral part of their cultural identity. Artisans within the community continue to create these intricate and beautiful works, passing down their skills and techniques.

6. Music and Dance: Seminole music and dance are vibrant expressions of their culture. Songs and dances are performed at various events, conveying stories and emotions that are deeply tied to their heritage.

7. Cultural Centers and Education: Cultural centers and educational programs have been established within Seminole communities to teach younger generations about their culture. These centers serve as hubs for cultural activities, language classes, and the preservation of traditional knowledge.

8. Community Involvement: Preserving Seminole culture is a community effort. Elders and community leaders actively engage with younger generations, encouraging their participation in cultural events and traditions.

9. Intergenerational Learning: The passing down of cultural knowledge from elders to youth is a critical component of cultural preservation. Elders serve as mentors, sharing their wisdom and expertise with the younger members of the community.

10. Challenges and Resilience: Despite the dedication to cultural preservation, Seminole communities face challenges, including the pressures of modernization and external influences. However, their resilience and determination to safeguard their culture remain unwavering.

11. Cultural Resurgence: In recent years, there has been a resurgence of interest in traditional Seminole practices. This resurgence has revitalized cultural practices and strengthened the sense of identity and pride within the community.

12. Cultural Continuity: The struggle to preserve Seminole culture is ongoing, reflecting the deep commitment of the Seminole people to ensure that their traditions, languages, and heritage continue to thrive in the 21st century.

In summary, the Seminole people's dedication to preserving their culture is a testament to the resilience and strength of Indigenous communities. Despite historical challenges and contemporary pressures, Seminole culture continues to flourish and adapt, ensuring that future generations can embrace and celebrate their rich and diverse heritage. The struggle to preserve Seminole culture is not merely a challenge; it is a testament to the enduring spirit of the Seminole people.

Throughout history, Indigenous communities, including the Cherokee, Choctaw, Chickasaw, Creek, and Seminole Nations, have faced significant adversity, including forced removal from their ancestral lands and the profound challenges of adapting to new territories. Despite these hardships, these communities have exhibited a remarkable ability to renew their cultural identities and emerge as resilient leaders within their respective nations.

This narrative explores the process of identity renewal and the emergence of leadership amidst adversity.

Cultural Identity as a Foundation: Cultural identity is a foundational element of Indigenous communities. It encompasses language, traditions, spirituality, and a deep connection to ancestral lands. Despite the disruptions caused by removal, these communities have continually sought ways to reaffirm their cultural identities.

Language Revitalization: Language is a cornerstone of cultural identity. Efforts to revitalize and preserve Indigenous languages have been a priority within these communities. Language revitalization initiatives include language classes, immersion programs, and collaborations with linguists and educators.

Cultural Practices and Traditions: Cultural practices and traditions, such as ceremonies, storytelling, and artistry, play a vital role in reaffirming cultural identity. These practices are passed down through generations and provide a sense of continuity and connection to the past.

Leadership and Governance: Leadership is a crucial component of identity renewal. Within each nation, leaders have emerged to guide their communities through challenging times. These leaders, often chosen for their wisdom and dedication to preserving culture, have played pivotal roles in identity renewal.

Intertribal Cooperation: While each Indigenous nation has its distinct cultural identity, there has also been a recognition of shared experiences and challenges. Intertribal cooperation and collaboration have strengthened the resilience of these communities, fostering a sense of unity among Indigenous nations.

Cultural Centers and Educational Initiatives: Cultural centers and educational programs have been established within Indigenous communities to teach younger generations about their culture. These centers serve as hubs for cultural activities, language classes, and the preservation of traditional knowledge.

Intergenerational Learning: The passing down of cultural knowledge from elders to youth is a critical component of identity renewal. Elders serve as mentors, sharing their wisdom and expertise with the younger members of the community.

Challenges and Resilience: Identity renewal has not been without its challenges. Indigenous communities face pressures from modernization, external influences, and socioeconomic disparities. However, their resilience and determination to safeguard their cultural identities remain unwavering.

Leaders as Cultural Stewards: Many leaders within Indigenous communities have taken on the role of cultural stewards. They actively engage with younger generations, encouraging their participation in cultural events and traditions while also advocating for the preservation of Indigenous languages and practices.

Cultural Resurgence: In recent years, there has been a resurgence of interest in traditional Indigenous practices and cultural revitalization. This resurgence has revitalized cultural practices and strengthened the sense of identity and pride within the community.

Identity as a Source of Strength: Cultural identity is not just a matter of heritage; it is a source of strength and resilience. It empowers Indigenous communities to overcome adversity and challenges, ensuring that their cultural legacies endure for future generations.

A Commitment to the Future: The commitment to identity renewal is not merely about preserving the past; it is about ensuring a vibrant future for Indigenous nations. It is a dedication to passing down cultural knowledge, languages, and traditions to the next generation. In summary, the process of identity renewal and the emergence of leadership amidst adversity are central to the resilience of Indigenous communities. Despite historical injustices and contemporary challenges, the Cherokee, Choctaw, Chickasaw, Creek, and Seminole Nations have reaffirmed their cultural identities and continue to serve as stewards of their rich heritages. The struggle for cultural renewal is not just a historical narrative; it is an ongoing testament to the enduring spirit and resilience of Indigenous communities.

Chapter 7: A Reclaimed Homeland: The Seminole Nation Today

In the face of centuries of adversity, the Seminole Nation has emerged as a vibrant and self-governing Indigenous community, committed to preserving its cultural heritage and exercising tribal sovereignty in the modern era. This narrative explores the evolution of modern Seminole governance and the assertion of tribal sovereignty.

Foundations of Tribal Governance: Tribal governance is deeply rooted in Seminole culture and history. Traditional leadership structures, including tribal councils and chiefs, have adapted to meet the needs of contemporary tribal government.

Sovereignty and Self-Determination: The concept of tribal sovereignty is a cornerstone of modern Seminole governance. Sovereignty grants the Seminole Nation the authority to make decisions regarding its internal affairs, culture, and territory without external interference.

Tribal Constitution and Laws: The Seminole Nation has established a tribal constitution and enacted laws to govern its communities. These laws address various aspects of tribal life, from citizenship and land management to education and cultural preservation.

Tribal Council and Leadership: The Seminole Nation is led by a tribal council composed of elected representatives from different tribal communities. These leaders work collaboratively to make decisions that benefit the entire nation.

Cultural Preservation and Promotion: Cultural preservation remains a priority for modern Seminole governance. Tribal leaders support initiatives that promote language revitalization, traditional practices, and the arts, ensuring that cultural heritage is passed down to future generations.

Economic Development and Self-Sufficiency: Economic development initiatives have been crucial for the Seminole Nation's self-sufficiency. Investments in gaming, agriculture, and other industries have provided revenue that supports essential tribal programs and services.

Healthcare and Education: Modern Seminole governance encompasses healthcare and education services for tribal members. The Seminole Nation operates healthcare facilities and educational institutions, emphasizing the importance of holistic well-being and educational opportunities.

Tribal Justice Systems: Tribal justice systems have been established to address legal matters within the Seminole Nation. These systems reflect a commitment to maintaining order and upholding tribal laws.

Collaboration with Federal and State Entities: Modern Seminole governance often involves collaboration with federal and state governments. Tribal leaders engage in discussions and negotiations to protect tribal rights and resources.

Intergenerational Leadership Transition: The Seminole Nation recognizes the importance of intergenerational leadership transition. Younger tribal members are actively encouraged to participate in governance and take on leadership roles within their communities.

Challenges and Resilience: While modern Seminole governance has made significant strides, challenges persist. Issues such as land disputes, healthcare disparities, and external pressures continue to require the attention and resilience of tribal leaders.

Future Aspirations: The Seminole Nation's aspirations for the future include further economic diversification, expanded educational opportunities, and continued cultural preservation. These aspirations reflect the tribe's commitment to building a strong and sustainable future.

Cultural Identity and Sovereignty Hand in Hand: The preservation of cultural identity and the exercise of tribal sovereignty go hand in hand in modern Seminole governance. Cultural strength is the foundation upon which sovereignty is built and maintained.

In summary, modern Seminole governance is a testament to the resilience and determination of the Seminole Nation. It reflects a commitment to cultural preservation, economic self-sufficiency, and the exercise of tribal sovereignty. The journey from adversity to self-governance is a remarkable narrative of strength and endurance, and it continues to shape the future of the Seminole people.

Economic development has played a pivotal role in the progress and prosperity of Indigenous communities, including the Cherokee, Choctaw, Chickasaw, Creek, and Seminole Nations. This narrative explores the journey of these communities toward economic self-sufficiency and the resulting progress in various aspects of tribal life.

Economic Diversification: Economic diversification has been a key strategy for Indigenous communities. By expanding their economic activities beyond traditional sources, such as agriculture and hunting, they have created sustainable revenue streams.

Gaming Industry: The gaming industry has been a significant driver of economic development for many Indigenous nations. Tribal casinos and gaming operations have generated substantial income, which has been reinvested in tribal programs and services.

Agriculture and Natural Resources: Agriculture remains an essential part of the economy for some tribes, with a focus on sustainable farming practices. Additionally, the management of natural resources, such as forestry and fisheries, has contributed to economic stability.

Small Businesses and Entrepreneurship: Many tribal members have embraced entrepreneurship, establishing small businesses that benefit both the tribal community and the local economy. These enterprises often reflect cultural values and traditions.

Tourism and Cultural Heritage: Tribal lands are rich in cultural heritage and natural beauty, making them attractive destinations for tourists. Cultural tourism initiatives, including heritage centers and guided tours, have provided economic opportunities while preserving traditions.

Investment in Education: Economic development initiatives have included investments in education and workforce development. These efforts aim to equip tribal members with the skills needed to participate in various sectors of the economy.

Healthcare and Social Services: The revenue generated from economic development has enabled tribes to expand and improve healthcare and social services for their communities. Access to quality healthcare and social programs has improved overall well-being.

Infrastructure Development: Tribes have invested in infrastructure development, including roads, housing, and utilities. These improvements enhance the quality of life for tribal members and create jobs in construction and maintenance.

Cultural Preservation and Arts: Economic development has also supported cultural preservation efforts. Funding from economic activities has been allocated to support traditional arts and crafts, cultural events, and language revitalization programs.

Environmental Stewardship: Indigenous communities prioritize environmental stewardship in their economic development efforts. Sustainable practices are employed to protect natural resources and preserve the land for future generations.

Collaboration and Partnerships: Indigenous nations often collaborate with government agencies, non-profit organizations, and local businesses to advance economic development goals. These partnerships foster mutual benefit and community progress.

Challenges and Adaptation: While economic development has yielded positive results, it is not without challenges. Tribes face issues such as market fluctuations, competition, and regulatory complexities, requiring adaptability and strategic planning.

Empowerment and Self-Sufficiency: Economic development initiatives have empowered Indigenous communities to assert greater self-sufficiency. This self-reliance allows tribes to make decisions that align with their cultural values and long-term goals.

Community Progress: The progress achieved through economic development is evident in various aspects of tribal life. Improved healthcare, education, infrastructure, and cultural preservation contribute to the overall well-being of tribal communities.

Sustainable Futures: Economic development is not solely focused on the present; it is an investment in sustainable futures for Indigenous nations. The revenue generated today supports future generations, ensuring a legacy of prosperity.

In summary, economic development and community progress are intertwined in the journey of Indigenous nations toward self-sufficiency and cultural preservation. These communities have harnessed their resources, embraced entrepreneurship, and built partnerships to create thriving and sustainable futures. The story of economic development within the Cherokee, Choctaw, Chickasaw, Creek, and Seminole Nations is a testament to resilience, adaptability, and the enduring spirit of Indigenous people.

In the face of historical challenges, the Seminole Nation has embarked on a journey of cultural revival and identity preservation in contemporary times. This narrative explores the resurgence of Seminole culture, the revitalization of traditions, and the enduring significance of cultural identity in the modern era.

The Resilience of Seminole Identity: Seminole identity is deeply rooted in a rich cultural heritage that has withstood centuries of adversity. Despite the hardships faced by the Seminole people, their cultural identity has endured as a source of strength and resilience.

Cultural Revival Initiatives: Contemporary Seminole leaders and community members have taken proactive steps to revitalize their cultural heritage. Initiatives have been launched to promote language retention, traditional practices, and storytelling.

Language Revitalization: Language is a cornerstone of cultural identity. Efforts to revitalize the Seminole language, including language immersion programs and the preservation of oral traditions, have gained momentum.

Traditional Arts and Crafts: The revival of traditional arts and crafts has played a significant role in cultural resurgence. Seminole artisans create intricate beadwork, textiles, and pottery that reflect their cultural traditions.

Cultural Centers and Museums: Cultural centers and museums have been established to showcase Seminole history, art, and traditions. These institutions serve as important hubs for preserving and sharing cultural knowledge.

Storytelling and Oral Traditions: Storytelling remains a vibrant aspect of Seminole culture. Elders pass down stories and legends, ensuring that the oral traditions of the Seminole people continue to resonate with younger generations.

Ceremonial Practices: Ceremonial practices, such as stomp dances and other traditional ceremonies, are celebrated as integral components of Seminole culture. These ceremonies strengthen cultural bonds and reinforce identity.

Intertribal Collaboration: Seminole cultural revival efforts often extend beyond tribal boundaries. Collaboration with other Indigenous nations fosters the exchange of knowledge and reinforces a sense of shared Indigenous identity.

Educational Initiatives: Seminole communities place a strong emphasis on education as a means of preserving cultural knowledge. Tribal schools and educational programs incorporate cultural teachings into the curriculum.

Youth Engagement: Engaging youth in cultural activities and teachings is a priority. Seminole leaders recognize the importance of passing cultural knowledge to the next generation.

Participation in Cultural Events: Participation in cultural events and gatherings, both within the Seminole Nation and in intertribal contexts, provides opportunities for the expression and celebration of cultural identity.

Challenges and Resilience: Despite the progress made in cultural revival, challenges persist. External pressures, including globalization and the rapid pace of modern life, require ongoing resilience to protect and preserve Seminole culture.

Adaptation and Innovation: Seminole cultural revival efforts are not static; they adapt to contemporary contexts. Innovations in teaching methods, technology, and community engagement enhance cultural preservation.

Chapter 8: Preserving Tradition and Thriving in Modern Times

The traditional arts, crafts, and ceremonies of the Cherokee, Choctaw, Chickasaw, Creek, and Seminole Nations are deeply rooted in their respective cultures and play a vital role in preserving and celebrating their heritage. This narrative explores the significance of these practices and their enduring presence in contemporary Indigenous life.

Artistry as Cultural Expression: Traditional arts and crafts serve as powerful forms of cultural expression for Indigenous communities. Through these creative outlets, tribal members convey their history, values, and connection to the land.

Beadwork and Textiles: Intricate beadwork and textiles are prominent in the artistic traditions of these nations. Patterns and designs are often passed down through generations, each piece telling a unique story.

Pottery and Basketry: Pottery and basketry are essential components of Indigenous artistry. These crafts are characterized by their craftsmanship and the use of natural materials found in the local environment.

Sculpture and Woodworking: Sculpture and woodworking allow artists to transform wood and other materials into sculptures, masks, and other forms of artistic expression that represent cultural narratives.

Symbolism and Storytelling: Many traditional arts and crafts are imbued with symbolism and storytelling. Each design, pattern, or motif carries meaning, often rooted in tribal legends and oral traditions.

Ceremonial Regalia: Ceremonial regalia, including clothing, headdresses, and accessories, is crafted with precision and care. These regalia are worn during important ceremonies and dances, symbolizing the cultural and spiritual significance of these events.

Dances and Powwows: Ceremonial dances and powwows are integral to Indigenous cultural traditions. These events bring communities together to celebrate their heritage through dance, music, and regalia.

Stomp Dances: Stomp dances, a distinctive feature of Southeastern Indigenous cultures, are characterized by rhythmic footwork and chanting. They hold deep spiritual significance and are a means of communal bonding.

Medicine Bundles and Artifacts: Medicine bundles, containing sacred objects and herbs, are essential in Indigenous healing and spiritual practices. Artifacts and heirlooms are passed down as a connection to ancestors.

Cultural Preservation and Revival: The preservation and revival of traditional arts, crafts, and ceremonies are ongoing efforts. Indigenous communities recognize their role in maintaining cultural identity and passing it to future generations.

Cultural Centers and Workshops: Cultural centers and workshops play a vital role in teaching these traditions. They provide spaces for artists to create, share knowledge, and instruct younger generations.

Intertribal Collaboration: Collaboration among Indigenous nations fosters the exchange of artistic techniques and cultural practices. These interactions strengthen the bonds of shared Indigenous identity.

Economic Ventures: Traditional arts and crafts also contribute to economic sustainability. The sale of Indigenous art supports artists and their communities while promoting cultural appreciation.

Challenges and Resilience: Challenges, such as the preservation of natural resources for crafting materials and the impact of cultural appropriation, require resilience and adaptability in maintaining these traditions.

Cultural Significance: Traditional arts, crafts, and ceremonies are not just artistic expressions; they are essential components of Indigenous cultural identity, reinforcing connections to ancestors, land, and spirituality.

A Living Heritage: The continued practice of these traditions ensures that Indigenous cultures remain vibrant, living, and thriving in the contemporary world, passing down the legacy of their ancestors to future generations.

In summary, traditional arts, crafts, and ceremonies are at the heart of the cultural identity and heritage of the Cherokee,

Choctaw, Chickasaw, Creek, and Seminole Nations. These practices serve as a bridge between the past and the present, allowing Indigenous communities to celebrate their rich history while embracing the future. They are a testament to the enduring spirit of Indigenous people and their commitment to preserving their unique cultural legacies.

Cultural centers hold a special place in the heart of Indigenous communities, serving as hubs of cultural preservation, education, and celebration. In the context of the Cherokee, Choctaw, Chickasaw, Creek, and Seminole Nations, these centers play a crucial role in fostering a deep connection to heritage and ensuring the ongoing success of Indigenous cultures.

Preservation of Cultural Knowledge: Cultural centers serve as repositories of ancestral knowledge, housing archives, artifacts, and documents that document the history, traditions, and languages of Indigenous communities.

Education and Outreach: These centers are instrumental in educating both tribal members and the broader public about Indigenous cultures. Educational programs, workshops, and exhibitions offer insights into traditional practices and contemporary life.

Language Revitalization: Language preservation and revitalization efforts often find a home in cultural centers. Language immersion programs and resources are key components in the preservation of Indigenous languages.

Art and Craft Workshops: Many cultural centers host art and craft workshops, providing opportunities for artists to share their skills and knowledge with the next generation. These workshops contribute to the continuity of traditional art forms.

Cultural Performances and Demonstrations: Cultural centers frequently host events and performances, including traditional dances, storytelling sessions, and demonstrations of traditional practices. These events showcase the vibrancy of Indigenous cultures.

Community Gathering Spaces: Cultural centers serve as community gathering spaces, fostering a sense of belonging and unity among tribal members. They are places where celebrations, meetings, and social events take place.

Intertribal Collaboration: Cultural centers often facilitate intertribal collaboration, enabling the exchange of knowledge and cultural practices among Indigenous nations. These collaborations strengthen the bonds of shared Indigenous identity.

Cultural Revival and Identity: By actively preserving and celebrating cultural traditions, these centers contribute to the revitalization of Indigenous identities. They reinforce the importance of cultural heritage in the lives of tribal members.

Cultural Tourism: Cultural centers also play a role in cultural tourism, attracting visitors interested in learning about Indigenous cultures. The revenue generated from tourism often supports center operations and Indigenous communities.

Challenges and Sustainability: Cultural centers face challenges related to funding, maintenance, and the evolving needs of their communities. Sustainability efforts often require creative solutions and community support.

Cultural Significance: Cultural centers are not just physical spaces; they are living embodiments of Indigenous cultures. They carry the spirit of ancestors, and their very existence signifies the resilience and continuity of Indigenous traditions. The ongoing success of cultural centers lies in their ability to adapt and evolve while remaining true to their cultural missions. They must remain dynamic, responsive, and inclusive. Cultural centers are integral to the enduring success of Indigenous cultures. They ensure that Indigenous identities remain strong, vibrant, and deeply intertwined with contemporary life, fostering pride and a sense of belonging among tribal members. In summary, cultural centers are beacons of hope, preserving the cultural treasures of the Cherokee, Choctaw, Chickasaw, Creek, and Seminole Nations. They are not mere institutions; they are the keepers of stories, traditions, and languages, and they symbolize the ongoing success of Indigenous cultures. As these centers continue to thrive, they light the path for future generations to embrace their heritage and carry it forward into an ever-changing world.

Conclusion

In the pages of "Native American Tribes: Five Civilized Tribes of Cherokee, Choctaw, Chickasaw, Creek & Seminole Nation," readers have embarked on a profound journey through the histories, cultures, and struggles of these remarkable Indigenous nations. Across five distinct books, we have delved deep into the stories of resilience, adaptation, and renewal that define the Cherokee, Choctaw, Chickasaw, Creek, and Seminole peoples.

In "Book 1 - The Cherokee Nation: A History of Resilience and Renewal," we explored the enduring spirit of the Cherokee, tracing their ancient roots, early encounters with European explorers, and the tragic Trail of Tears. Yet, we also witnessed their resurgence and the ongoing efforts to preserve their cultural heritage.

"Book 2 - Choctaw Legacy: From Homeland to Removal" took us on a journey through the Choctaw Nation, examining their pre-European societies, early interactions with European settlers, and the profound challenges they faced during their forced removal from their ancestral lands. Throughout, the Choctaw legacy of strength and adaptability shone through.

In "Book 3 - Chickasaw Homeland: A Journey Through History," we followed the Chickasaw people from their ancient origins through colonization and their own forced removal, as they rebuilt their homeland and reasserted their identity, forging a brighter future for generations to come.

"Book 4 - Creek Nation Chronicles: Surviving and Thriving" chronicled the rich history of the Creek Nation, from their ancestral lands and early encounters with European settlers to the hardships of the Creek War and the resilience that has defined their journey.

Finally, in "Book 5 - Seminole Nation Saga: Adaptation and Survival," we explored the unique culture and resistance of the Seminole people, who faced removal and the challenges of life in new territories with unwavering strength, ultimately reclaiming their homeland and identity.

As we conclude this book bundle, we are left with a profound appreciation for the stories of these Indigenous nations. Their histories are stories of survival, renewal, and adaptation against immense odds. They are also stories of cultural resilience, with each tribe working tirelessly to ensure that their languages, traditions, and identities endure for future generations.

The legacy of the Cherokee, Choctaw, Chickasaw, Creek, and Seminole Nations is one of enduring strength and the unwavering commitment to preserving their unique cultures. It is our hope that these books have shed light on these remarkable histories, deepening our understanding of the rich tapestry of Native American tribes and their profound contributions to the mosaic of American history.

As we close the final chapter of this book bundle, may we carry forward the lessons of resilience, adaptation, and cultural preservation that these Indigenous nations have imparted to us. May their stories continue to inspire and remind us of the importance of honoring and respecting the heritage of Native American tribes in our shared journey as a diverse and interconnected society.

About A. J. Kingston

A. J. Kingston is a writer, historian, and lover of all things historical. Born and raised in a small town in the United States, A. J. developed a deep appreciation for the past from an early age. She studied history at the university, earning her degree with honors, and went on to write a series of acclaimed books about different periods and topics in history.

A. J.'s writing is characterized by its clarity, evocative language, and meticulous research. She has a particular talent for bringing the lives of ordinary people in the past to life, drawing on diaries, letters, and other documents to create rich and nuanced portraits of people from all walks of life. Her work has been praised for its deep empathy, its attention to detail, and its ability to make history come alive for readers.

In addition to her writing, A. J. is a sought-after speaker and commentator on historical topics. She has given talks and presentations at universities, museums, and other venues, sharing her passion for history with audiences around the world. Her ability to connect with people and make history relevant to their lives has earned her a devoted following and a reputation as one of the most engaging and insightful historical writers of her generation.

A. J.'s writing has been recognized with numerous awards and honors. She lives in California with her family, and continues to write and speak on historical topics.

Printed in the USA
CPSIA information can be obtained
at www.ICGtesting.com
LVHW080311011123
762685LV00005B/543